MW01138967

Behind
FRENEMY
LINES

Behind
FRENEMY
LINES

Zen Cho

BRAMBLE

TOR PUBLISHING GROUP

NEW YORK

BEHIND FRENEMY LINES

Copyright © 2025 by Zen Cho

All rights reserved.

A Bramble Book
Published by Tom Doherty Associates / Tor Publishing Group
120 Broadway
New York, NY 10271

www.torpublishinggroup.com

Bramble™ is a trademark of Macmillan Publishing Group, LLC.

The Library of Congress Cataloging-in-Publication Data is available upon request.

ISBN 978-1-250-33047-5 (trade paperback)
ISBN 978-1-250-33048-2 (ebook)

Our books may be purchased in bulk for promotional, educational, or business use. Please contact your local bookseller or the Macmillan Corporate and Premium Sales Department at 1-800-221-7945, extension 5442, or by email at MacmillanSpecialMarkets@macmillan.com.

First Edition: 2025

Printed in the United States of America

0   9   8   7   6   5   4   3   2   1

To Max

Behind
FRENEMY
LINES

PROLOGUE

Kriya

I knew I was in trouble the moment I opened my eyes. It was the morning of my first-ever training contract interview, and someone had started drilling in the road outside the window of my tiny student room.

I rolled over and grabbed my phone, panic rising in me. It was a full hour past the time I'd set my alarm to go off.

"Oh no no no no no!"

My big mistake had been spending all those hours the night before reading up on the firm I was interviewing with. Swithin Watkins was highly ranked in all the legal directories, a *Times* Top 50 employer for women, and one of the biggest law firms in the world, raking in over £2 billion in revenue the previous year.

It was also, according to several online forums for disaffected lawyers, "hell on earth," "evil. fucking evil," and "full of people I wouldn't piss on if they were on fire."

"Everyone who works there missed their vocation as a Spanish inquisitor circa the 1500s," said one memorable comment.

After reading all of that, I hadn't been able to fall asleep till two a.m., despite climbing into bed at 9:30 p.m. like an old person. Which was why I was now throwing on my clothes in mad haste, about to be late for the most important job interview of my life.

My phone pinged. I seized it as I raced around the flat, brushing my teeth. Tom had texted, like a good boyfriend:

Good luck today! You'll smash it xx

Which should have cheered me up. Except my best friend Zuri had texted ten minutes earlier:

Interview today right? Good luck!

Eh do you need your shoes

I froze.

I'd forgotten I'd lent my smart shoes to Zuri, to wear to her dissertation presentation the week before. The shoes were sensible low-heeled black pumps Amma had bought me from Bata, and I didn't have anything else suitable to wear.

Unless I wore my party shoes. They were pointy-toed patent stiletto heels I'd bought mostly because it was nice to imagine myself as the kind of person who would wear stilettos. They made my toes go numb after two minutes, but I was going to be on the bus for most of the way anyway.

Except turned out the bus terminated two stops early. I found myself hurtling down Farringdon Road in those heels, dodging commuters, students, and the remains of someone's kebab smeared over the pavement. I got to the firm with three minutes to spare.

I took a moment to catch my breath, staring up at the imposing grey office building. I straightened my blazer, exhaling. Then I took a step towards the building, caught that damned stiletto heel in a grate, and came crashing down on the steps leading up to the entrance.

As I was picking myself up, feeling like a bloody idiot, I heard someone clear their throat. Towering above me, outlined against the white English sky, was the most beautiful East Asian man I'd ever seen in my life.

Not beautiful like a kpop idol. More like an Asian American

actor who starts out playing the scene-stealing comic relief in a quirky sitcom, then all of a sudden he's a sex symbol and cast as the lead in the "this one's for the Chinese market" instalment in a huge Hollywood franchise. He had designer stubble and a tiny mole under his right eye, and beautiful, glossy, thick black hair. He could have been in an advertisement for hair tonic.

"I'm fine," I said, yearning for death.

I scrambled to my feet. Only then I realised he hadn't asked.

He was cradling four bulging lever arch files in his arms. He squinted at me over them, as though I were a half-eaten pavement kebab he'd almost stepped in by accident.

"What are you doing here?" he said.

He had a British accent. When you've lived in the UK for a while, this stops being sexy, but because my life sucks, his was really sexy.

I flushed. Luckily no one can tell. "I, uh, I was invited to the assessment centre. For the, um, for a training contract? At the firm?"

It struck me that maybe he was looking at me like that because he didn't expect someone like me to be interviewing for a training contract somewhere like Swithin Watkins. Probably I should have puffed up with defiance. Instead I felt even more like something nasty on the pavement you'd be annoyed about having to clean off your shoe.

"You're in the wrong place." He started going up the steps.

"Is this not Swithin Watkins?" I pointed at the sign next to the large glass doors. "It says 'Swithin Watkins' right there."

"There are two buildings," said the beautiful but unfriendly man, without pausing. "You want the one over there." He jerked his head.

I looked across the street and saw another imposing building, this one sand-coloured, with a sign next to the glass revolving doors. That sign *also* said "Swithin Watkins."

"Shit!"

I ended up being eight minutes late to the assessment centre. As I sidled in, the other candidates glanced at me before looking away quickly, as though worried the no-doubt terrible impression left by my unpunctuality might somehow rub off on them if they stared for too long.

We were in a light-filled meeting room on the fourteenth floor, with large windows looking out on the City of London. From where I was sitting, I could see the towers of Smithfield Market, with their green domes.

That wasn't the only thing I saw. There were five other candidates waiting for the assessment centre to start—all women, but that was where any resemblance ended. Not only was I the sole candidate who wasn't white, I was the only person who wasn't blonde, or thin.

I was beginning to wonder if it had been a mistake to apply to the firm. And a mistake to study law. And a mistake to come to the UK in the first place. Maybe I should have stayed in Malaysia. At least I had the right to work in Malaysia.

I gazed out at the City skyline while the Graduate Recruitment lady droned on about their international secondments. It was hard not to yearn after all the jobs I could've gone for if not for needing a visa. Jobs that were meaningful, that weren't simply about the preservation of wealth.

I could have joined a nonprofit, like the refugee rights organisation I'd interned with last summer. I could have applied to the Government Legal Department. I could have joined a normal law firm that helped actual people with their problems.

Those types of employers weren't prepared to sponsor a visa, though. For that, you needed a big firm like Swithin Watkins, one that wouldn't notice the cost.

Except it didn't seem likely Swithin Watkins would be volunteering to sponsor me. There were two Hannahs in the cohort of candidates. That meant there were more Hannahs than nonwhite people of any background present.

I shrank into my chair. The memory of Beautiful East Asian Guy from earlier didn't help. He was probably an aberration, the exception that proved the rule. And our encounter had hardly been one to boost my confidence. Remembering it made me want to wither up with sheer embarrassment.

At least I'd probably never see him again. Looking around me, I had a feeling the firm wouldn't be taking me on.

Charles

Went to court today. Urgent application on the Oldham matter. Print Room came through with the bundles, but it was tight.

Counsel said to client in conference, "Of course it's finely balanced." Meaning, *We're going to lose.* Client didn't get it.

Told supervisor we should tell the client their case is weak: "That's what they're paying us for. To advise on the merits of the case."

Jamie: "No. Clients pay us to tell them what they want to hear. Oldham went with us over Brown, Rosenburg and Cushway because we said we'd win the case for them."

Jamie pointed out that by the time the court hands down its ruling, even if it goes against Oldham, the fees will have been paid. I said Oldham could sue us for negligence and claw the money back.

Jamie, unimpressed: "You never know what will happen in litigation anyway. The judge may decide in our favour. Who knows?"

That's true. The rest, I disagree with. Jamie: "It's not your job to disagree. Your job is bundling."

Good thing about Jamie, you know where you stand with him. Good quality in a supervisor. Tact also a good quality, but can't have everything.

Should have helped that girl when she fell on the steps. I could have put the files down. Didn't think of it till later, when I was home having dinner with Loretta.

Loretta didn't want to hear about Oldham: "There must be something going on in your life other than work, Charles."

Couldn't think of anything, so told her about girl on the steps. Didn't say anything about girl's looks, but Loretta immediately said: "You fancied her, didn't you? That's why you did the awkward turtle thing. Being rude to girls you like doesn't work in real life, you know. You're not Fitzwilliam Darcy."

Made the mistake of saying: "What are you talking about?" She forced me to watch highlights video of BBC *Pride and Prejudice*. I begged off. Fourteen hours per day of staring at a computer at work more than enough screentime for me.

Loretta: "This is why you're going to die alone. You're Darcy without the pool scene."

Didn't know what she meant, but knew it was insulting.

Tact also a good quality to have in a cousin. Arguably more important in an in-house cousin than a supervisor. Loretta does not cook, do laundry, or pay market rent. While she cleans the flat sometimes, her standards for hygiene are significantly below what is pleasing. The least she could do is be nice to me. Jamie may not be nice, but at least he explains Part 36 offers.

I pointed this out to Loretta. Realised, since she's not familiar with the Civil Procedure Rules, she wouldn't know why Part 36 offers are so complex and why you've got to get them right. Started explaining the costs consequences.

Loretta said: "Oh my God, Charles."

She's not wrong. I *am* going to die alone.

CHAPTER
ONE

THIRTEEN YEARS LATER

Kriya

I paused outside the entrance to Swithin Watkins, gazing up at the building's sandstone façade.

I was waiting for the traumatic flashback to hit. I hadn't been here since the day I interviewed for a training contract, in the summer of my second year at university.

That had been more than a decade ago. I was coming to Swithin Watkins now as a senior lawyer, with a track record of court cases won; matters brought to a successful close; difficult clients wrangled into contentment. But the memory of that interview still made me cringe.

I took a deep breath as I stepped through the revolving door, stale apprehension shivering over my skin. Maybe I shouldn't have followed Arthur here.

When my boss pulled me aside for a chat, a month ago, I didn't think anything of it. Arthur and I spoke, on average, three to sixteen times a day. I assumed he wanted to talk about the class action we were defending for a car manufacturer, or the business development trip we were planning to Hong Kong.

Or it might just have been a check-in. Arthur was going

through a divorce with his wife of twenty-five years and it was making him especially alive to the issue of workplace well-being. We'd had more pastoral chats in the past month than we'd had in the preceding eight years total.

"Kriya, I wanted to ask you something," he said. He shut the door to his office and sat down.

He looked nervous, but that was part of Arthur's vibe. He was lean, silver-haired, and high-strung, with piercing blue eyes and the kind of nose you'd find on a Roman coin. Trainees always had guilty crushes on him, until they started working with him.

"I've accepted an offer to join Swithin Watkins," said Arthur. "And I'd like you to consider moving with me. It would be a step up in terms of pay. More importantly, it would be on the understanding that you'd be promoted to Of Counsel within the year."

"Oh," I said. I was so taken aback I felt winded.

I hadn't been thinking about promotion. I knew I should—I'd made senior associate as early as the firm allowed, four years after qualifying, and I was now eight years out from qualification. I needed to start preparing for the next step, or be marked as lacking ambition. But my attention had been elsewhere for the past few months.

I'd gone too long without saying anything.

"What do you think?" said Arthur.

I didn't know what I thought. For lack of anything better to say, I said, "You know I interviewed for a training contract at Swithin Watkins? I didn't get an offer."

"Their loss." Arthur tried to smile, fidgeting with a pen. "Joining them as their top new senior associate would be the best revenge."

His nervousness was starting to infect me. I pushed away the temptation to say yes just to calm him down.

"Can I think about it and come back to you?"

"Yes, of course," said Arthur. "It's a big decision. Take all the time you need."

He leant back in his chair. "So what—I mean, do you have any questions? I don't have details of the compensation package to hand, but I can dig them up. Give me a moment."

He started scrabbling around in the chaos of papers on his desk.

"Your phone's on top of that filing cabinet," I said absently. "Can I ask . . . ?"

Arthur sat up. "Yes, of course. Fire away."

"Why move?"

It was the obvious question. Arthur was prepared for it.

"You know I have issues with some of the ways we work here. I want to do things differently, but there isn't scope for that here. We're losing clients to firms that are willing to be more innovative, more flexible. Swithin Watkins recognises how the market is changing. I'll be able to be more entrepreneurial, tailor our offering to what clients are looking for. It's a great opportunity. And," said Arthur, "and I have to say, you know, I've been at this firm for more than fifteen years, and I'm ready for a change."

I knew about Arthur's frustrations with the firm—I'd heard most of this before, at one time or another. But I thought, of everything he'd said, the very last line was the truth.

"Are you planning on bringing anyone else over?"

Arthur shook his head. "We've got some great lawyers here. If they decide to apply to join us, I'll be thrilled. But my move is already going to ruffle feathers. I'm picking my battles." He fixed me with an intense blue stare. "You're worth fighting for, Kriya."

I squirmed. Post-divorce, Arthur was given to saying things like this—nothing you could call out as being inappropriate, but uncomfortable all the same. Maybe his therapist had told him he should express appreciation for the people in his life.

If so, I wished his therapist had clarified that I didn't count as "people in his life." The firm consumed enough of my life as it was. I was fully committed to compartmentalising my work and personal spheres. All I wanted from colleagues was for them to return the favour.

Arthur looked away.

"You have to decide if it's the right choice for your career, of course," he said.

So here I was now, back at Swithin Watkins. Funny how life worked.

My friends had doubts about the move. ("So because your boss is having a midlife crisis, you've got to uproot yourself?" said Zuri.) But it made sense. I'd worked almost exclusively with Arthur since qualifying into the Product Liability team at Brown, Rosenburg and Cushway. I didn't have the same relationship with other partners in our department—they didn't know and trust me the way Arthur did. And when he moved, he'd be taking his clients with him. If I stayed at my old firm, either I'd be fighting him for business or I'd have to find myself a new client base.

Whereas if I followed Arthur to Swithin Watkins, I got a pay rise and a guaranteed promotion, and I'd be well placed to make partner.

If I wanted to. I wasn't sure I did. Arthur wasn't exactly a great advertisement for the life of a City law firm partner. Sometimes, working with him, it was like there were three of us in the office: me, Arthur, and his divorce.

Hopefully the change would do us both good. Arthur wasn't the only one reeling from a catastrophic breakup. It had been six months since Tom had broken up with me, and I still felt raw.

Waiting in the lobby of Swithin Watkins while a receptionist searched for my newly issued staff pass, I felt a glimmer of hope. This was what I'd been needing: a fresh start.

I'd been feeling stuck ever since Tom had flown off to California without me, for a dream job—and, it turned out, a dreamy coworker. In fact, if I was being totally honest with myself, I'd been feeling stuck even before Tom left. Maybe that was why he'd decided to blow up our relationship, after more than a decade together. He could see I wasn't going anywhere he wanted to be.

Thinking about Tom made me too sad. It was easier to think about work. I had to go pick up my new laptop, and then I was headed for the sixth floor, where Swithin Watkins' nascent Product Liability team was based.

Arthur had been pleased with himself for managing to secure me an office.

"They revamped the building a couple of years ago, it's mostly open plan now," he'd said. "Offices are like gold dust. You'll be in with someone from their Commercial Litigation practice, they've got the desk by the window. But at least it's an office."

I hadn't shared an office in a while. The junior associate I used to share with at my old firm had left to go in-house the year before, and the firm hadn't got around to allocating her desk to someone new before my own departure. It would be nice to have company again, even if I was going to have the desk closest to the door, traditionally assigned to the less important occupant.

My new office was pretty similar to the one I'd had at my old firm. Against one wall, two large L-shaped desks faced each other, with matching monitors and docking stations tucked into the corner of each L. Filing cabinets and shelving ran along the opposite wall.

The window was behind my new roommate's desk, so I had the better view. He was sat looking out on the corridor.

Though he was on a call when I walked in, his back turned to me. It was the back of someone who worked out, the shoulders broad under the crisp white shirt. The hair under the headset he was wearing was thick and dark.

I'd registered this much when he swivelled around in his chair, raising a hand in greeting.

Our eyes met.

The man across me was East Asian, with perfect skin and absurdly long eyelashes. He was wearing glasses with thick black rims, the kind a Hollywood starlet playing a nerd wears when the film's pretending she's ugly. The glasses obscured the tiny mole under his right eye, dropped by an overly generous god along the line of one high cheekbone. But I knew it was there.

My smile froze. He lowered his hand, giving me a look of unalloyed horror.

It was a look I was used to by now, after ten years' worth of run-ins with Charles Goh.

I turned around and walked right back out.

Arthur had a spacious office to himself at the end of the corridor: lots of space, floor-to-ceiling windows. The light was nice, though the windows didn't yield much of a view. Grey streets, office buildings, and people walking fast, with their coats buttoned up to their chins and Pret bags dangling from their hands. It had been chilly all the past week, even though it was early June.

Arthur had already put up a couple of family photos. I'd grown used to the one he used to have on his old noticeboard, featuring him, his now-ex-wife, Kelly, and the two kids bundled up and beaming, on a skiing holiday.

It took me a moment to realise what was different. The pictures he had up now were of the kids alone. Kelly was gone.

Arthur himself was looking cheerful, as though the move

had already given him a new lease on life. It was all right for some.

"Morning," he said. "Got your kit? How's the office?"

"Er, yeah, about that," I said. "Is the room allocation definitely fixed? Or is there any scope for flexibility, do you think?"

Arthur's smile dimmed. "Is there a problem?"

I hesitated.

I could try explaining that Charles Goh and I were bound together by an evil fate, from our first encounter at this very firm. But Arthur would think I was nuts. He didn't know what it was like to keep running into a hot lawyer employed by the firm that rejected you and have it be a disaster *every single time*.

It wouldn't sound plausible. The City of London was actually pretty large. There was no reason I should have seen anything more of Charles Goh after that ill-fated assessment centre. We didn't even do the same kind of law, apart from the fact that we were both litigators. Yet Charles had kept turning up, over the years.

("He's your good friend," said Zuri.

"He's my bad luck charm," I said. "He's like the omen you see when something terrible is going to happen. Like flocks of birds flying backwards. Rains of frogs."

"You won the case what," said Zuri. "The one where he spilled his coffee on you at the big strategy meeting. Eh, and didn't you win the other court application? That time you were late to court and had to run there with the files on a trolley and he was sitting up there with the judge, watching you, when you went in and rolled the trolley over the client's foot."

"That's the claimant's lawyer's fault. If he didn't leave his laptop cable trailing on the floor there, I wouldn't have tripped over it, and the trolley wouldn't have gone anywhere near the client." I rubbed my face. "That kind of thing only happens when Charles Goh is around. Like I said, my bad luck charm."

"Your good friend," Zuri intoned. Which was how she and all our mutual friends had started calling him Kawan Baik.)

I said to Arthur now:

"The office is right by the kitchenette. It gets pretty noisy, with the coffee machine and people chatting. I don't suppose there are any other offices going free?"

"They're tight on office space here," said Arthur. "Firm policy is to move towards open plan. No fixed desks for anyone, since everyone's doing hybrid working. The room you're in was only available because the other guy comes in five days a week. He managed to negotiate for his own office."

"Five days a week?" I said faintly.

I'd been thinking that if I couldn't switch offices, I'd aim to come in on Kawan Baik's "work from home" days. At least I could minimise exposure to him that way.

Typical of Charles Goh. It was like he purposely wanted to thwart me at every turn.

"It doesn't look too busy out there," said Arthur, peering out of his office. "You could use one of the empty pods if you need to focus? Or a meeting room?"

"Yeah," I said, without enthusiasm. "I could do that."

Arthur ran his hand over his hair, looking harassed. His air of good cheer had vanished.

I felt bad. I knew intellectually I wasn't responsible for Arthur's feelings, but my job *was* about making him—and by proxy, our clients—happy. The instinct was ingrained in me by now. Besides, there was no denying my life was easier when Arthur was in a good mood.

"I can't promise anything," he said, "but I'll speak to Farah."

Farah was the group managing partner. I'd only met her once—a British Asian woman with a cut-glass accent, silvering hair, and a mind like a steel trap. I didn't want her to know me as the new joiner who was complaining about having to hear people talk in the office.

"It's fine," I said. "I wanted to know what the options were. But it doesn't sound like it would be straightforward to relocate me."

"No," agreed Arthur. "Sorry. I can talk to Farah if you want, but I doubt she'll be able to do anything . . . No? If you're sure." He settled back, looking relieved. "Anything else I can do for you?"

I shook my head, suppressing a sigh. It had always been a long shot. Arthur never really helped solve my problems. That wasn't what our relationship was about. "I'll let you get on with your day."

"Wait," said Arthur. "Since you're here—you've met our PA, right? Victoria's very nice, she sits in the pod down by the lifts. Can you talk to her about sorting our travel to Hong Kong for the conference?"

I stared. "What conference?"

"The one we're speaking at," said Arthur. "I'm going to ring the clients we were going to see, set up some meetings."

I opened my mouth before closing it again.

We'd liaised closely with our old firm's Hong Kong office when making our original arrangements to travel out there. It was our Hong Kong colleagues who'd helped set up most of the planned meetings with clients. I had been the one who'd had to email them to explain about us moving to Swithin Watkins and apologise for pulling out.

Arthur had been cc'd on the emails. He hadn't said a word to indicate the trip was *still on*.

"I didn't think we were going anymore," I said. I'd planned to travel on from Hong Kong to Malaysia to visit my parents, but when I'd given notice at the old job, I'd postponed my flight to Malaysia and resigned myself to eating the associated charges.

"Yeah, I assumed we'd be calling it off. But when I mentioned our move to the chair of the conference, he said we could keep our speaking slots. They'll update our bios. I think it's a good idea. We need to get out there, let clients know where to find us."

I took a deep breath. "Were you thinking of a similar agenda? Will we be delivering training for clients?"

Arthur nodded. "We've got to set out our stall. It's an opportunity to show what we've got to offer. All the preparation's been done, it'd be a shame not to use it."

That was true. Except that the slides and speaking notes I'd spent weeks preparing had been left behind at our old firm.

"I don't have access to the materials anymore," I said hollowly. "If I'd known we were still going . . ."

Arthur had to be aware of the abyss that had opened in my soul, but he was dealing with this in a typically Arthur way, pretending he hadn't noticed the shimmering waves of rage rolling off me.

"Those materials belong to BRC anyway," he said. "But we should be able to reconstruct the contents pretty easily, I would have thought. I'll have a word with Farah about getting a trainee to help. We've got plenty of time. The conference is two weeks away. All right?"

He met my eyes, expectant.

It is not fucking all right, Arthur, what the fuck? Could you not have told me, oh I don't know, any time within the past four weeks? Did you have to land this on me on my first day at a new firm?

I swallowed that answer down.

It wasn't that bad, I told myself. Arthur was right: I should be able to re-create the slides from memory. The next two weeks should be quiet. Some of our long-standing clients had indicated they'd follow Arthur over to Swithin Watkins, but with a couple of exceptions, we weren't bringing over any active matters.

It wasn't that there wasn't enough time to prepare. It was the waste of all the preparation I'd done already that hurt.

At least I should get a trip to see my parents out of this. I'd have to see if I could book annual leave and reschedule the flight to Malaysia again.

"Sure," I said. "We'll make it work."

"Great," said Arthur, his eyes already drifting back to his inbox. "You're a star."

CHAPTER TWO

Charles

Came into the office early before my nine a.m. client call, so I could look over the file. Anne-Laure was travelling, so we were doing an old-fashioned phone call.

Should have been straightforward. She didn't want anything complicated, just an update on the lawsuit against them, so she could brief her CEO. I explained we were awaiting the claimant's reply to our last letter.

Anne-Laure: "Why the delay on their end?"

Didn't say, *I don't know, I don't have a psychic bond with the claimant that tells me what they're thinking*, despite the temptation. "They could be instructing external lawyers. We've been dealing with their in-house counsel so far."

Anne-Laure, hopefully: "Maybe they're planning not to progress the case? I have never found the claim convincing. How can we be responsible for their future profits? They have no way of knowing they would have earned all that money."

Always amazes me how clients sign contracts promising to take responsibility for all sorts of things, and then are surprised when they're held to it.

CG: "Unfortunately the contract is explicit that the claimant is entitled to loss of profits. And it's not a matter of dispute that you failed to meet the SLAs. We haven't seen their evidence on quantum yet, but from what they've said, £1 million doesn't seem an unrealistic estimate of their losses—"

Anne-Laure: "Oh shit!"

CG, taken aback: "Anne-Laure?" No response. "I think there's a problem with the line. Can you hear me?"

Line crackled. Removed the receiver from my ear to inspect it. Was wondering if I should end the call and try ringing again, when I heard a noise at the door. Looked up and saw Kriya Rajasekar.

Her hair had grown out since the last time I saw her. (When was the last time? Conference where she gave that talk on privilege, must be.) Her curls were halfway down her back now. Big gold hoops in her ears, tiny gold stud in her nose. She was wearing a black dress, long-sleeved and high-necked.

And fitted. Very fitted. Kriya had a lot to fit. In a good way.

Averted my gaze, hoping she hadn't caught me looking. Not appropriate to stare at a professional contact—competitor, in fact. But what was a competitor doing in my office?

My eyes, searching for somewhere safe to land, alighted upon my computer screen. There was a new email from my PA, sent at nine a.m. sharp. Subject line:

Don't forget your new office mate Kriya is starting today! :)

Gaped at screen.

I'd known I was going to have to start sharing my office. It had been framed as a request, but saying no had not been an option. (Checked with Farah, thinking she might have leverage as group manager. She said: "Thank your stars you've got an office at all, Charles. I practically had to threaten to go on strike to get it signed off. You don't want to risk reminding Facilities and HR they made a concession. They'd be all too happy to walk it back.")

No one had told me who was going to be sharing my office, though. I knew they were coming over with the Product Liability partner we'd poached from Brown, Rosenburg and Cushway. But I hadn't bothered asking their name. Hadn't thought it would make a difference.

Kriya looked at me, then went away.

Anne-Laure's voice said, from the phone: "Hello? Are you there?"

CG, after a pause: "Yes. I'm here. You cut out for a moment."

Anne-Laure: "Yes, sorry, it was not the line. There was a little bit of an incident. I was driving, and when you said we might have to pay £1 million . . . however, it is all fine. Nothing is damaged, and I have pulled over. Did you say they are suing us for £1 million? The contract says they are entitled to the money?"

Managed to complete the call without making Anne-Laure drive into a tree (again). Only casualty was my ego. This is what Farah means when she says I must improve my bedside manner with clients.

Kriya nowhere to be seen. She'd taken her things with her, instead of leaving them at the desk opposite me. Maybe she wasn't going to be sharing my office after all, notwithstanding PA's email. But it wasn't like my PA to get something like that wrong.

Found myself wishing Loretta had been there to interpret Kriya's reaction upon seeing me. Loretta also not great at bedside manner—must be genetic—but you can trust her to be forthright. Told her once, after that conference where I last saw Kriya:

"I think Kriya Rajasekar doesn't like me."

Hoping for reassurance: You must be imagining it, you barely know each other, etc.

Loretta: "You did correct her mistake. In the middle of her talk, in front of everybody."

CG: "She mixed up the case names. It was nothing personal. Probably a trainee put the slides together. Though she should have checked."

Loretta: "Nobody asked you to raise your hand while she was speaking and tell the whole audience. You could have mentioned it after she was done, one-on-one."

CG: "But then the audience might not have caught the error."

Loretta: "Well, there you have it. You were devoted to the truth, so that's what you get. If you were devoted to getting Hot Lawyer Who Hates You to like you, you should have made a different choice."

Loretta is a five on the Kinsey scale, or a two, or whatever number means she is primarily attracted to women but would make an exception for Gong Yoo. She stalked Kriya online early on in our acquaintance, and again whenever I happened to run into Kriya over the years. She found Kriya's Instagram account a few years back and made inappropriate noises, disgusting to hear from a cousin. (Loretta: "You have good taste, Charles, but no game. That is your tragedy.")

CG: "You think she does dislike me, then?"

Loretta: "Biu Gor"—only calls me this when she's taking the piss—"I have never met this woman in my life. I have no idea what she thinks of you."

Suspected I didn't need her insight just then, anyway. Kriya hadn't exactly looked delighted. She probably could have competed with Anne-Laure in a Most Horrified Expression contest.

Leaned back in my chair, pinching the bridge of my nose.

Luckily (or not), I didn't have the chance to brood, because Ma rang. Told her I was at work.

Ma: "You're always at work. If I don't call because you're at work, I'll never get to speak to my son."

Could see her point. "OK, but I've got a meeting in an hour's time. What's up?"

She hesitated. Showed she felt some shame, at least. "I've been talking to Ba."

Head started throbbing. Took off my glasses so I could massage my temples.

CG: "Why are you talking to Ba? I told you to block him."

Ma: "I don't know how to block him." (Keeps refusing my offers to walk her through it.) "Anyway, he's your father."

CG: "Let me deal with him, then. The whole point of divorcing him was so you don't have to worry about him anymore."

Drives me round the bend. They split almost twenty years ago. Ba didn't worry about Ma when he cut and ran, leaving her with a mountain of debt and a son to raise on her own. He fucked her over and all she says is, *I only had one husband. It's not so easy to stop worrying.*

Ma: "He's having problems with his business."

I was going to need fresh air for this conversation. Told Ma to hold on and grabbed my coat.

Went down via the stairs to the back entrance, opening on an alley. Smelled of cigarette smoke and piss as usual. Importantly, nobody there. Kicked a couple of cigarette butts away and leaned against the cold wall after checking it was free of pigeon shit.

CG: "Which business is this?" Ba always has some "business" cooking. "The instant coffee thing? Or is it some new wheeze?"

Ma: "No, but this was very promising. You know gwaat saa? 'Gua sha' in Mandarin. You can use it to scrape the face, the body, a lot of benefits. My friend had neck pain and the doctors only told her to take painkillers. She used gwaat saa, no more pain. Now it's becoming popular among the gwai lo, they're putting it on their TikTok. You haven't seen the videos? A lot on my phone."

Put Ma on speaker and Googled while she was talking.

Gua sha are flat stones you rub on yourself. Said to cure everything from acne to liver inflammation. Load of bollocks, obviously.

CG: "Don't people say 'gwaat saa' to mean 'can't make money'?"

If we'd been talking about anyone else, I might have suggested he should "gwaat lung." Get rich doing something shady. Except Ba's tried that. No one wants him going down that road again.

Thing is, Ba's probably not wrong there's money in gua sha. Ba being Ba, he's not going to be the one to make it.

CG: "Has Ba ever thought about just getting a normal job?"

Ma: "He set up the company already. A big Western company ordered a lot of units. But there was some issue—I'm not sure what happened—Ba said somebody bad-mouthed him to the company—anyway, the buyer pulled out. But Ba already confirmed the order with the factory. Now the factory is saying they will sue him if he doesn't pay. He's at his wits' end. You know, the oldest girl, what's her name—"

CG: "Teodora."

Ma: "She'll be finishing secondary school soon. How is he going to manage her education? He says she wants to study art. Art!"

CG: "Teo's interested in animation. She's looking at universities in the Philippines. I'll sort Teo, don't worry—"

Ma: "But it's not only her. It's everything. Ba's had such bad luck, these past few years. He's thinking of borrowing from loan sharks. If he does that and they come after him because he cannot pay, what is going to happen to Iza and the children?"

CG: "He's the one who decided to marry Iza and have another family. How is it your problem?"

Ma: "You always say this is not my problem. How can I not think about them? I know how Iza feels. And she has three children. I only had one, and you were so good, you didn't cause me any trouble."

Ma always knows where to stick the pins in. Felt guilty for being exasperated, which made me even more exasperated. Why is she like this? I've got nothing against Iza and I get along with the kids, but they're my half-siblings. Ma doesn't have to give a shit about them.

After what happened last time, I swore I was going to push back with Ba. Loretta says if I let him fend for himself, he might learn his lesson and stop sinking funds he doesn't have in pie-in-the-sky ventures.

But I've seen what happens when Ba fends for himself. If he didn't learn from three years in jail, what's me cutting him off going to do?

Ma: "We can't punish the children because Ba is not practical."

Maybe if she got a dog, she'd have less time for Ba. Opened inbox on phone, tapped out *MA DOG?* and emailed it to myself.

CG: "How much is he in the hole for?"

She told me.

Took me a moment to find my voice. "But that's *fifty thousand pounds.*"

Ma, tragically: "Now you see."

CG: "How do you spend that much on stones?! What are they made of, pure gold?"

Ma: "For the best ones, must be jade. Not cheap."

CG: "No kidding!"

Ma: "It wasn't just buying the gwaat saa. He invested in a website, hired a designer. Shopping is all online now, so that's very important. He hired some young people to advertise the product on their Facebook—"

CG: "Oh my God!"

Ma: "That's not even everything. If you knew it all, you would be so stressed. I knew I wouldn't be able to sleep tonight, after talking to Ba. That's why I called you."

CG: "Right. OK. I'll handle it. All right? There's no need to worry about it."

Ma: "But can you manage? It's so much money."

CG: "If I said I can cover it, I can cover it. What's the point of doing this job if I can't afford to fund whatever idiotic get-rich-quick scheme Ba comes up with?"

Ma: "You sound stressed out. Are you stressed out? I think you work too hard."

No arguing with that. What does Ma want me to do? I could quit my job and go mountaineering in the Andes, but then what would happen to her and Ba and Iza and the kids?

CG: "I'm fine. But can you do one thing for me?"

Ma: "What?"

CG: "Go and find . . ." Wasn't sure who to suggest, then remembered Loretta's younger brother was home on a "gap year," i.e., skiving and leeching off his parents. "Go and find Freeman—"

Ma: "Why Freeman?"

CG: "He plays so many video games, he should be good at tech. Get him to block Ba's number on your phone. OK? It's my birthday in five months' time, it can be your present to me. Bye, Ma."

Went back up the stairs to sixth floor. Felt like I was dragging a boulder behind me, weighing down every step.

I could come up with fifty grand. Would blow a hole in my savings, such as they are. Cleaned them out when I bought the flat from the landlord a few years ago, even with the massive mortgage I took out. Could have got somewhere cheaper if I'd moved farther out, but I was used to the flat by then—had been renting it for years.

Throat felt tight. Felt like I'd been running all my life and looked up to find myself in the same bloody place. No progress, no possibility of change. Just me doing the same thing over and over again, hoping for a different outcome each time.

Feeling was familiar. Get it whenever I have to deal with Ba.

He doesn't contact me directly, even though I don't have him blocked. He spends all day long online, gambling and getting scammed by dodgy Facebook accounts with profile photos of attractive young women. He could WhatsApp me, email, whatever. But he's never the one to break the news about his latest crisis. Last time, it was Iza.

She didn't ask for money. They don't have to. They know I'll understand why they've got in touch.

Good old Charles. Reliable as the Bank of England.

Relief to get back to my desk, to the deluge of new emails in my inbox. Anne-Laure wanted a note on why I thought the claimant was entitled to £1 million in damages. Already did this for them—twenty-seven pages of closely argued analysis— but she wanted a two-hundred-word summary she could ping on to the Board.

And there were directions from the court on the DLP case, setting dates for the hearing. Farah had forwarded a request from the client for an urgent meeting to discuss next steps.

It was looking like I'd be staying late at the office. Needed to text Loretta, or she'd wait for me to have dinner and probably forget to eat.

Fumbled on desk for my phone. A noise from the other side of the room made me look up.

The noise was the chair at the desk opposite me creaking. Because Kriya was sitting in it.

She must have been there when I came back from my call with Ma. And I hadn't acknowledged her.

It had been at least ten minutes since I'd got back. We'd been sitting in silence the whole time.

If Kriya hadn't disliked me before, she definitely disliked me now. Even I knew blanking people was commonly considered impolite. You were supposed to say hi to them. Especially if they were your new colleague you were sharing an office with.

But it would be weird to greet her now. Too late. Wasn't it?

Sneaked a glance across the room. Kriya was staring at her screen. Maybe she hadn't noticed?

CHAPTER THREE

Kriya

Charles wasn't at his desk when I got back to what, like it or not, was now my office.

I could hot desk in the open plan area, as Arthur had suggested, but then I wouldn't have such luxuries as shelves for my client files, or a permanent noticeboard, or a drawer to keep spare pens and Post-it notes in. Even sharing with Kawan Baik was better than that.

I sighed, slung my coat over the back of my chair, put down my bag, and plugged in my new laptop. The computer was booting up when I heard a step behind me.

Charles stalked past and sat down at his desk. He did not say hello, or look at me. I might as well not have been there.

To be fair, I hadn't said hello to him either, when I'd come by earlier. But he'd been in the middle of a call. If you thought about it, it had been *more* polite not to interrupt him.

In any case, we were colleagues now, and we were going to be sharing an office. I had to put this weird whatever you wanted to call it—antipathy, tension, evil fate binding us together— behind me. Forget the fact that something bad happened every time I bumped into Charles Goh, whether it was me bombing my training contract interview, screwing up my conference talk, or dousing my firm-provided laptop with sparkling water. (This last had happened at the joint strategy meeting we'd attended as junior lawyers, moments before Kawan Baik had chucked his coffee over my lap, supposedly by accident.)

I had to let it go. I was never going to be good friends with Charles Goh, notwithstanding my nickname for him. But there was no reason why we couldn't have a civil working relationship.

I was opening my mouth to say something friendly when I caught Charles sneaking a look at me out of the corner of his eye.

What was *that* about? I'd thought he hadn't noticed me and that was why he hadn't said anything on coming into the office. But had he blanked me on purpose? Was that why he was checking for my reaction now? Was this all some kind of mind game?

If that was the case, Charles was about to find out it wasn't easy to intimidate Kriya Rajasekar. Growing up in Ipoh had given me a working understanding of spoken Cantonese, a reliable craving for mooncakes at Mid-Autumn and tang yuan at Winter Solstice, and a skin thicker than a rhinoceros hide. A light spot of workplace bullying was nothing compared to the crap I'd got back at primary school, as a chubby, dark-skinned Indian girl.

I said, "I don't know if you remember me. My name's Kriya." I smiled, bright and steely. "We worked together on the sugar labelling JR?"

That was the case for which we'd had the strategy meeting years ago, where I had ruined my firm laptop and Charles had ruined my dress. I'd been an NQ: newly qualified as a solicitor, overawed by the fact I was being allowed to talk to clients in my first two weeks on the job.

Charles had qualified a couple of years earlier than me, according to his LinkedIn, so the meeting was probably less significant to him. It was entirely possible he had no memory of it, or me.

Charles twitched like he'd been zapped by static. "Yes. I know."

I let a few seconds pass, but that seemed to be all he had to say.

I said, determinedly normal, "You guys were acting for G&O, right? Do you still do work for them?"

"I believe the Food Law team do," said Charles. "It was Mackintosh Cereals who were your client."

I wasn't sure if that was meant to be a question. "Yes?"

His eyes flicked to me and back to his monitor. I could practically hear his mind whirring.

Was Charles Goh actually a robot? It would explain a lot about his approach to social interactions.

"I'm sorry about the coffee," he said stiffly. "I spilled some on you at the first meeting. You might not remember."

"I remember," I said.

Silence descended.

Charles broke it. "Hopefully that wasn't the reason why you stopped appearing at the strategy meetings."

Was that a joke? Who knew Kawan Baik had a sense of humour?

"Oh no," I said. "The client decided they didn't want to pay for me to attend the meetings. I was on the case all the way through, though. For all the good it did Mackintosh."

I could joke about it, because we'd won the case. The court had struck down the regulations our clients had challenged. Unfortunately, judicial reviews being what they were, the government had simply turned around, tweaked the regulations to nullify any further challenge, and passed them regardless.

"Bought them time," said Charles.

For a while, neither of us said anything. Charles tapped

away at his keyboard, his forehead furrowed in concentration. I set up my Westlaw login, following the instructions from IT. I was going to need it to re-create the slides for the client training sessions I'd be helping to deliver in Hong Kong in two weeks' time.

I jumped when Charles spoke.

"It was a good witness statement," he said.

"What?"

"The one Mackintosh filed in the JR," said Charles. "It was well drafted."

"I drafted that! My first ever witness statement." I grinned. "I'm surprised you remember it. It's been, what, eight years?"

"The judge quoted it extensively in her judgment," said Charles, and after that he said nothing more.

CHAPTER FOUR

Charles

W*hy did I* mention the Mackintosh witness statement? Don't have to ask Loretta to know Kriya thought it was weird I remembered it. It is objectively weird.

Considered explaining I have a photographic memory, but decided that would only make me sound insufferable. Anyway, don't remember every witness statement I've read. That one stuck out to me because I knew Kriya must have been involved in drafting it.

Office smells different after she's been in it. Hard to pin down the scent. Not floral. More bracing. Citrus? Lemongrass?

It's not unpleasant.

CHAPTER FIVE

Kriya

Rosalind Wijanarko of Sanson followed me and Arthur when we moved to Swithin Watkins, but we had known she would. Rosalind was the one client I would have retained if I had refused to move with Arthur.

Rosalind was from a fabulously wealthy family, in accordance with the usual stereotypes about Chinese Indonesians. She could have afforded her Chelsea flat, her black cab habit, and her extensive collection of designer fashion even if she never did a day's work.

With that kind of family money, I would happily have done my degree in obscure genres of wayang kulit and devoted the rest of my life to perfecting my kaya recipe. But Rosalind was driven by different demons. She worked maniacally hard as a senior compliance manager at Sanson, a multinational conglomerate that produced everything from highlighter pens to industrial laminates. She treated me as a combination of typist, oracle, favourite niece, therapist, tax accountant, and spiritual confessor.

Besides listening to her dating woes, the main thing I'd done for Rosalind was draft a compliance protocol that she was trying to roll out across her company. Eight months on, it hadn't been implemented yet. Rosalind was too busy arguing with her Board, as well as the seventy markets in which San-son operated, most of which didn't see why they should give a flying fuck about regulatory requirements in far-off Europe.

She relied heavily on me for support, which mostly con-sisted of me making soothing noises and drafting emails for her to send on to obstructive internal stakeholders. It wasn't exactly the sort of work I'd envisioned doing when I was study-ing for my law degree, but Rosalind seemed to find it helpful. We spoke at least twice a week—sometimes twice a day, if her stakeholders were being particularly difficult.

She gave me a brief break after the firm move. But on the Wednesday of my second week at Swithin Watkins, Rosalind rang, raging about "those bastards in Malta."

"I need you to write me an email citing chapter and verse of the legislation, so I can send it to that cow over there and copy her GM. You tell her—"

"Hold on. Give me a second." As I was putting Rosalind on speaker so I could type, I caught a twitch of the lips from Charles.

Shit. I wasn't used to having a roommate anymore. I couldn't have long conference calls with Rosalind on speaker while poor Kawan Baik was trying to work.

"Wait," I told Rosalind. I ducked under the desk to fumble in my bag for my headset.

Rosalind kept talking, ranting about the Maltese Head of Legal and her various deficiencies of personality, intellect, and appearance.

"Rosalind," I hissed. "You can't use that language. I share an office now!"

"Oh? With who?"

"With, um—" Where had I put that damn headset? It had to be in my bag somewhere, underneath the layers of crap it turned out I'd been carrying around. How many packets of tis-sues did one person need? "With, you know, another lawyer."

"Male or female?"

"Why does it matter?" My fingers closed around the plastic band of my headset. I yanked it out of the bag, scattering forgotten receipts and Boots vouchers all over the floor.

Charles was sat straight-backed at his desk, pretending to be engrossed in his screen.

"It's a bloke, is it?" said Rosalind knowingly. "Is he attractive?"

"He can *hear you*," I said.

"Ask him to give me his number if he's between the ages of twenty-five and sixty-five," said Rosalind, undeterred. "I haven't dated a lawyer in a while. He can Google me to see what I look like, I'm on LinkedIn. My cousin took the photo. She did Photoshop it, but you can tell him I got fillers after the shot was taken, so it's 99 percent accurate."

We were both laughing by now. Even Charles was grinning, his ears pink.

I plugged in my headset. "Thanks for that. Turning to the email . . ."

I ended up talking to Rosalind for an hour and getting a new instruction from her: I was to get our US colleagues to provide a note of advice, to help persuade her stakeholders over the pond that the protocol did not conflict with the laws of their jurisdiction.

I'd have to be careful telling Arthur about it. He got dog-in-the-mangerish about new instructions, even for work he wasn't remotely qualified to undertake. But so long as I could figure out how to handle Arthur, being able to pass on business to my new colleagues at Swithin Watkins was a good thing. It would help establish me as a desirable addition to the firm.

"Sorry about that," I said to Charles, taking my headset off. "Rosalind's incorrigible."

"Long-standing client, I take it."

"Yeah. She's a real character. I apologise in advance for all the boundary-crossing conversations you'll be overhearing." I hesitated. "Actually, is there somewhere I can go to take her calls? Rosalind can go on for a bit. I don't want to disturb you."

Charles reflected. "There are meeting booths, but they're always in demand. I wouldn't bother. The point of having an office is so you don't have to worry about taking calls."

"It was your office first, though."

"And now it's yours as well," said Charles. "I've got noise-cancelling headphones. I can put them on if I need to."

"OK. Thanks. Just let me know if it gets too much," I said. "I promise I won't take it the wrong way."

Charles smiled, shaking his head. The smile made him look totally different from his usual forbidding self—sweet, a little goofy, a little vulnerable.

Kawan Baik didn't seem so bad. Maybe this office-sharing business was going to work out.

I was returning to my emails when Farah came into the office.

"Hello, Kriya, how are you? Settling in? Good." She looked over at Charles. "Charles, what's the rest of the day looking like for you? From, say, two p.m.?"

Charles checked his computer screen. "Relatively free now Marcus has cancelled our three o'clock. I've got that note for DLP to finalise, but the client's said tomorrow would be fine. Why?"

"I've got a favour to ask." Farah paused. "Kriya, would you mind closing the door?"

I glanced from her to Charles. "Should I go out?"

"No, stay. I don't want gossip spreading, that's all." Farah leaned back against a filing cabinet, sighing. Her shoulders slumped.

This was a new side to the unflappable Farah. Even Charles, who presumably knew her well, looked concerned.

"What's happened?" he said.

"You know our work experience programme—oh, Kriya won't know about this." Farah turned to me. "The firm runs an annual work experience programme for students from under-represented backgrounds who are interested in law. First from the family to attend university, low SES and so on. Four weeks, they rotate around a couple of practice areas, they're paired with a trainee, go to talks—Charles has kindly delivered a few in his time. The feedback is very good and we've had a number of excellent trainees come to us through the programme."

"Sounds like a great initiative," I said.

"We have a new cohort starting today," said Farah. "Fifteen students, all very promising. There was also an induction this morning for new canteen staff. The catering company did a recruitment drive recently, and there were fifteen new joiners."

There was a silence as Charles and I joined the dots.

"Oh my God!" Charles coughed. "I mean . . ."

"Oh, I said much worse when I heard what had happened," said Farah. "Apparently they had all been put in aprons and caps before the confusion was found out. I've got our DEI manager, Amy, lying flat on the floor of my office. She may never get up again, and she really is very good, you know.

"We must do something to remedy the situation before it all goes on RollOnFriday. And that," said Farah, "is where you come in. Everyone has been put back in the right place. The work experience students are doing a moot this afternoon, but the partner who was going to be the judge has dropped out—wretched man. Can you step in? I'll get Amy to peel herself off the floor to brief you, but there isn't much to it. You merely have to listen and be encouraging. You won't have to assess their performance, the Graduate Recruitment lot will do that."

"Of course," said Charles.

"Great." Farah went on, a little too casually, "We've laid on a nice dinner for them on fourteenth floor after the moot. Once that's over, I want you to take them to the wine bar across the street and charm them. I'll give you a firm credit card to put behind the bar and we'll do our best to blot out their memories of the morning. Is that all right?"

"Oh," said Charles, looking like a stuffed fish. "I, um, I might have something on this evening. Let me check my diary."

"Charles."

"But I'm not *good* at charming people," Charles protested.

"You won't have to do anything to charm them. They're university students and you will be paying for their drinks. You can wrap things up by half nine, we don't want them to bankrupt the firm."

"But—"

"We have talked about the importance of soft skills," said Farah. "Your technical skills can't be faulted, but that's not enough in a lawyer of your seniority. Isn't that right, Kriya?"

I hesitated. If I said yes, wouldn't that be an implied criticism of Charles? It didn't seem fair to gang up on him with Farah.

Looking at his horrified face, I felt a surge of pity. I already knew Charles had no problem pulling late nights. Farah could have asked him to sacrifice his evening to the production of an advice note, or to a call with an overseas client, and he would have obliged without a murmur. But it was clear he couldn't imagine anything worse than being trapped in a wine bar with fifteen university students.

"I can do it," I said.

They stared at me.

Farah recovered first. "Would you? Are you sure?"

"Yeah. I used to do a lot of outreach at my old firm," I said. "Gave talks at schools, manned our stall at university careers fairs, that sort of thing."

"You're a star. That would be fabulous."

"You don't need to," said Charles, looking stricken. "I don't really—I mean, my evening plans can be rearranged."

"It's fine," I said. "I'm not doing anything else this evening. You can go ahead with your plans."

Charles made a show of looking at his phone. "Looks like I got it wrong. It was tomorrow I was thinking of. This evening is free."

"Perfect! You can both go," said Farah. "Two lawyers to fifteen students is a much better ratio. Thank you so much for volunteering, Kriya. I'll go and tell Amy. She'll email you the details of the moot, Charles, and perhaps you can let Kriya know when you're all done and ready to move across the road. You should know," she said gravely, "that you are making one DEI manager very happy."

She swept out of the room, leaving us gaping after her.

"Is she always like this?" I said.

Charles looked resigned. "Pretty much. I'm sorry, I didn't mean for you to lose your evening. I'm not very keen on networking events. As I'm sure you are astonished to hear."

There was something endearing about how terrified he was at the prospect of having drinks with a bunch of twenty-year-olds. I'd always liked men who weren't afraid of showing their emotions. That was one of the things I'd liked most about Tom, his open-heartedness.

Well. That hadn't stopped Tom from sticking the knife in *my* heart.

At least I didn't have to worry about that with Charles. I had thought him good-looking, once upon a time, but that was before he'd become Kawan Baik.

But the better I was getting to know Kawan Baik, the more I found myself liking the man beneath the nemesis. It had been nice of him to try to claw back my evening for me.

"It's fine," I said. "It'll be fun. You'll see."

CHAPTER SIX

Charles

Moot went off without a hitch. There were a couple of decent arguments run, one or two good speakers, and one genuine entertainer among the cohort. Might not make a lawyer, but I wouldn't be surprised to see him in a film some years down the line.

Could have stayed on for dinner, but I've had enough dinners at the firm's expense. Crept away to check my emails instead, until the Graduate Recruitment lady messaged that the students were done with dinner. It was time for Kriya and me to do our duty as hosts.

It was awkward to start out with—contrary to Kriya's assurances, but entirely consistent with my expectations. Stood staring at the university students while they stared back at us. After a while, one of the students said:

"So . . . do you guys do any human rights law?"

CG: "No. It rarely comes up in my practice."

Student: "Oh. Right."

She looked a bit squashed. Didn't mean to squash her. Remembered her from the moot: Razia, British Bangladeshi, first girl in her family to go to university. Round, earnest face under a black headscarf. Reminded me a little of my oldest half-sister, though Teo's younger.

CG: "I have done a case where we sought to rely on the EU Charter freedom to conduct a business, but it didn't take us very far. The limitations on the right are such that—"

Kriya: "But you do a lot of pro bono work, right, Charles? Like that CICA case you've got on." To the students: "That's a government scheme that allows victims of violent crime to seek compensation. Charles has got a tribunal hearing—is it next month? He's representing a woman who was trafficked."

CG: "Yes. But that's a statutory scheme. It's got nothing to do with the Human Rights Act."

Razia, perking up: "It sounds interesting. What does CICA stand for?"

Turned out she was doing her dissertation on how the Human Rights Act 1998 has shaped litigation. Interesting topic. When I'd explained the Criminal Injuries Compensation Act to her satisfaction, we went on to discuss the deployment of rights-based arguments by corporates.

Evening was significantly less painful than expected. Was surprised when I glanced at my watch and saw it was past nine. Hadn't noticed the time passing. Never happened at a social event before.

The difference, I concluded, was Kriya, even though she'd moved away to mingle. Her presence seemed to make the whole thing easier. Couldn't tell how she did it.

Watched her surreptitiously, trying to figure it out. She talked a lot, but not too much. Asked questions. Looked people in the eye while listening. Smiled and laughed at the right times.

I went through a phase of trying to make eye contact, early in my career. Resulted in supervisor telling me people found me "a bit intense." Allowing for softening effect of British corporate speak, what that meant was I was coming off like a serial killer.

Probably helped that Kriya was attractive. People are nicer to attractive women. I read an article about it, there are studies.

Was mulling on this when Razia said:

"Can I ask you a question? It's a bit personal."

CG: "Yes?"

Razia: "To be honest, I feel like some of the lawyers I spoke to today, they were fronting when they talked about enjoying their work. But you seem to really like your job. Like, genuinely."

CG: "I suppose so. It can be demanding, but it's interesting work. And it's well paid."

Razia: "You mentioned Swithin Watkins does a lot of pro bono and corporate social responsibility stuff. That's great, but . . . at the end of the day, your clients are, well, they're big companies, right?"

CG: "We represent a few private individuals, but yes, they are in a minority among our fee-paying clients."

Can't be helped. Most human beings can't afford our fees.

Razia: "I was looking through the list of clients on your website. And it was all these businesses in, like, oil and gas, and tobacco, and finance, and tech. Industries that arguably don't do much for society, that are, you know, exploitative. Have you ever wondered if—I mean, do you ever worry about that?"

So taken aback I stood there blinking. Not the sort of thing anyone would say out loud at Swithin Watkins.

Of course, Razia not employed by Swithin Watkins. Not learned the norms.

Rest of the group shooting looks at one another, like school kids worried about getting a telling off.

Razia, nervously: "I'm not trying to catch you out. It's just . . . with my family circumstances, I'm going to have to prioritise financial security when I'm looking for a job. Which means going into one of those industries, or something related. I don't know how I feel about that."

CG: "Yes. I was . . . similarly placed. It sounds like you've thought more deeply about these issues than I did, at your age."

Hesitated. Not used to talking about this sort of thing. At work, focus is on how to do the job, not why one does it.

Anything I said risked sounding false, given my position. Self-justifying. But I felt she deserved a real answer.

CG: "It must be right that everyone is entitled to legal representation. That is a fundamental right. One could question whether it is correct for corporations to be afforded that right. But that is not a decision for you and me. That is a decision of Parliament and the courts. We live in a democracy. We have the good fortune to be able to criticise those decisions freely, to challenge and test them. But the best way to test a legal principle is to apply it to a set of facts. You saw that today, at the moot. What you and I can do, as lawyers . . ."

Next part was a little embarrassing to say out loud.

But Razia and the other students' eyes were fixed on me, as though what I said might hold the key to the secret of their lives. Perhaps it did.

CG: "What we can do is the best we can. In acting for our clients, in discharging our duties to the court, we serve the rule of law. Which means no dictators." Thought of everyone back home. Ma doesn't want to leave Hong Kong—she says she's too old to make a new start in a foreign country—but you can see why people do. "It means no one's above the law. We contribute to that, in a small way."

Palms were damp. Something quite mortifying about admitting one believes in one's work as a corporate lawyer. It's far less exposing to pretend one's simply doing it for the money.

Behind me, Kriya said: "That's a good argument."

I started. Might not have been quite as sincere if I'd known Kriya was listening. Had a feeling she didn't have a high tolerance for corporate apologism.

There was a gleam in her eyes, as though she was tempted to argue the case for the opposition. But all she said was:

"We've got to finish up here. They've got another booking coming in."

Ought to have been relieved. Had an eight a.m. with an Australian client the next day. But the sensation I felt—so unexpected it took me a moment to identify it—was disappointment.

I'd hardly got to talk to Kriya all evening. True, I'd see her in the office, but that wasn't the same.

Heard myself saying:

"Do you want to go on to Cittie of Yorke for a drink?"

Kriya looked surprised. Not nearly as surprised as me. I've spent most of my career trying to avoid going to the Cittie of Yorke. Passed too many endless evenings there as a law student and trainee, until I worked out I could decline the invites.

Kriya: "Sure, let's go." Glanced around the group. "Anyone else want to come?"

Not what I'd intended. Most of them said they'd come along, vexingly. (Didn't they have essays to write? Exams to prepare for?)

But Razia said: "I'm heading home. Thanks so much."

She was looking at Kriya, despite muggins having laid himself open to ridicule, holding forth on the rule of law. Kriya smiled back at her.

My resentment receded. Could see Razia's point of view, to be fair. I'd gaze at Kriya as goopily as she was doing, hit with a smile like that.

Razia, shyly: "I wanted to say, it's really meaningful to see Asian people in senior positions in law. Thanks for answering my questions."

This time she was talking to me, too.

CG: "It was my pleasure."

CHAPTER SEVEN

Kriya

The work experience students made me feel about a million years old. They reminded me of what I'd been at their age. Ignorant and insecure, but also idealistic, full of hope and promise.

Had I made good on that promise? Best not to ask. I could look after myself and my parents, and I didn't have to do anything more strenuous than sit at a desk to do it. My Thaatha would have thought I'd got it made. He'd supported seven children on a rubber tapper's wages. Who was I to complain?

Only around half of the programme cohort ended up coming with me and Charles to the pub. They clumped together, chatting about coursework, tutors, and friend drama—nothing we aged senior associates could comment on.

I'd been on all evening and I didn't mind taking the move as an excuse to relax, too. I cast up next to the bar with Charles, a little way away from the rest of the group.

"I liked what you said to Razia, about how our work contributes to the rule of law," I said. "I've never seen it in that light before."

Charles blushed right up to his hairline. "Oh, I don't know. It was a bit earnest."

"There's nothing wrong with being earnest."

"No. I suppose not."

I looked down at my G&T. Charles had got both our drinks; he was having a beer.

"I know what you mean, though," I said. "I think it's easier to be cynical about what we do. It's that or trotting out the approved corporate lines, right?" I shook my head, rueful. "You know, Razia asked me what I was working on and I told her about this corporate acquisition we're supporting. I said, 'It's very interesting.' Which, if I'd said that to anyone in the firm, they would have nodded along, right? Razia looked at me, astonished, and said, '*Really?*'"

Charles joined in the laugh with me. He had a nice laugh.

"She's going to have to improve her poker face if she wants a job in the City," I said.

Charles nodded. "To be fair, it does sound interesting, the matter you're working on."

"It is," I said judiciously, "compared to some of my other matters. But I don't think I've got your passion for the work."

Charles blinked, as though taken aback at being accused of being passionate about anything. "I don't know if I would call it that."

"But you're really interested in what you do, right?" I looked at him wistfully. I'd drunk enough to sand off the rough edges of the world. I felt loose-jointed, relaxed. "I don't know that I have that. I applied for a training contract because I needed a stable job that would pay me well and meant I could stay in the UK. I like some things about it—the intellectual challenge, and some of my clients, like Rosalind. But there are a lot of things I could do without."

Charles looked thoughtful. "What else would you have done? If money and the rest weren't a consideration."

He'd abandoned his jacket and pushed up his sleeves. My eyes skipped from his forearms to the line of his collarbone, visible through the open collar of his shirt. I swallowed and looked away.

"I would have liked to do something that was more about helping people," I said. "I pick up pro bono work when I can, but it's hard to juggle with the billable stuff."

Plus, Arthur got shirty if I filled up my time with too much do-gooding. But I didn't mention that, out of an obscure sense of loyalty.

"What would you do, if you could do anything else?" I said.

"Well . . ." Charles hesitated.

Was he about to reveal dreams of running away to the circus? Maybe he secretly yearned to be a Zumba instructor, or an oncologist?

"I did a seat in Tax Law as a trainee," he said. "It might have been interesting to specialise in that. But there were no jobs when I qualified, and I found Litigation equally stimulating."

I laughed despite myself.

Charles ran a hand through his hair, sheepish. "Not a very imaginative answer, I know."

"No, it's good," I said. "There are so many miserable lawyers. It's refreshing to meet someone who loves it. What do you do outside of work?"

"I, uh, I go to the gym."

I waited, until Charles's expression turned from sheepish to hangdog. I realised he didn't have anything else to add.

"That's cool," I said encouragingly. "I'd like to get back into working out. I was doing pretty well for a while, but I fell off the wagon." When Tom dumped me and my life went down the toilet. But that was too much to disclose, less than two weeks into sharing an office.

"Do you have any hobbies?" said Charles.

"Hmm, they mostly revolve around food." I laughed. "I like cooking, baking, trying out new restaurants with friends. I was experimenting with making kaya from scratch for a while, doing different flavours, like salted caramel and coffee—oh, kaya's this spread we have in Malaysia. It's made from coconut milk and eggs."

"I know kaya," said Charles. "My dad's from Malaysia."

My eyes widened. "Really? I'm from Malaysia. Where's your dad from? My parents are in Ipoh."

"Kuala Lumpur. He moved to Hong Kong before I was born, but I'm familiar with the cuisine," said Charles. "My dad used to take me to the JW Marriott in Hong Kong for nasi lemak."

I opened my mouth to remark on going to a five-star hotel to eat *nasi lemak*—that humblest and most everyday of Malaysian meals—then closed it. It was hardly a revelation that Charles came from money. His public school accent gave that away. I didn't want to disrupt the nice conversation we were having, if it turned out he was sensitive about it.

"I think Arthur and I are staying at the JW Marriott," I said instead. "You know we're going to Hong Kong for a conference next week? I didn't realise you were from there, or I would have asked for food recommendations."

Up till now, Charles hadn't struck me as being particularly Asian. I'd pegged him as being British-born and fairly assimilated. But now he straightened up, a new light coming into his eyes.

"You should go to Yat Lok and have roast goose and lai fun, that's noodles. Dim sum, of course—Luk Yu is not bad, that's also in Central. If you like milk tea, Lan Fong Yuen is famous. It's a cha chaan teng. You could have French toast, or a pork chop bun, those are classics. Though it's probably not worth waiting, if there's a queue."

"Hold on. Give me a second," I said, laughing. "I need to take notes. What was the first one, Yat . . . ?"

"'Y,' 'A,' 'T' . . . If you give me your phone, I can type it out for you."

His fingers brushed mine as I passed him the phone. There was a jump in my stomach, fierce and unexpected.

I whipped away my hand like I'd been scalded, cheeks warming. Was I really so touch-starved that any encounter with a man in a remotely appropriate age range would get me going?

Admittedly, it had been six months since I'd had a boyfriend, and a year since I'd seen him in person. But I hadn't noticed missing sex. I'd been too busy missing my life with Tom, the future I'd thought we were going to have together.

At least Charles didn't seem to have clocked anything. He was scowling down at my phone as though it had stolen a price-less family heirloom from him.

After a week and a half of sitting opposite Charles while he worked, I knew this was the default expression his face assumed when he was concentrating. I was even starting to find it charming.

"You miss Hong Kong, huh," I said.

"The food," said Charles, with feeling.

"Would you ever go back? Is your dad still there?"

Charles handed my phone back to me. This time we didn't touch, to my relief.

Though if I were being honest with myself, that relief had a distinct undertone of disappointment to it.

I had to get back on the dating apps. Clearly my body was waking up again, after six months of being too sad to have a libido. It was a natural development, the blurring effect of the passage of time. Nothing to do with Charles himself. I probably would have responded like that to being touched by any reasonably attractive man.

"Most of my family lives there, yes," Charles was saying. "I might go back some day. I came over here when I was eleven, for school, so it's comfortable. But my mum's back in Hong Kong, and she's getting older."

"Yeah," I said. "I know what you mean."

Though it wasn't likely I'd ever go home, much as I worried about my parents. Amma and Appa would have a fit. I worked so hard to get a good degree and a good job in UK, what for did I want to go back to Malaysia? So I could have estate agents turn me down for being Indian when I wanted to rent a place? So I could be passed over for promotions at work, in favour of my Malay (if government) or Chinese (if private sector) colleagues?

Hong Kong had its own problems, but any issues Charles had with Hong Kong were going to be very different from my animus against Malaysia. Or, more accurately, Malaysia's animus against me.

Charles's eyes flicked to a point above my shoulder. One of the students had come up to us.

"We're going to head off, but thanks for speaking to us. It was really helpful," she said. "Um, we put our drinks on the tab. What do we owe you?"

"Nothing. Don't worry about it," I said. "Are you guys all right to get home? OK. Enjoy the rest of your time with the firm. We'll try to make it to the closing drinks."

When we'd waved them off, I turned to Charles. "Can I have the firm credit card? They needed a card behind the bar to set up a tab, so I gave them mine. The bill comes to around £180."

I hadn't expected this to be controversial, but Charles hesitated.

"Farah said it was just for the wine bar. I don't think she meant for the firm to cover us if we went on anywhere else."

"Oh. OK." I supposed it was consistent that Kawan Baik should be scrupulous about the firm's budget. It fit with everything I'd seen of him so far—the surprising idealism about his work, the tendency towards rigidity. "Fair enough. Shall we split it, then?"

Charles wouldn't meet my eyes. A bad feeling unfolded in the pit of my stomach—a harbinger of disappointment.

"I assumed everyone was going to cover their own drinks," he said.

Charles had to be on at least £150,000 a year, same as me, not including bonuses. He was probably on more, given he'd been with the firm for longer and he was a man. He was single, with no dependents; he'd gone to boarding school; and his father used to take him to the JW Marriott for nasi lemak. Ninety pounds was nothing to him. Small change.

I was the one who'd told everyone we'd cover their drinks, I reminded myself. I hadn't given Charles the chance to disagree.

But it was the accepted convention at social occasions like these that the most senior person paid. Partners and senior associates covered the drinks of trainees, who were on what were, by any measure, healthy salaries. The rule had to apply all the more to university students from traditionally underrepresented backgrounds.

To be fair, I could afford to drop £180 on everyone's drinks. It wasn't about the money.

"OK," I said. "I misunderstood. I'll cover it."

Charles looked wretched. "Sorry."

I half expected him to row it back, or offer to cover some of the bill, even if he wasn't up for splitting it fifty-fifty. But he didn't.

"No worries," I said.

There was no reason to feel upset about it. I'd volunteered us to pay the bill. Charles didn't want to. That was his prerogative. Just because he was rich didn't mean he couldn't be stingy. That was how rich people hung on to their money, by refusing to share it with anyone else.

But I'd been starting to *like* Charles.

I thought wistfully of Tom. Money had never been an issue with him. Sure, I'd paid for both of us most of the time, when we ate out and went travelling. But then, he'd earned a fraction of what I did. It simply hadn't mattered.

Or so I'd thought. When Tom moved to California, it had been for a six-figure salary—a huge step up for him. Maybe he'd no longer wanted me, once he was earning that kind of money himself.

Wow, thanks, brain. That was super helpful.

"I'll go settle up," I said.

At least Kawan Baik and I were going to have a break from each other after this evening. I worked from home Thursdays and Fridays, and I was flying to Hong Kong on Sunday. I was going to be away for two weeks: four days in Hong Kong, then the rest of the time on leave in Malaysia.

I'd be over this by the time I saw Charles again, in a better place to make nice. I was going to be sharing an office with him for the foreseeable future, after all. I needed to keep things civil.

I'd tried to keep my tone pleasant, but something of my real feelings must have filtered through. Charles's face fell.

I felt bad for him, despite my irritation. Poor Kawan Baik. It was like he couldn't even help himself.

"Good night, Charles," I said, more gently.

"Good night," he said.

CHAPTER EIGHT

Charles

Loretta had made noodles for dinner when I got home from work. A week had passed since my ill-starred drinks with Kriya at the Cittie of Yorke.

Loretta was on a healthy eating kick, so she'd left out the seasoning packet and added cabbage. Soup tasted like water, but not as good. Poured out most of the soup while she wasn't looking.

Ate the remainder on the sofa next to her, watching some anime thing on the telly. Cabbage was decidedly al dente.

Loretta angsting about her wedding, as per usual.

CG, crunching: "Why do you need to get married anyway?"

Loretta, waspish: "I don't know, Charles, why do straight people get married?"

CG: "Because of societal convention. Their parents would get upset if they didn't. But your parents are upset anyway, so why bother?"

Good thing I'd got rid of the soup. Loretta hit me on the arm, which would have resulted in a spill if there had been any liquid left in the bowl.

Loretta: "I know you're an ally, but sometimes you talk like a dickhead." Shook her hand vigorously. "Ow! Why's your arm so hard?"

CG, swallowing a noodle: "I've switched up my arm workouts. I do cable lateral raises, four sets of twelve to fifteen reps, and a bicep superset of three sets of six to twelve reps EZ bar preacher curls, with standing dumbbell hammer curls at a weight I can normally do ten reps at, but for—"

Loretta: "It was a rhetorical question, Charles. Anyway, you've forgotten Hayley needs a visa."

Loretta's fiancée is American. They met on some obscure gay social networking site called Tumblr.

CG: "She's transferring to the London office of her company, isn't she? Aren't they sorting the visa?"

Loretta: "Have you seen the news about immigration policy recently? We need a backup." She dropped her head back on the sofa, letting out a gusty sigh. "We should have eloped."

CG: "Yes."

Loretta: "It's too late now. Only two weeks to go. We've spent all this money on the wedding, I owe you rent—"

CG: "I told you, don't worry about it."

Though I could have done with the rent, in all honesty. Mind went back to that exchange with Kriya over the bill, for the eighty-second time since that evening at Cittie of Yorke. Cringed down to my soul at the memory, again.

Should have thought of the fact we'd be expected to cover the students' drinks. Didn't occur to me until Kriya said it, and then was too busy reeling from sticker shock to think of saying something sensible, like that I'd owe her the ninety pounds. Would have been better than saying I wasn't going to pay at all.

Problem was, I was skint. Transferred £25,000 to Ba the day before the drinks with Kriya. After putting aside money to cover the mortgage and lai see for the wedding, I had enough to see me through to the end of the month, but just barely. And I still had the next £25,000 looming over me.

But Loretta had enough stress to contend with from the wedding. Didn't need me hassling her for rent. She's a postdoc, she never has any money anyway.

Loretta: "I'm going to pay you back."

CG: "I said you don't have to—"

Loretta: "I'm mid-complaining, don't interrupt. What was I saying? Oh yes, I can't cancel the wedding now. Ba's coming. That means so much to Hayley. Her parents always talk about wanting to meet my family."

CG: "I would have thought the one advantage of being gay and Chinese is your partner doesn't have to suffer the nightmare Chinese in-law experience."

Loretta: "Yeah, I know. But she *wants* to. My parents live in Hong Kong and they're scared of speaking English anyway. What's the most they can do to traumatise her? She's lucky. She's only having to meet them now, when she's well past her formative years. Not like us suckers." Gestured at me and herself.

CG: "What's the latest with your mum? Is she coming?"

Loretta's mum—my mother's younger sister—has been one of Loretta's chief sources of wedding stress. At the last count, Ah Yi has changed her mind about whether or not she's attending the wedding five times.

Loretta: "Oh, that's a new drama. Ba's saying now the only reason why she's reluctant to come is because she's scared of upsetting your mum."

That *was* a new one.

CG: "What's Ma got to do with it? She's not even coming."

I offered to book Ma's flights, but she gave some excuse about having to be at home because the neighbours were going to be away visiting their daughter in Australia and she'd promised to water their plants.

Don't think she disapproves of the wedding. More that it's delicate with Ah Yi. Ma knows about Loretta and Hayley, but the rest of the extended family don't. Loretta's parents keep it quiet.

Just as well Ma's not coming. Couldn't afford the flights now, with Ba's bloody gua sha debts to pay off.

Loretta: "Brace yourself. This is the most fucked up thing you'll have ever heard in your life."

Made a non committal noise. Prepared for anything when it comes to Ah Yi. She's bonkers.

Loretta: "Ma thinks your mum thinks I've turned you gay, and that's why you haven't brought a girlfriend home in a million years."

CG: "It's only been six years."

Loretta: "That was not the important part of what I said!"

CG: "How are you supposed to have turned me gay?"

Loretta: "I don't know. Osmosis?"

CG: "Osmosis is specifically the passage of water molecules through a semipermeable membrane. You're thinking of diffusion."

Loretta: "I'm thinking of *homophobia*, Charles."

CG: "Right. Sorry."

Loretta: "But I only have one mother. Even if she is insane, I want her at my wedding. Ba hasn't travelled anywhere by himself in the past ten years, he'd probably get on the wrong plane without her. And you know, having them both there at the wedding, it would make Hayley happy. What's the point of getting married if I don't make my fiancée happy?"

CG: "Indeed."

Loretta: "You have got to stop saying things like that, this is why you've not gotten laid in six years. Anyway, you want my wedding to go well, don't you?"

Alarm bells went off in my head. Loretta looking smarmy, the way she does when she wants a favour.

CG, suspicious: "What do you want me to do?"

Loretta: "I have a plan. Before you say anything, I want you to bear in mind that this plan is for the advancement of family harmony, my marriage, *and* your love life."

CG: "What is it?"

Loretta: "You need to bring a date to the wedding. A female date. Although if you are into men, I support you—"

CG: "I am not into men."

Loretta: "If you're asexual, that would be fine too. There's a whole world of options out there other than 'straight,' you know."

CG: "I am not asexual. We've discussed that."

Loretta: "But you know it would be fine if you were gay or asexual. Or anything else. I would support you, like you supported me."

She meant the time, almost fifteen years ago now, when her parents said they weren't going to pay for her education anymore and she needed to come back to Hong Kong and be straight. Loretta chose to stay in London and finish her degree, but she didn't have anywhere to stay. And I happened to have a spare room.

CG: "That wasn't—I needed someone to oversee the works to the flat."

Loretta: "Why do you always have to pretend it wasn't you being nice? The 'works' was one day while they replaced the carpet. You could have managed without taking me on as a tenant. Accept that you did a good deed and take the thanks."

CG: "Technically you're probably a licensee, rather than a tenant. You don't have the right to exclude people from the property, as a tenant would."

Loretta: "Forget about it, you win. The point I was trying to make is, if you're still insisting you're straight—"

CG: "I'm not *insisting*. I just am."

Loretta: "Then this is the time to prove it. You need to bring a girl to my wedding as your plus one and do straight things with her. Like kiss and hold hands and, I don't know, explain films to her. Get her to manage your social calendar. Rely on her to help you process your feelings . . ."

CG: "Remind me, are you asking me for a favour? Because it feels quite a lot like you are insulting me."

Loretta: "Sorry." Her apology was somewhat undermined by the fact it could barely be heard through the giggling. "What do you think?"

CG: "I don't see the point. How does me bringing a plus one to your wedding help?"

Loretta: "It means I can tell my mum, 'I haven't turned Charles gay, he's got a girlfriend. He's bringing her to the wedding.' And then she can tell your mum. And—another pro—your mum will be happy."

CG: "Because I'll have lied to her about seeing someone."

Loretta: "You don't have to lie to her. You could ask someone out."

CG: "I'm not going to find someone to ask within the next two weeks. It's not enough notice."

Loretta: "So I had an idea about that. But you have to be open-minded. And not a gutless loser."

CG: "What is it?"

Loretta: "You know how you're sharing an office with Hot Lawyer Who Hates You now?"

Took me a moment. Then her meaning dawned on me, in all its horror.

CG: "No. No, no, no."

Loretta: "Oh, come on! You've always fancied her. This is your moment. You guys are working at the same firm, sitting across from each other every day—"

CG: "It's only for three days a week. Firm policy is for people to spend 60 percent of their time in the office. Most people don't do more."

Loretta: "For you, 60 percent of your work time is like 60 percent of your life. You're already spending 60 percent of your life with her. It's fate. It's yun fan!"

Thought of Kriya's expression when I'd said I wasn't going to pay for everyone's drinks. Felt like crawling underneath the sofa and never coming out again. "She really doesn't like me. It wouldn't go well."

Loretta: "She doesn't know the true you. You have to win her over, give her the chance to get to know you outside of work."

Didn't see how that followed. *I* barely knew me outside of work.

Saying that would only provoke an argument, though, so I tried a different tack. "Asking her to a family wedding is a bit much for a first date."

Loretta pulled a face, but conceded: "Fine. Ask her as a friend. Explain the situation with my mum and your mum. She's Asian, she'll understand about family drama. She'll probably be up for coming along. It's one day, free food and alcohol, and anything might happen with my mum. Besides, I bet she's never been to a wedding where the brides will be reading out *Duke of Badminton* quotes during their vows."

Duke of Badminton was the terrible anime of Loretta and her fiancée's heart, and indeed—or rather, not "indeed," strike out the "indeed"—the anime that united their two hearts. Over the years, I have watched far more of it than I personally would have volunteered for, through Loretta constantly having it on in the background. I have not yet caught up with all 227 episodes, but I have had sufficient exposure to the dialogue that I knew its inclusion in the wedding vows was not a selling point.

Was about to point this out when Loretta said: "It would be cool to meet Kriya. You've talked so much about her over the years."

CG: "Don't tell her that!"

Loretta: "What am I, an idiot? I won't say anything. So you're going to ask her?"

CG: "No. I don't want to make her uncomfortable."

Loretta: "It doesn't have to make her uncomfortable. Just make it clear you'd be going as friends, nothing more."

Stared at the TV. Hadn't really been watching, but the anime girl onscreen appeared to be turning into a car. Maybe it would have made sense if I'd been paying attention.

CG: "We're not friends."

Loretta: "Colleagues, whatever you want to call it. It's not a big ask. Who among us hasn't attended a wedding where you don't know the people getting married, because somebody's dragged you along?"

CG: "I'm not asking her, and that's final." Picked up remote. "Are you still watching this?"

Loretta snatched the remote from me. "Yes."

I didn't try to take it back. Best to pick your battles, living with Loretta. Could count myself lucky I'd won this one, for now.

CHAPTER NINE

Kriya

We were going to Hong Kong for business, not fun. Arthur was giving a talk and I was speaking on a panel at the conference. Around that, we'd booked in client meetings and training sessions. Every spare moment was crammed with networking coffees, drinks, lunches, and dinners. For the next four days, I was basically going to be a dancing bear with legal training and horrendous jet lag.

Yet I still felt a thrill of excitement as the island came into view through the plane window: clusters of tall buildings, winding roads amid verdant hills. It was all kdramas and BTS nowadays, but when I was growing up, it was Hong Kong my Chinese friends had looked to. That was where *cool* came from, in those days. (It was very clear to us that "cool" was not locally produced in Malaysia.)

I remembered the little girl I'd been, playing on the scuffed parquet floor of our old house, while some Hong Kong cops and gangsters movie blared from the TV. Appa preferred English and Tamil movies, but he'd watch Hong Kong films if they were on, like at Chinese New Year. It would have blown tiny Kriya's mind to know she'd be coming here someday.

What with the bustle and excitement of arriving, it took

me a while to clock that Arthur was being weird. His luggage came out first on the carousel at baggage reclaim. Then I spotted my purple hard-shell suitcase. "That's mine."

"I'll get it," said Arthur, and took it off the conveyor belt for me.

Arthur had never bothered helping with my luggage before, on the several business trips we'd taken together. But I was too tired from the flight, and too distracted by the novelty of being in Hong Kong, to take notice.

There was something intensely familiar about the place, though it was my first time visiting. The deep green hills, the bright sunshine, the blast of air-conditioning as we walked through the airport, the red-threaded charm dangling from the rearview mirror in the taxi. Cantonese was being spoken all around us. Hearing it was triggering and soothing at the same time, like being back home.

Arthur didn't get a chance to be weirdly chivalrous at the other end of the journey. As the taxi pulled up outside the hotel, a uniformed attendant leaped to open the door for us. He passed us on to a second fellow, who led us through the hotel lobby to reception. I glanced over my shoulder to see our luggage being wheeled in on a trolley, pushed by yet another attendant.

I'd never stayed at such a fancy hotel before. The floors were tiled in shining red marble. Light streamed in through vast floor-to-ceiling windows. There were giant Chinese paintings and lush potted plants everywhere, contrasting with the gleaming reflective surfaces of floors and walls and mirrors.

I should have pushed Amma and Appa harder to fly over to join me here, after the conference. I could have got a room for the three of us for a couple of nights. But then again, they would have tormented themselves the whole time, calculating the cost of every second spent breathing this rarefied air, and converting it into ringgit. Maybe it was for the best.

I couldn't wait to get to my room, have a shower, and crawl

into the soft, roomy batik kaftan rolled up at the bottom of my suitcase. An evening vegging out in bed with room service sounded like bliss.

After we'd checked in, I was turning towards the lifts like a sunflower towards the sun, when Arthur said:

"Do you want to get a drink?"

"Right now?" I said. The vision of my hotel room slid away, a mirage in the desert. "Oh, do you want to talk through the training slides?"

I'd sent Arthur the slides for the training sessions we were going to be doing a week ago, but he hadn't looked at them. I'd been prepared for this, so I'd brought along printouts for him to review on the flight. Presumably he'd had the chance to glance at them at some point during the thirteen hours we were in the air. Luckily we hadn't been sat together, so I had been able to relax and watch a couple of movies.

"We should probably talk about timing, and who's covering which slides," I said.

Arthur blinked. Then he said, "Yes. Let's talk about the slides."

We found a table in the lounge, a flight of stairs down from the lobby. The high ceiling arched above us, held up by vast mirrored pillars. The guests at the tables were reflected in the glass: people in suits; affluent families on holiday. Through the windows I glimpsed the leafy tops of trees, snaking roads, high-rise buildings, and in the distance, behind the Hong Kong skyline, the vague shapes of hills.

Arthur had a beer. I ordered chrysanthemum tea.

The vibes were off. I couldn't put my finger on what it was. Arthur was being normal enough: He'd got our drinks and was now flipping through the slides, scribbling notes as he went.

But hadn't he been taken aback when I'd assumed he wanted to talk about work? Did that mean he'd had something else in mind, some other motive for suggesting drinks?

The hairs rose on my forearms.

I shook myself internally. Arthur *wouldn't*. I'd worked with him for eight years and I'd never seen him do anything inappropriate. He was old enough to be my father—a young father, but still.

Even the thought was unsettling, unlikely as it was. I'd never been one of the parade of trainees and NQs who got crushes on Arthur. I knew too much.

I rubbed my arms.

"Cold?" said Arthur. "They've really got the air-conditioning on blast."

"Yeah, I should have layered up." I opened my laptop. "I'll make the amendments now. What was the change you wanted to the title?"

My unease faded as we worked through the slide deck. Arthur was being fine, not leaning in too close or anything like that.

Why should the poor man come under suspicion simply because he'd helped me with my bag and wanted a chat? If his ex-wife was any guide, I was nothing like his type. I was dark, fat, and frizzy-haired. Whereas Kelly looked like a rich man's wife: a slim, blonde woman who'd made all her clothes look exactly as expensive as they were.

I shut my laptop when we'd got through the slides, getting up. "I'll go ask about getting these printed off." Arthur preferred having hard copy notes to refer to when delivering presentations.

Arthur seemed disconcerted. "There's no rush. You haven't finished your drink."

I glanced down at my glass, half-full of chrysanthemum tea.

"I've had enough," I said. "It's a bit too sweet for me."

The weirdness with Arthur faded away after that first day. He was being completely normal. We talked exclusively about work.

We kicked off each morning with a pre-brief over breakfast, running through the agenda, talking about what we were going to do and who we were going to see.

This was Arthur's idea. I would have preferred to have breakfast by myself. The breakfast buffet was amazing, a holy grail of fancy Asian hotel buffets. Besides the cereals and English breakfast and cured meats and cheese you might have found at any decent English hotel, there was fried rice, fried noodles, fresh tropical fruit, congee, eggs cooked to your liking by a man in a giant chef's hat, dim sum, mini pastries, waffles, spring rolls, deep-fried bao, a salad bar, a juice bar, and another man in a giant chef's hat who would make you noodle soup to your precise tastes, from your choice of a dizzying selection of noodles, green leafy vegetables, mushrooms, meatballs, fish balls, and wonton.

Faced with all this bounty, Arthur chose to eat, every morning, a bowl of oat porridge with a banana sliced into it. White people!

I made sure I ate well, since we didn't always get to have lunch. The days were long. After the conference panels and training sessions and networking events and coffees with people who might at some point prove useful, there was always a dinner to entertain some client or other. After that, we went on to drinks—our local contacts all seemed to have some hip bar in Lan Kwai Fong they took proprietorial pride in showing us.

Arthur gave a good impression of enjoying himself. He might never have heard of jet lag. I could only do my best to keep up, swallowing my yawns and my yearning for my hotel room. It was an incredibly nice room. I had a king-size bed all to myself, and a view of the sea.

Our final client dinner, on our last day in Hong Kong, was with the GC of a Chinese tech company, a Dutch woman who'd been hired in recently and was still making sense of local office culture. At eight p.m., she did something miraculous. She looked at her watch and said:

"I must get going. Thank you for dinner."

"Oh," said Arthur. We'd only just finished our mains. He'd ordered a second bottle of wine, which hadn't even arrived yet.

"You carry on," said Karin airily, getting up and settling her handbag on her shoulder.

After she left, Arthur looked over at me. "Do you want dessert?"

I was pleasantly buzzed. I'd drunk my fair share of the first bottle of wine, but it was mostly the relief of being nearly done with the trip. Now, thanks to Karin, it was even looking like I might get back to my room before ten p.m., for once.

So I said, "I'll take a look at the menu."

I decided on tiramisu. Arthur deigned to order a scoop of lemon sorbet.

We chatted idly about Karin and the job she had ahead of her, whipping her company's in-house legal function into shape. The conversation drifted on to the conference and the various people we'd seen over the past week.

Arthur was feeling optimistic about the business we were going to get from the trip. We had already had a couple of verbal instructions, as well as an invitation to deliver training to a client's European colleagues.

"Can you make a note of all of that?" he said. "I'll send it on to Farah. She'll want to know what we've been up to."

I opened Outlook on my phone, saving a reminder in my diary. "I'll do it before my flight tomorrow."

"Oh, don't worry about it now. It'll keep till you're back in the office." Arthur poured himself another glass of wine. "Got any plans while you're in Malaysia?"

"Just spending time with my parents. I don't have many friends left in my hometown, most people have moved away."

I'd got Appa and Amma to swear not to tell the auntie-uncle

contingent I was coming, so I wouldn't have to entertain everyone in Ipoh and its environs who remembered me as a child. I'd have nothing to do other than eat and try to fix the way my parents' TV kept logging them out of my Netflix account.

"It should be nice," I said.

"Good," said Arthur. Something about the way his eyes flicked to me and then skittered away made me nervous.

But he only said, "How are things generally? All right?"

I'd had half an hour to look through my inbox in my hotel room before we'd had to leave for dinner. "Everything's under control. Rosalind emailed wanting advice, but nothing urgent. The partner in New York who's going to do the US law advice for her dropped me a note to say thank you for the introduction to Sanson."

Arthur's face twitched at the idea of another partner getting work from his client. But he couldn't reasonably object, and luckily for me, he didn't seem to be feeling unreasonable that day.

"That's great," he said. "But I meant more, you know, outside work. I know it wasn't easy, with Tom . . ."

"Oh, let's not talk about Tom." I kept my tone light, but I meant it.

"Right. I know what you mean," said Arthur. "I hope he didn't leave you too bruised, that's all." He met my eyes. "You're a very special person, Kriya."

Goose bumps popped up all along my arms and the back of my neck.

"Thanks, I appreciate that," I said, as though it were my appraisal and Arthur had passed on some nice client feedback.

I had never felt so grateful for a table as I was now. If only the one between me and Arthur were bigger. "How are the kids?"

"They're good. Coping better than me." Arthur's mouth quirked in a wry half smile. "Margot's at uni, so she has some distance from it all. And Lachlan doesn't seem bothered. I think they could see the smash-up coming."

He knocked back his wine and picked up the bottle, making to top up my glass. I shook my head. Arthur poured the remainder of the bottle into his glass.

"It was probably a relief for everyone else," he said. "That it finally happened. I was the only one it came as a shock to. What's the saying? The last to know."

I thought about Tom and the way Zuri had said "Shit" when I'd told her about him dumping me. Angry, but not surprised.

I had felt like I'd sallied out of my front door on a fine blue-skied day and stepped straight into a pit. Half a year later, I wasn't sure I'd climbed out yet.

I wasn't about to share that with Arthur, though. On a normal day, he wouldn't have been interested.

I missed normal Arthur. Weirdly intense Arthur who kept trying to make eye contact was freaking me out.

"It's good that they're not taking it too hard," I said. "Shall we make a move?"

Arthur was quiet in the taxi back to the hotel, and as we waited for the lift in the hotel lobby.

The lift arrived. We both got in. I was beginning to think I might get away without having to endure any further awkwardness, when Arthur said:

"Kriya."

I should have taken the stairs. "Yeah?"

Arthur didn't say anything for a moment. The lift pinged as it arrived at my floor.

"Good work," he said. "Enjoy your break. I'll see you back at the office."

"Thanks. Good night." I stepped out of the lift with a sense of escape.

I wouldn't be seeing Arthur now till we were both back in the UK, the week after next. He was leaving at seven a.m. for his flight the next morning. My flight to Malaysia was later in the day. I'd be able to have breakfast by myself. Maybe I could even go for a swim in the hotel pool. Once I sent Arthur the note for Farah that he'd asked for, I'd be on holiday.

He'd be normal by the time we were back in the office, I told myself. It was being abroad and sad about his ex-wife and drinking too much wine. He probably didn't realise how he'd been coming off. I couldn't believe that Arthur might really have been . . . No. I'd worked with him for so long. He wasn't like that.

My hotel room was dark when I let myself in. I could see Hong Kong through the bank of windows, lit up in the night.

Ant-like cars and buses and trams sped along glowing roads. Beyond them was the dark expanse of the sea. Ferries and junks moved to and fro, cutting through the wavering reflections of the city's lights on the surface of the water.

The fruit bowl on the side table had been refilled, as it was every day, with one orange, one honey-scented apple, and one crisp yellow pear. I collapsed into an armchair, biting into the apple, watching the lights outside and thinking about nothing in particular.

There was a knock at the door.

Arthur was standing in the corridor, in the same suit he'd worn all day. He looked sweaty and dishevelled, more like a man you'd swerve away from in the street than a successful law firm partner.

"Er," I said. "Is everything all right?"

Everything was obviously not all right. But it wasn't like I had anywhere I could run to. I could shut the door in his face, but I had to work with the guy.

My best strategy was to pretend everything was normal and hope that shamed Arthur out of whatever it was he'd come here to do.

"I'm sorry," said Arthur.

I could smell the alcohol fumes coming off him. I shuffled back, wishing I'd left the door chain secured.

"I couldn't stop thinking about you, all evening," said Arthur huskily. "What would happen if I took a chance and came to your room."

"Oh," I said. It was the kind of noise you let out when you put your hand in the kitchen cabinet to grab a mug and a lizard ran over it.

My brain engaged just in time to stop me from saying anything else. But the tone had been enough.

Arthur blinked several times. "I've screwed up, haven't I. I'm sorry." He passed his hand over his eyes. They were less piercing than usual, red from tiredness and alcohol. "It's been such a busy week, and then I turn up here. You must be thinking I've lost it."

I wasn't sure what to say. Agreeing was too risky. Arthur might be drunk enough to be making bad decisions, but he didn't seem *quite* drunk enough not to remember my reactions the next day. "Arthur . . ."

"I couldn't let you go without at least giving it a shot." He took a deep breath. "I need you to know, you're the most important woman in my life. I just thought I'd ask if you thought . . . in case it was something you'd, you know, be open to exploring . . ."

This was in some ways a very familiar situation. Arthur was fumbling for a thought. My role was to step in and clarify it, help him grasp the idea he was reaching for.

Except this time, the thing he was reaching for was *me*.

I'd been mad at Arthur before, for many legitimate reasons. I knew all his foibles: his possessiveness with clients; his insistence on taking all the credit even if he'd done none of the work; his tendency to swing between micromanaging and disengagement; the fact his inbox was perpetually two thousand unread emails deep.

But he'd always been a decent boss, as partners went. I understood how he worked, and he understood me. So I'd thought.

Arthur was still talking. "I want you to think about it. Take all the time you need. We make a great team. I think we could be good together, you know?"

The silence stretched out. Arthur looked expectant, and also like it would take a literal earthquake to move him.

"I have a boyfriend," I blurted.

"You what?" Arthur looked like someone had upended a bucket of cold water over his head. Maybe I should have tried that. "I thought you broke up with Tom."

"Yes, it's, uh, it's someone else," I said. "Look, Arthur, I've always had so much respect for you." *Before you hit on me.* "I think of you as a friend." *A friend who is also my boss, so I have to do what you tell me to, whether I like it or not.* "And you know, I value our professional relationship and all the support and leadership you've shown. I don't want anything to come in the way of that, or to risk—" *my career and my family's financial stability.*

I paused to think of something I could say out loud.

"Who is it?"

"What?"

"This guy you're dating," said Arthur. "It can't have been— you only broke up with Tom a few months ago." He paused. Suspicion crossed his face. "Why didn't you mention you've been seeing someone before?"

I couldn't let Arthur go on like this. I pulled myself together. "Arthur, I'm sorry, but my personal life is not your business."

I resisted the temptation to soften or caveat what I'd said further, holding his gaze. He looked away first.

"You're right," he said. "I'm sorry. That was out of line."

The words were right, but Arthur didn't mean them. He was angry, already on the way to resenting me.

"That's not what I meant," I lied. "But this isn't the time to talk about it. It's late, you've got an early flight tomorrow."

His shoulders slumped. "Right. I'll let you get to bed."

But he didn't move.

"Good night, Arthur," I said, and shut the door on him.

It was a heavy door. The floors were thickly carpeted, absorbing sound. But as I waited with my ear to the door, I thought I could hear his footsteps, moving away.

I locked the door and slid the chain through the track. Then I dragged a chair across the room and put it against the door, feeling ridiculous.

What did I think was going to happen? Arthur wasn't going to come back and kick the door in. All he had to do was knock, and I'd open the door myself. It wasn't like I could afford to ignore him. He was my boss.

I felt sick.

Why had I said I had a boyfriend? Arthur was already going to be mad at me for turning him down. He was going to be even more annoyed if he caught me out in a lie. And it was bound to happen. I spent too much of my life at work for it to be plausible that I was seeing someone. There wasn't *time* for me to have found anyone new. I should have told him I wasn't interested, full stop.

I collapsed in the armchair, staring at the half-eaten apple on the side table.

Who was I kidding? I couldn't even say no to Arthur when he wanted me to cancel an evening engagement with friends so I could turn around urgent client work. I was too well trained. You didn't say no to a partner. If you weren't biddable and hardworking, if you got branded as a troublemaker, there was always plenty of fresh young blood to replace you.

What if Arthur decided to hold a grudge over this evening? Swithin Watkins had courted him, not me. If Arthur wanted me gone, he could make it happen easily. I was still on probation. They only had to give me a week's notice to fire me. My career—ten years' worth of working long hours, handling Friday evening client emergencies, slogging through tedious documents—destroyed in an instant.

I could try to defend myself, but so far as the firm was concerned, I was an appendage to Arthur. I had no other allies at Swithin Watkins. The only two people I had more than a passing acquaintance with were Farah, with whom I'd had all of one conversation, and Charles, who mostly knew me as the person who'd tried to stick him with a bill for ninety pounds he had no intention of paying.

A chill washed over me. I'd assumed it was a spur-of-the-moment pass from Arthur—a fleeting lapse of judgment, born of exhaustion and alcohol. But was it deliberate that it had happened now? If he'd tried it before, at our old firm, I would have known who to go to, in HR and the partnership. I'd have had a sense of who would take me seriously if I confided in them, who might be willing to stick their neck out for me. That wasn't the case at Swithin Watkins.

I didn't have those relationships at our old firm anymore, though, so it wasn't even like I could return. They hadn't been happy about my departure. The split between Arthur and the partnership had not been amicable, and I had very much been *his* associate.

I couldn't see any good choices, any clear way out of the situation. Had Arthur counted on that?

I shook myself. I couldn't reconcile the picture I was building up of a coolly calculating predator with the Arthur I knew. And I knew Arthur—surely I did, after eight years. He had his issues, no one knew that better than me, but he'd been good to me, over the years.

Like when Tom had broken up with me. HR had made a stink about the fact I was failing to meet my billable hour targets in the immediate aftermath—I'd had 16 percent utilisation the month after I received that final message from Tom.

Arthur had told me not to worry: "I'll square it with them." And I'd heard no more of it.

That kindness, the Arthur I knew, was real. It had to be.

This evening had simply been an aberration. Arthur had had the best part of two bottles of wine and it had gone to his head. He'd go to bed and wake up with a headache tomorrow, regretting everything. The next time we saw each other, we could pretend nothing had ever happened. Things would go back to normal.

I took my long-delayed shower, dragged on my kaftan, and climbed into bed. I was bone-tired, but I didn't fall asleep for a long time.

CHAPTER
TEN

Kriya

I was alone in the office when Arthur came in, my first day back after my holiday in Malaysia.

"Morning," he said.

I whipped around, my heart going into overdrive. It was the first time I'd seen Arthur since the night he'd hit on me in Hong Kong, more than a week ago.

I wasn't feeling great. I'd struggled to get to sleep the night before. I was too anxious about seeing Arthur again, after what had happened. I'd thought about working from home, so I wouldn't have to come in, but Swithin Watkins were strict about being in on your office days—any variation to your working pattern had to be approved in advance, by a partner. And I would have just been putting off the inevitable, anyway.

Arthur seemed nervous, too. He picked up a ballpoint pen off my desk and started fiddling with it, glancing at the empty desk opposite mine. "Is Charles around?"

"He's in a meeting. He should be back at eleven. Shall I tell him you're looking for him?"

Maybe we *were* pretending nothing had happened. I was very happy to go along with that, if it meant reverting to the safely professional relationship we'd had before.

Arthur shook his head. "I was looking for you. Can we talk?"

There was a rushing in my ears. I said, as steadily as I could, "Sure."

Arthur leaned against the bank of filing cabinets lining the wall. I had to stop myself from rolling backwards in my chair, so as to put more space between us.

Arthur said, with studied casualness, "How was your trip to Malaysia? Parents well?"

"Yeah." Though it would have been more accurate to say they were as well as could be expected. There was always something going on with Amma and Appa. This time, when I'd presented my usual gift of a bundle of family-size Cadbury fruit and nut bars—Amma's favourite—she had said:

"Oh, thank you, thank you, that's very nice. We should give to Auntie Chew. She can keep in her fridge."

"They're for you," I said. "I didn't buy so you can give away to the neighbours. Keep them in our fridge." You didn't keep chocolate out of the fridge in Malaysia, unless you preferred licking it off the wrapper.

"Oh," said Amma. "We don't have a fridge right now."

It turned out my parents' fridge had broken down several months before. They'd been doing without by switching to tinned milk powder, going without butter, visiting the wet market twice a day, and—in extremis—having to resort to their long-suffering neighbour Auntie Chew's refrigeration facilities.

"Why you all didn't tell me?" I said. "I call you guys every week!"

Amma looked vague. "I forgot. You're so busy, there's no time to talk about every single thing."

I knew and she knew and Appa knew the reason they hadn't told me was because they didn't want to admit they couldn't afford to replace the machine themselves. Appa received a pension as a retired government servant—it wasn't that much money, but it should have been enough, especially as I covered their housing costs.

But Appa had never been able to hang on to money. The eldest in a large and improvident family, he was always being touched for loans that the relatives saw no need to repay. Appa could never bring himself to say no, or to ask for the money back.

I dragged him and Amma out to buy a replacement straight away. But the incident had been a salutary reminder that I didn't have a safety net that would catch me if I lost my job. I *was* the safety net.

I had to stay on good terms with Arthur. Not only could he fire me, he could make it difficult for me to land another job. It wasn't like I was an employment or data protection lawyer—every company needs one of those. My legal specialism was niche. It was a small market, and Arthur was one of the most prominent people in it. He could poison the well for me, if I pissed him off badly enough.

I stared up at Arthur, prepared for anything.

"I wanted to apologise," said Arthur. "For what happened in Hong Kong. I crossed the line."

I'd been so braced for the worst that it took a moment for the words to sink in. I didn't say anything. Arthur hurried on:

"It was a mistake. I'd had a bit too much to drink. I thought you were giving off signals that you were interested . . ."

Every fibre of my being was saying, *Really?!* It must have been obvious from my expression, because Arthur broke off and said, "Anyway, I misread the situation." He cleared his throat. "I hope I didn't make you uncomfortable."

"It was uncomfortable," I said, though my heart was thumping so loud I thought Arthur must be able to hear it. "Our relationship has always been strictly professional. It never occurred to me that you might have anything else in mind. I've never seen you in any light but—I mean, you're my boss."

Arthur said, "I don't see it that way." He was clicking the ballpoint pen he'd nicked from me, compulsively. "You know I don't care about status in that way. If we're in the same team, we're equals. I've always seen you as a friend. It's not about me being the boss and you being my subordinate."

I couldn't help thinking about all the evening plans cancelled at Arthur's behest, all the articles I'd written that he'd put his name to, all the work I'd done to prepare him for meetings and conferences so he could impress clients with his legal expertise. I didn't resent him for it—it was how the system worked. But how could Arthur look me in the eye and say, with a straight face, that he didn't see status when it came to me?

I couldn't doubt Arthur meant what he was saying. I'd simply never realised how far his ability to deceive himself went.

"But I want to assure you, it won't happen again," said Arthur. "I would never have approached you if I'd known you were seeing someone."

"I appreciate it, Arthur," I said. It was a good thing I'd made up a fake boyfriend, after all.

Of course, what he'd done would have been inappropriate whether I was coupled up, or as forever alone as I actually was. But it wasn't my job to teach Arthur unwelcome truths. My job was to keep my head down, not rock the boat, and survive. I'd learned that much from my childhood.

I was lucky Arthur was being conciliatory. If he hadn't felt inclined to accept he was in the wrong—if he'd decided to take offence at how I'd behaved—he could have blown up my career. He could still do it, if he was so minded.

Just two weeks ago, I wouldn't have said Arthur would do something like that. But now—after years of anticipating what Arthur was thinking, jumping in to meet his demands before he'd even expressed them—I could no longer predict what he might do.

Arthur said, "I don't want this to affect our relationship. I wasn't thinking straight in Hong Kong, but I was being honest when I said you're important to me. I want to put this behind us, if you feel able to do that."

There was nothing I wanted more.

"I'd like that," I said. "And I appreciate the apology."

Arthur looked relieved. "Good. Great."

He couldn't have been more relieved than I was. This was why I'd invested so many years—almost the whole of my adult life—in working for Arthur. At the end of the day, despite his idiosyncrasies, he *was* trying.

Everyone made mistakes. Surely what mattered was whether they were willing to acknowledge them and try to do better?

I thought he'd leave, now we'd cleared the air. But Arthur lingered, putting my pen down on Charles's desk.

"So, this person you're seeing," he said. "When did it start? You haven't mentioned a boyfriend, other than—" He caught himself before saying Tom's name. "I mean, is it quite new?"

"Er, yes," I said. "It's new."

"How'd you meet?"

I gave him an incredulous look. Arthur's smile wavered.

"I'd rather not talk about that," I said, repressing the impulse to apologise. He had forfeited the right to talk about our personal lives for at least the next twelve months or so.

Besides, the more we discussed my mythical boyfriend, the greater the likelihood that Arthur was going to figure out he was a figment of my imagination. I didn't want him finding out I'd lied to him, when we'd just made things up.

"Right," said Arthur. "Sorry."

Awkwardness hung between us, so thick I could practically touch it. Arthur looked woeful, but he also didn't look like he was going anywhere.

I could feel the expectation, hovering in the air, that I should say it was all right, downplay how he'd broken my trust, soothe his feelings. I was used to managing Arthur's feelings—it was a big part of managing him, which was a good 40 percent of my job—but for once, I didn't feel like playing my role.

Before either of us could decide to break the silence, the door opened and Charles came in. He had his laptop tucked under one arm and a plate of cookies in his other hand.

"You like salted caramel, right?" he said, without precursor.

I blinked. "Yeah?"

Charles placed the plate of cookies on my desk. "Leftovers from the meeting. Do you want some? I've got to go back up to fourteenth floor later, I'll return the plate then."

"Oh," I said. "Thanks." Was this because I'd mentioned salted caramel in passing when we'd had drinks at the Cittie of Yorke?

I hadn't spoken to Charles since getting back from Hong Kong, apart from exchanging perfunctory greetings when I got in. I still felt a little sore about getting stuck with the bill at the pub. But it was sweet of Charles to remember the salted caramel thing.

"These are the famous Swithin Watkins meeting room cookies, right?" I said. "They look great. Don't you want them?"

"I've had one, thanks," said Charles. "They're pretty good, you should try them."

He looked up and spotted Arthur, apparently for the first time. "Oh, hi. Sorry, I didn't see you there." He hesitated.

There was no way for Charles to get to his desk unless he squeezed past Arthur. But Arthur was leaning against the filing cabinets as though he'd been hit with a freezing ray, staring at the cookies on my desk.

"Would you like one?" I said, offering him the plate.

"No," said Arthur, after a moment. He glanced at Charles, then back at me, his brow furrowing. "No, I'm fine. Thank you."

Arthur straightened up. He said to Charles, "Let me get out of your way."

CHAPTER ELEVEN

Charles

W as in and out of meetings the Monday Kriya was back in the office, so I didn't see much of her at first. But a feeling crept up on me, that something was wrong.

Couldn't say what it was. Kriya seemed different. Subdued.

Maybe annoyed with me about that ninety pounds? But she wasn't acting annoyed. Seemed to like the cookies.

Didn't know her well enough to ask if she was OK. When she came in the next day, I asked how she'd found Hong Kong, instead.

Kriya: "It was good. Busy. I didn't make it to any of the places you recommended. The breakfast at the hotel was really good, though."

Small talk ensued: "Where did you stay?" "Marriott, near Admiralty." "Oh yes, you said. Were you there the whole two weeks?" "No, I went to Malaysia to visit my parents."

Asked where she'd recommend eating out in Malaysia. Not that I'm planning a visit any time soon, though no reason not to: Ba's creditors unlikely to be waiting for me at the airport. It had the effect I was aiming for, anyway, i.e., cheered Kriya up.

She was getting into a level of detail that was well over my head ("if it's itik salai you want, there's a place in Kajang that's

good, but it's a bit of a trek for a tourist"), when the new partner showed up at our door. Kriya's boss, the one that looks like
a greyhound with anxiety in a suit. Can never remember his
name.

Partner: "Have you guys got a moment?"

He was addressing both me and Kriya. Surprised, I said:
"Uh, yeah."

Partner (James? Richard?) shut the door and took the chair
in the gap between our desks, pushing it out so he was sat facing
me and Kriya.

Partner: "I wanted to talk to both of you."

I glanced at Kriya, but she didn't meet my eyes. She was
watching him, warily, like she was braced for him to do something alarming.

Puzzling. Thought they had a good relationship. Partner always coming by the office to chat with Kriya. She clearly runs
the show for him.

Classic dynamic: Female associate does all the work; male
partner gets all the credit. Makes Farah huff and puff. Never
noticed it before she pointed it out, but once you see it, you
can't stop. Really is everywhere.

Having started, Partner didn't seem to know how to go on.
He looked around the office, as though searching for something to help him. Took a Post-it note off Kriya's desk and
started fidgeting with it, folding it into rectangles.

CG: "What did you want to talk about?"

Partner: "The fact is, I—well, what I wanted to talk about
was—well, it's—it's about your relationship."

Thought I must have misheard. Looked over at Kriya.

Kriya looked as baffled as I was. "What relationship?"

Partner: "I won't beat around the bush. You told me you're
seeing someone. It's fairly clear who it is." Looked at me, before
turning back to Kriya. "I don't want to overstep. Obviously,
what you do in your personal life is your business. But I've

worked with you for a long time, and I feel it's my duty to raise it with you if you're doing something that may have an impact on your career."

Kriya gaping. So was I, but Partner wasn't paying attention to me. (What *was* he called? Nick? Chris?)

Partner: "You'll have read the firm policy on relationships between colleagues. As you know, there's no ban on it, but the policy does advise that you inform the group manager as soon as reasonably possible. I'll leave that to your judgment, but—"

Kriya: "I am not in a relationship with Charles!"

Had started to wonder if I'd somehow fallen into an alternate universe where I'd summoned up the nerve to ask Kriya out. Relief to hear Kriya reassert reality, where we were not in fact dating.

Though it was also a little worrying, how firm she was about it. As if there was no chance she'd consider it.

Partner, reasonably: "I'm not saying there's anything wrong with it. I'm glad you've met someone, after . . ." Cleared his throat. "But we need to think about the implications for your work. The two of you sharing an office—it's likely to be detrimental, both personally and professionally. If you'd told me about the nature of your relationship earlier, I would have made sure you weren't assigned to the same office."

Kriya: "Look, there's been a misunderstanding—"

Partner: "I've spoken to Farah. As I thought, there isn't another office available. But we discussed it and—"

Kriya: "You discussed it? Arthur, did you tell Farah Charles and I are seeing each other?"

(Arthur! Knew it was something like that.)

Arthur: "No, no. Like I said, it's for you to make Farah aware of it, when you see fit. But I told her you've asked to change offices, since you raised it with me." (She did?)

Arthur went on: "Since there isn't another office you could use, Farah suggested you do as the other fee earners do. Book a desk in the open plan space on the days you come into the office. The pod outside my office usually has free desks, Victoria works there—"

Kriya: "Are you telling me that I'm being reassigned from this office?"

Her voice was low, but it was somehow more ominous than if she'd raised it.

Arthur: "It's not about forcing you, or anything like that. I'm thinking about what's best for everyone concerned. Working in such close quarters with your partner—it can put a lot of pressure on a relationship. We don't want that to impact your work."

Kriya, exasperated: "Oh, this is—Charles and I don't even work together! We have different clients, different specialisms. Neither of us manages the other, so there's no supervisory relationship. Even if we were dating, why would that be a concern?"

Arthur: "I'm not saying it's a concern. But our line of work is stressful. It's important to be able to maintain a division between the personal and the professional."

Kriya: "I agree."

She said it like she was sliding a knife between his ribs. Arthur flushed.

Dawned on me, all of a sudden, why Kriya had seemed off since getting back. Something must have happened in Hong Kong. From the emphasis she'd placed on *supervisory relationship*, it was becoming clear what that must have been.

Had to suppress a sudden impulse to pick Arthur up by the collar and chuck him out of the room. Been training regularly this year. Reasonably confident I could do it. Lucky for him that the windows don't open.

Kriya: "Given I am *not dating* Charles, I don't see a problem here. I'd prefer to have an office, I don't work as effectively in open plan. Since there isn't another office I could use, I'd rather stay here."

Arthur looked, disconcerted, but after a moment, he rallied: "All the other fee earners are in the open plan area. That's standard practice. The arrangement Charles has, where he has his own office, is by exception. And it's not set in stone. If it's known what the position is, with your relationship, things may well change."

Kriya: "There is no relationship! Right, Charles?"

CG: "Yes. I mean, no. I mean—did Farah say they're going to take away my office?"

Arthur: "No, but—"

Kriya: "I accepted the offer to join Swithin Watkins on the basis that I would have an office. That was highlighted to me as a benefit. Can I clarify—are you saying it's been decided that I can no longer use this office? In other words, the firm has gone back on our original agreement?"

Arthur: "No, that's not what I'm saying. It's your decision. But this is about making sure the situation works for everyone. We're all grown-ups here. We know emotions can affect our objectivity—"

Kriya: "So it's up to me?"

Arthur: "Well—yes. But I'm asking you to think about the implications. For Charles, as well."

He looked over at me, as though he thought I might help him out. Couldn't deny the idea of having my office back to myself was appealing, but Kriya looked at me, too, and it wasn't difficult to decide whose side I was on.

CG: "I don't find sharing an office with Kriya affects my work."

Kriya: "Great! So we're agreed. Thanks for raising your concerns, Arthur. I appreciate the chance to discuss the options, but I'm happy with the current arrangement. I can assure you, you won't see any impact on performance."

She smiled at Arthur, steely, until he stood up.

Arthur: "If you're sure. I just wanted to flag that there are other options." Plucking up some spirit: "We'll keep an eye on the situation. If there are any issues . . ."

Kriya: "I'm sure there won't be."

Arthur was almost out of the door when he turned and said: "Oh, one more thing. I don't think I've seen the note for Farah yet, can you get that to me?"

Kriya: "Sure. You'll have it within the next hour."

She kept smiling until Arthur was gone. Then she sprang up, closed the door, and turned to me.

CHAPTER
TWELVE

Kriya

"I am so, so sorry," I said. "I know that was super weird."

Kawan Baik seemed remarkably unfazed for someone who had just discovered he was apparently his office roommate's boyfriend now, at least in Arthur's mind. Probably in Farah's mind, too, despite what he'd said about not telling her. Arthur was never as sneaky as he thought.

"I owe you an explanation," I said.

Charles said, "Did something happen with Arthur in Hong Kong?"

"Oh my God, you've heard?" A horrific thought struck me. "Have people been talking about it?"

Shame crashed over me. It was no good telling myself I hadn't done anything wrong. Arthur's behaviour wasn't my fault. But if there was a rumour going around that something had happened between us, I knew which of the two of us would have the worst of it. Who was going to believe the Indian woman with the funny accent over the senior white guy?

"What are they saying?" I said. I didn't want to know—I could imagine it, all too easily—but if people were gossiping, I couldn't afford not to know what they were saying.

Charles shook his head. "I haven't heard anyone talking.

Made me wonder, that's all." He gestured at the door through which Arthur had vanished.

My heartbeat slowed. "Oh. Yeah. I guess he made it obvious." I scrubbed my face, sinking down into my chair. "Arthur's his own worst enemy."

I couldn't believe the unhinged conversation we'd had. All Arthur had needed to do was apologise and go back to treating me as he had before. I was fully on board with moving on and forgetting Hong Kong had ever happened.

No doubt he'd told himself he was questioning my office setup out of concern, that it was no more than a good boss would do. I knew better than anyone how good Arthur was at justifying himself.

"He approached you?" said Charles, tentatively.

"Sexually harassed me. Yeah." It was the first time I'd said it out loud, in those terms. The words felt so stark I found myself hastening to caveat them. "He didn't touch me, or anything like that. He just, you know, he came to my hotel room and hit on me. So I told him I had a boyfriend."

"And you told him this boyfriend was me?"

It was almost funny how carefully non-judgmental Charles's voice was. I wished I felt like laughing.

"No! I don't know where he got that from," I said. "He knows I broke up with my ex recently, but I have no idea why he thinks I'm dating you."

Even as I said it, an image rose up before me—of Arthur, in our office the day before, staring at the plate of cookies Charles had placed on my desk.

I covered my eyes. "Oh God, of course. It was the cookies."

"The what?"

"The meeting room cookies you offered me," I said. "Arthur's gone round the bend. One perfectly normal human interaction and he decides we're in love."

Charles made a strange choking noise.

I lowered my hands, worried. "Are you all right?"

"I'm fine. Frog in my throat." Charles took a sip from his mug of green tea. He looked a little flushed, but he did seem fine. "Quite a leap on Arthur's part."

"Right? I mean, the cookies would have been thrown away otherwise."

"That's what I thought," agreed Charles. "Are you going to report him?"

I stared at him. "What?"

"I'd be happy to be a witness, if you're planning to raise it with HR," said Charles. "Obviously I wasn't present for the original incident. But the conversation we just had with him makes more sense with the added context of what he did in Hong Kong."

"I . . . thank you."

It wasn't like I didn't know going to HR was an option. But it held at least as much risk for me as for Arthur, even with Charles on my side. As Charles said, he wasn't in a position to corroborate my account of what had happened in Hong Kong. And even though he could vouch for the fact Arthur had been unhinged about us sharing an office, that on its own wasn't self-evidently out of order. Maybe firm policy did frown upon romantic partners sharing an office. I hadn't read the policy, since it wasn't relevant to my situation—or rather, it hadn't been, until Arthur had decided it was.

"I thought about it," I said. "But what would I be reporting? Nothing really happened."

Charles raised an eyebrow. "You said he hit on you."

"Yeah. And when I said no, he went away. He didn't try to force me, or push back, or anything."

Charles's forehead wrinkled. "I'd hope HR would have a more nuanced view than that. He came to your hotel room, you said? It was inappropriate."

"He's apologised," I said. "Maybe I should have recorded it.

If you think about it, it was an admission." I rubbed my temples. I couldn't believe this was my life now, that I was regretting not taping my boss. "Say HR take our view of it—I agree with you, by the way, that it wasn't a great thing for him to do." Understatement of the year.

"Arthur's going to deny it," I said. "He's going through an expensive divorce, he's moved firms because he wants to reset his career. He can't afford to be labelled a sexual harasser. And if it's my word against his, who are they going to believe?"

Charles didn't try to reassure me. "You're not obliged to report it, if you don't want to. It's your decision."

"It was a single incident," I said. "He did back off after I told him I was seeing somebody. All of this is really out of character for him. I've worked with him for eight years, and he's never done anything like it before. Definitely not to me, and not to anyone else that I know of. He's been under a lot of pressure recently . . ."

My voice trailed off. I could hear how unconvincing I sounded.

But what could I do? If I was wrong, if this *wasn't* a one-off I could put behind me, that would mean my career, as it was, was over. Even if I went to HR and they believed me, and it was Arthur who lost his job instead of me.

I didn't know what my career would look like without Arthur. I'd have to rebuild it from scratch, and I didn't have a model for that. I wasn't prepared to sink my career as I knew it over one mistake—a mistake Arthur had owned up to and had promised not to repeat.

"I think he's learned his lesson," I said.

I could tell Charles wasn't buying it. But all he said was, "It's up to you. My offer stands. I won't say anything about it without your agreement."

"Thank you," I said.

Charles was being so decent. I felt bad for calling him

Kawan Baik all those years, though it was barely an insult. After how he'd behaved today, it didn't feel like he deserved to be the object of a running joke.

"I'm sorry you got dragged into this," I said. "I'll tell Arthur he got it wrong, since he's got it stuck in his head that you're the guy I'm seeing." I sighed.

"Can't you tell him who it is you are seeing?" Charles recollected himself. "Of course, you probably don't want to share personal information with him."

"I mean, yeah, that. But I'm not seeing anybody! I only said it because I wanted to let him down gently." I ran my hands through my hair. "I'll tell him I met somebody on the apps. That should sound plausible. He probably thought it was you because he knows all I've been doing is working lately. I've hardly had time to keep on top of my laundry, much less meet someone new."

"You don't have to," said Charles.

"Don't have to what?"

Charles was pink. "If it makes things easier with Arthur, you don't have to clarify. I don't mind."

I wasn't sure if I'd understood him. "You mean . . . let him keep thinking we're dating?"

Charles shrugged. "You've already denied it. If he doesn't believe you, that's his lookout. It makes no difference to me either way. I'm not in a relationship, so there's nobody to object. I wouldn't have to do anything differently, it sounds like. Arthur seems perfectly capable of inventing the evidence to prove his hypothesis."

"Oh." It would be one less thing to worry about. I didn't even know how I was going to persuade Arthur I wasn't dating Charles, given that several outright denials hadn't worked.

If anything, the denials I'd issued had probably cemented it as truth to Arthur. I could see everything I'd said to the contrary was exactly what I *would* say if I were dating Charles and didn't want him to know.

There was no way to win. Even if I'd agreed to surrender my office, that would simply have confirmed for Arthur that he was right. And it would have left me out of an office, simply because Arthur had decided to go on a weird interfering rampage.

"Are you sure?" I said. "People might gossip."

"They won't to me."

I could see people wouldn't. There was a kind of natural severity about Charles's manner. You felt that if you were to talk about anything other than work, he'd judge you.

"But they might talk behind your back," I said.

"So?"

That was hard to counter.

Charles looked away, at his screen. I thought he was about to wind up the conversation so he could get back to work, but instead he said, quietly, "I'd like to help, if I can. It seems to me you're in a difficult position."

My eyes stung, my vision going blurry. I bent my head, glad Charles wasn't looking at me. He'd dealt with enough drama for the day. He didn't need to have me dripping tears on my desk, on top of it all.

"It would help," I said, when I was sure I could speak without my voice going wobbly. "Just till Arthur's through this phase. I'm sure he'll get over it and things will go back to normal."

I wasn't sure. But I wasn't ready to look at what it would mean for my life if Arthur kept acting like this and made it impossible for me to continue working for him. I had to hope he'd get . . . whatever this was out of his system, and go back to being the guy I knew.

"Hopefully it won't take long," I said. "But if you start feeling uncomfortable about it, or if you change your mind, for whatever reason, I can let him know we've broken up. Does that work?"

Charles nodded.

"Thank you." I took a deep breath, letting it out slowly. "Sorry for all the drama."

"Really," said Charles. "Don't worry about it. It's fine."

It was fine. It would be fine. I just had to believe that.

CHAPTER THIRTEEN

Charles

W as in the thick of drafting a complex piece of advice, three days before Loretta's wedding, when the phone on my desk started ringing. Assumed it was a client: Everyone internal sends Teams messages when they want a call.

CG: "Hello, Charles Goh."

Got a start when Loretta's voice issued from the receiver: "Charles, are you avoiding me?"

Didn't think Loretta would notice. Hayley arrived from the States last weekend. Staying with us until the day before the wedding, when she and Loretta will be going over to spend a couple of nights at the hotel where it's happening. They've been floating about in a haze of romantic bliss, and I've been busy at work.

That's my excuse, anyway. Been keeping away so Loretta won't hassle me about bringing a date to the wedding. Only need to survive a few more days. Should have known Loretta would track me down.

CG: "I'm in the middle of something. Can we talk later?"

Loretta: "Who's the girl you're bringing to the wedding? Ma's asking."

I shot a surreptitious glance at Kriya, sat across me at her desk. She was working, of course, her eyes fixed on her monitor.

Lowered my voice, switching to Cantonese.

CG: "I'm not bringing any girl. I told you. Why's your mother even asking?"

Loretta: "Why are you speaking Cantonese—*oh*. Kriya's there, isn't she? Have you asked her?"

CG: "No."

Loretta: "Come on, Charles. You know what Ma's like. She's not on the plane yet. She could change her mind at any moment. I'm relying on her nosiness. She's so curious about your new girlfriend, it's the main reason she wants to come."

CG: "You told her I have a new girlfriend?"

Loretta: "I had to lure her over somehow."

CG: "I can't ask Kri—my colleague to the wedding." Looked over at Kriya again. She was absorbed in her screen, showing no sign she'd noticed I'd almost said her name. "It's not the right time. She's in a difficult situation."

Loretta: "How so?"

Gave her a potted history. Left out the part where Arthur is convinced Kriya and I are dating, despite Kriya's denials. Loretta would get too excited.

As it was, she was suitably appalled. "Shit. That's so bad. Why doesn't she report him to HR?"

Had reflected on this myself.

CG: "I think she's hoping it will blow over. My impression is her boss has been good to work with, till now. If she speaks up, that's the end of working with him. Even if he left, and she got to keep her job, it would mean having to rebuild all her relationships. Losing clients. Clients are hierarchical, they want a partner to talk to. They'd probably stay with him, even if she's the one doing the actual work. And that's if HR support her. They might not, if it's her word against his. You'd have to be sure reporting was the right thing to do."

There was silence on the line. Thought the call had dropped. "Hello?"

Loretta: "Wow. That's the most words I've ever heard you say on a topic that wasn't boring law stuff."

CG: "The point is, I can't ask her to your wedding. Bad enough the boss is chasing her. If I start trying it on, there's nowhere for her to run. We share an office."

Loretta: "Yeah, no. I see."

CG: "You need to tell your mum I'm not bringing anybody to the wedding."

Loretta sighed. "This is so sad. I can't believe Fate put you in the same room and then made it so you can't ask her out. You'd make her such a good boyfriend."

Didn't point out I was currently being exactly the boyfriend Kriya wanted, i.e., one in name only, to shield her from Arthur.

Spotted him earlier, wandering down the corridor to come speak to Kriya. I met his eyes through the glass and thought hard about how satisfying it would be to give him a kick. Arthur turned green and kept on walking.

Best thing he could do for her is leave her alone, in my opinion. Kriya's already picked up a pro bono case with Farah.

CG: "I need to get back to work. Bye, Loretta."

Put down receiver before she could say anything else. Turned back to my draft note of advice. Was about to start typing when Kriya cleared her throat.

She said: "Um. This is awkward, but I should probably have mentioned earlier, I understand Cantonese."

I froze.

CHAPTER FOURTEEN

Kriya

I hadn't eavesdropped on Charles's personal call on purpose, but his expression was almost worth the awkwardness of the moment.

"What?" said Charles.

"I'm not fluent," I said. "But I can follow most of what's said to me. A lot of people speak Cantonese in Ipoh, and I watched TVB growing up. And I did lessons for a while here in London, one of my friends wanted to go and she asked me to come along."

Charles looked like someone had smacked him across the face with a dead fish. "Was it obvious that—."

"That you were talking about me? It was pretty obvious." Charles looked so despairing I added, "You didn't say anything *bad*."

Though it had stung a little, hearing some of the things he'd said. I hadn't followed all of it, but what I'd picked up of his account of recent events hadn't cast me in the most flattering light. I sounded utterly spineless. The obedient little dogsbody, keeping her head down and hoping the unpleasantness would blow over.

Charles hadn't mentioned that Arthur had apologised for his behaviour—though, OK, he'd tried to kick me out of my office right after. But I could believe he'd genuinely thought that was for the best, for all concerned.

Arthur had done a lot for me, over the years. Charles wasn't to know that.

It wasn't a topic I felt like delving into. I said, "Whose wedding is this?"

Charles passed a hand over his face. "My cousin."

His tone was so tragic I laughed. "I thought it must be somebody you're related to, from the way you were bickering with them."

"I wasn't bickering," said Charles, with dignity. "Loretta doesn't know where to stop. Her mum can be very difficult, to be fair," he added.

"Why does she want you to bring me to her wedding? Did I get that right?"

Charles hesitated. "This will sound completely mad."

"Well, you've *got* to tell me now."

He told me.

"Wow," I said.

"Yeah."

"You know, it sounds like Loretta's mum may be looking for problems," I said. "Like, if it wasn't this, there'd be some other reason she can't come to the wedding."

"It's an excuse," Charles agreed. "It's not pure invention, though. That's the challenge, what she says always has some basis in the truth. My mum does worry about me. Though she'd be fine if I brought a boyfriend to the wedding, probably. That's the irony, my mum's more relaxed about all of that. She's only not coming because she doesn't want to embarrass my aunt."

I shook my head. "Asian family dynamics. My relatives would be just as bad. Poor Loretta."

"She hasn't had an easy time of it," said Charles. "I'm sorry I told her about, you know, what's going on. She wasn't letting it go."

I shrugged. "Family's complicated, I get it. When's the wedding?"

"Saturday."

"In London?" When Charles nodded, I said, "Why don't I come with you?"

His head swivelled on his neck like an owl's. "What?"

"I haven't got anything on that day," I said. "And we are supposedly dating." I grinned.

Charles blushed.

Was I flirting with Kawan Baik? I shouldn't flirt with Kawan Baik. Goodness knew there was enough going on at work as it was, without me making it weird with my office roommate and long-time work nemesis.

Well, making it weird*er*. It was already pretty weird, what with the fact Charles was the only other person who knew about Arthur hitting on me, and the fact Arthur believed he was my boyfriend.

A thought struck me. "Wait, does Loretta think we're together? Is that why she wants you to bring me as your date?"

Charles went from pink to brick red. "No! No. She just—er—I told her I wouldn't be able to find a date at such short notice. She knows I'm sharing an office with you—that is, with a female lawyer. So she suggested I ask you, as—as a friend."

He stumbled a little over the word "friend."

It wasn't a word I would've thought to use of Charles before, despite the nickname. And yet it wasn't wrong. We weren't work nemeses anymore, but he was something more than a mere colleague. "Friend" didn't feel that far off.

"That makes sense," I said. "How about it? Shall I come?"

Charles scrunched up his forehead, looking at me. "You wouldn't mind?"

"I'm Asian. It's not the first time I've been to the wedding of someone I don't know, let's put it that way."

Plus, I owed Charles. He'd been so supportive about the whole Arthur situation.

And—the thought came despite myself—if I shared photos of myself at a wedding with an attractive guy on social media, maybe Tom would hear about them, even if he didn't see them. We'd blocked each other after the breakup, by mutual agreement.

No, what was I thinking? I couldn't share photos of myself with an attractive guy on social media. Tom probably wouldn't hear about them, but I knew who definitely would. My one million aunties, uncles, cousins, former neighbours, ex-schoolmates, old teachers, and everyone they knew. There was a global network of spies I was only ever two steps away from stumbling into. They would guarantee that the next thing I knew, Amma would be on the phone asking, "Who is this Chinese boy ah, you put the photo online? Is he your friend?"

Amma had been more broken up about Tom dumping me than even I was. Despite my first-class education and good job, she seemed to think the fact I was unmarried at thirty-four meant I was a failure destined for a ruinous old age.

It would be feeble-spirited of me to try to use Charles to fend her off. And it wasn't a long-term solution anyway. What was going to happen when Amma started asking when she was going to get to meet Charles?

"What's the dress code?" I said.

"Oh, it's very open-ended. There will be a range of costumes." Odd choice of language, but presumably Charles meant "outfits." He went on, "I'll be dressed to match the wedding theme, but standard summer wedding attire would be fine for you. But are you sure? You don't have to come. I'm sure it'll be fine with Loretta's mum. Or—well, even if it isn't, it won't necessarily be because of this. There's no point trying to entertain all of my aunt's whims. I've told Loretta."

"I'd like to come," I said. "I love weddings. So long as you don't mind the company."

"It would be nice to have you there," said Charles.

He met my eyes, then looked away. My cheeks warmed.

"Good," I said.

"Thank you. It'll mean a lot to Loretta. And she'll be very excited about meeting—" At this point Charles was briefly overcome with a coughing fit. "About getting married, I mean," he said, when it had passed.

"All very exciting," I said. "I'm looking forward to it."

CHAPTER FIFTEEN

Charles

Kept it low-key, the morning of Loretta's wedding. Went to gym, had tuna on rice, drafted a witness statement. Wanted to get it done while the witness interviews I'd conducted during the week were fresh in my mind.

Weird going about my day without being trolled about my lunch and working at the weekend ("How can you live like this, Charles?"). Loretta and Hayley had gone over to the hotel in Mayfair the night before. They'd booked two separate hotel rooms for the wedding party to get ready in, plus a suite for the two of them for their wedding night.

Hayley and her parents paying; they're minted. Loretta says she's looking forward to being a trophy wife: "It'll be a change from being a trophy cousin."

Speaking of trophies, time to get dressed.

Had a qualm when I opened the wardrobe and saw my suit hanging in it. Took a deep breath and grabbed it, along with the accessory I'd bought to go with it.

Got contact lenses, too, so I could forgo my spectacles. Never worn contacts before. Had to get a special prescription. But they were necessary for the look. Am going to be judged by people who will notice any incorrect detail, however minor.

Almost lost my nerve when I saw myself in my getup in the mirror, accessory in hand. Looked a right wally.

Not that I was going to stand out on the Tube. People get on with much stranger things. Saw a bloke carrying a life-size Dalek on the Jubilee line once. I was merely going to look like a fitness enthusiast, which, after all, I am.

Still, I might have got an Uber, if I had any money. Reviewed my outgoings that morning to see where I could make savings. Gym membership was the biggest recurring expense, after mortgage and groceries. But unluckily, or luckily, I paid for the year up front. Can't cancel till next March.

It'll be all right once I'm paid at the end of the month, but Ba and his creditors will have to wait for the next £25,000. Would be easier to get it together if I broke into my ISA, but that's a last resort, in event of emergency.

Ba needing money from me not an emergency. Just a fact of life.

Decent of Kriya to say she'd come to the wedding. Agreed we'd meet at Regent's Park station so we could walk to the hotel together. Glanced at my phone before leaving the flat, to check she hadn't texted to change plans.

Nothing from Kriya. But there was a text, from a number I didn't know.

Hey, Charlie, all well? Shaw Boey here. My dad passed me your number. Might have a job for you. In Provence for the weekend, but give me a bell on Monday, will you?

Gave me a start to see Shaw's name. Haven't seen him in years. Not in touch with anyone from school except the Odds & Sods (name of WhatsApp group), bunch of foreign misfits everyone else hated. We meet biannually, which means either twice a year or once every two years, depending on how busy people are.

Shaw was foreign too—Malaysian, but his family was based in Hong Kong for a while. His dad was a friend of Ba's in the old days. Ba used to ask after Shaw, as though we were mates.

He didn't understand that Shaw was different. People at school liked him. He kept well away from the rest of us. Couldn't blame him, considering. It was understood among the Odds & Sods that nobody spent time with us unless they had no choice. Strange to hear from him like this, out of the blue.

Put away my phone without answering. I'd find out what it was all about on Monday. In the meantime, I had other things to worry about.

Regent's Park is the second-least-used Tube station in Zone 1. (Least used is Lambeth North.) Went up a narrow passage with green-tiled walls, up a flight of stairs, and into the sunshine. Kriya was waiting by the cream wall by the station exit.

She was wearing a sleeveless green dress with a square neckline, a shawl draped loosely over her arms. Dress fabric was some sort of satin, draped around the bust, nipped in at the waist and hugging her hips. Lower-cut than anything she'd ever worn to work. Hair loose over her shoulders. She was wearing earrings like gold bells with small white pearls hanging from them, and her lips were dark red, like the flesh of a black plum.

She looked incredible.

Stopped so suddenly the bloke behind me walked into me and shouted, inexplicably: "Fuck off! Wee Willie Winkie!"

Kriya looked around and spotted me. Her jaw dropped.

CG: "Hi."

Kriya was wearing a thin gold chain around her neck, with a crescent-shaped gold pendant that drew the eye down to her frankly amazing breasts. If you were so incautious as to let the eye be so drawn. Which I was not.

Kriya: "Charles, what are you *wearing*?"

Right. Forgot about my outfit.

Kriya looking anxious: "Am I going to be overdressed? You said it was standard wedding attire, so I went with this."

Charles: "No, it's fine. What you've got on is perfect. You look really, really good."

Shut my mouth, two seconds too late. Should have cut it off at the first "really." Should have avoided intensifiers altogether. Not appropriate language to be using with a colleague. All your office roommate wants to hear from you is unadorned adjectives.

CG, hurrying on: "It is standard wedding attire, for most of the guests. I'm just matching the theme."

Kriya staring at me like I was an alien. "You look like you're about to play badminton."

I was in a blue jersey, white shorts with black stripes, and blue trainers. Could have been dressed to play anything from table tennis to squash, but the badminton racquet I was holding was probably a giveaway.

CG: "Yes. It's based on the Japanese national men's team uniform for the 2012 Olympics."

Kriya: "So . . . it's a badminton-themed wedding?"

CG: "Not quite." Paused. "Have you ever heard of a TV series called *The Duke of Badminton*?"

CHAPTER SIXTEEN

Kriya

Charles was lucky it was a warm, sunny day. I stuffed my shawl in my tote as we walked along the elegant curve of Park Crescent, lined with a semicircle of cream-coloured Regency-era houses.

I wasn't sure I was so lucky. Charles's top was sleeveless—presumably it was the Japanese national men's badminton team summer uniform. It was the first time I'd ever seen his upper arms.

I'd thought his forearms were good when I'd seen them at the pub, but that was before I'd been treated to a sight of his biceps. They made me feel slightly faint.

His shorts also revealed far more of the thigh than was comfortable in a colleague. Not to mention his calves. Charles was evidently not in the habit of skipping leg day.

Stop perving on the poor man, Kriya.

It was all a little difficult to reconcile with the Kawan Baik I knew. Charles wasn't wearing his glasses, which made him look different—younger, undefended. He didn't look like everyday Charles who shared an office with me, who had a protein shake at his desk every morning and glowered through his Teams calls and told me about the latest case law on limitation.

It felt like I was hanging out with some other guy altogether, on a date.

"Can I carry that?" said Charles.

I yanked my eyes up to his face. "Sorry?"

Charles gestured at the tote slung on my arm. I had a tiny gold clutch as well, into which I'd crammed my phone, a lipstick, tissues, and face wipes.

"It looks heavy," he said.

"It's not that bad," I said.

But Charles was looking embarrassed, like he was feeling foolish about having made the offer. And it wasn't like I *wanted* to lug a tote around. It didn't go with the rest of my outfit—whereas Charles's outfit was pretty much impossible to spoil.

"But sure. If you don't mind," I said. I passed the bag over.

Watching the muscles in Charles's arm flex as he hoisted it onto my shoulder, I decided not to feel bad. Presumably he'd worked on those muscles. It was probably nice for him to get a chance to use them.

"Thanks," I said. "You were saying, you're dressed as the main character of this anime series, *Duke of Badminton*. So it's an anime-themed wedding?"

"It's more that Loretta's life is anime-themed," said Charles. "*Duke of Badminton* is important to her and her fiancée, Hayley. The cake toppers are figures of the main characters, Yamaguchi Kiichiro and Beaufort Mirrikin. Beaufort has blond hair, like Hayley, and Kiichiro has black hair, like Loretta.

"I'm dressed as Kiichiro," he added. "Thought I'd save on a wig."

"I see," I said, though I wasn't sure I did. "I've been looking for something new to watch in the evenings. I'll have to check it out."

"You shouldn't," said Charles definitely. "It's one of the worst things I've ever seen. In one episode, a character wins a match by smashing a shuttlecock through the centre of the Earth."

I laughed. "It's nice of you to do this, if that's how you feel about the show." I waved at his costume.

"Oh well, you know. Loretta will find it funny."

"You guys seem close."

"She's my best friend." Charles went pink, as if he hadn't quite intended the admission. He added, with an attempt at lightness, "I'm not great at making friends. You may have noticed."

I felt a pang of guilt. Not that Charles knew about all the times I'd bitched about him to my friends, and our code name for him.

To be fair, he'd legitimately been a dick in the past—the recent past, at that. That £180 bill at the pub floated to the top of my mind.

But my soreness about that had faded, three weeks on. I'd had ample proof of Charles's decency, his kindness and integrity, over the weeks we'd shared an office. It wasn't merely how he'd treated me, with the Arthur situation. I'd seen how hard he worked for his clients, how much partners and peers valued his opinion, how courteous and considerate he was with paralegals and PAs.

Sure, Charles might be a little socially awkward, a little funny about money. That didn't change the fact he was a good guy.

"You're too hard on yourself," I said. "You're obviously a great friend. I'm sure your cousin's going to love the outfit."

Charles went even pinker. He said, "Are you busy at the moment?"

I shook my head. "There hasn't been much coming through."

We were still waiting to hear back from our leads in Hong Kong. The usual stream of work from Rosalind had slowed to a trickle, as it did from time to time. Either she'd found a new boytoy—that always distracted her—or she was caught up with some project that didn't require legal support.

I hadn't seen Arthur since our disagreement about me sharing an office with Charles, though we'd been in touch via email, strictly on work matters. I couldn't help suspecting Arthur was avoiding me on purpose.

But perhaps that was for the best. We needed a reset. If this break in interaction was a sign Arthur was trying to redraw our working relationship within more professional bounds, I was all in favour.

I'd chased a couple of people who had promised us instructions when we met in Hong Kong, and I'd picked up a pro bono case, working with Farah. But otherwise I was making the most of the lull—closing my timesheets, doing the induction training sessions I hadn't had time to do before now, even meeting my friends for dinner on weeknights.

Charles and I chatted idly about work until we got to the hotel—a large, stately Victorian building, in yellow brick and white stone. The entrance was through an imposing portico. An attendant in a grey morning suit nodded as we approached. He didn't bat an eyelash at Charles's outfit.

I was starting to feel a little less overdressed. Charles waited for me to pass through the revolving door before following me into the hotel lobby. The floors and pillars were tiled in shining black-and-white marble. An ornate chandelier lit the room. Charles seemed in his element.

Maybe that was the difference between people who grew up rich and the rest of us. The wealthy were used to the staff being better dressed than them. They'd never be challenged about their entitlement to be in a place because they were wearing the wrong shoes. The shoes didn't matter—so long as you could afford any kind you liked.

The woman at reception said, "Oh yes, you're the best man? The brides are doing photographs in the Tower Suite. We'll let them know you're joining them."

"I can wait down here," I said to Charles.

"Come on up," said Charles. "Loretta will want to see you."

I hesitated. It didn't seem the moment for a stranger to intrude. Surely Charles's cousin wouldn't want her wedding photos to include a random Indian girl he wasn't really dating.

But Charles was twirling the badminton racquet in his hand, at real risk of beheading a potted plant or smashing a vase. I realised he was nervous.

"Sure," I said gently. "I'll come."

CHAPTER
SEVENTEEN

Charles

Plan was for Loretta and Hayley to have their "first look" photos in the suite, capturing the moment they saw each other in their wedding clothes for the first time. An intimate moment: just the two of them, the photographer, the photographer's assistant, the videographer, and the videographer's assistant.

The brides had done all their looking by the time we got there. Room was full. Loretta's parents were there, along with a white couple—a slim grey-haired woman and a burly red-faced man. Hayley's mum and dad, presumably.

Hayley was glowing in a huge white dress, looking like a bride in a magazine. And Loretta, but not everyday Loretta. Loretta in makeup (weird), with her hair up (weird), and dressed in something other than a sweatshirt and tracksuit bottoms (extra weird).

A friend had made her outfit—Hayley and Loretta have a lot of friends who know how to sew, it comes from all the cosplay. She was wearing a cheongsam-style top and fitted trousers in a sheeny off-white fabric embossed with flowers, with purple jade buttons across the chest and up the ankles. And gold heels. Loretta never wears heels.

Nothing about the outfit was like anything Loretta usually wore. Yet somehow she looked more herself than ever, like someone had turned her Loretta-ness up to eleven. Looked happy.

Was on the verge of embarrassing myself, by welling up or something horrific like that. But everyone's jaws dropped as we came in, and I remembered I'd already embarrassed myself in a different way.

Loretta and her mum: "*Charles!*"

Ah Yi, in Cantonese: "What is that you're wearing? Why haven't you changed for the wedding? It's starting in an hour's time!"

Was worried for a second. Pretty sure my costume was accurate. Had confided in Hayley, and she'd enlisted the help of their cosplay seamstress friends. One cosplay friend had even sent me a step-by-step guide to hand-painting the racquet so it'd match the one in the series. (Did it on a Saturday morning. Loretta never gets up before eleven on a Saturday.)

But this was the first time Hayley, or anyone, was seeing the results on me.

Hayley: "Oh my God. Charles . . . you're *attractive*." Clapped her hand to her mouth. "I'm sorry! I don't know why I said that."

My eyes slid to Kriya despite myself. She looked amused.

Loretta, hollowly: "No, no. I see it too. He looks *hot*. Why'd you do this to me, Charles?"

CG: "I thought you'd find it funny!"

All parents present looked baffled. Loretta's dad the only one who seemed to have got a sense of what was going on. Unfortunately, he tried to help.

Yi Cheung: "Maternal cousins, in Chinese culture they can get married. It's not considered a stigma. The surname is different. If the surname is the same, that can be an issue."

Loretta was blinking the way women do when they're wearing

too much makeup to cry. Looking up at the ceiling, she said: "Ba, are you saying it's not too late for me to swap Hayley for *my own cousin?*"

Ah Yi, to me: "Now, you see, she's upset! What are you doing, going to play sports on the day of your cousin's wedding? You can play badminton any day!"

Loretta, sweeping her palms under her eyes: "It's OK, Ma, stop scolding him. I'm not upset, I'm *touched.* Come here, Charles, let's take a picture!"

She flung her arms around me when I got to her. Smelled familiar.

CG: "Did you nick my cologne?"

Loretta: "I'm borrowing it. You can have it back if you want. Do you want it?"

CG: "It's my cologne! Did you go in my bathroom without asking?"

Loretta: "There was only a little bit left in the bottle. You've got a new one waiting, I saw it."

CG: "That's not the point. My bathroom cabinet is not a bloody Superdrug—"

Hayley, grinning, through her teeth: "I love you both, but you need to stop squabbling, or we're going to be late for our own wedding."

I shut up. Bride's prerogative to burgle her relatives, I suppose. Also, I'd forgotten Kriya was there and watching the whole thing.

She flashed me a smile when she noticed me looking at her. Seemed to be enjoying herself, at least.

The photographer was taking it all in her—their—stride. They had teal-streaked hair and wore stripy knee-length socks, a fuchsia dress covered with round-eyed anime frogs, and a "they/them" pin. No doubt they'd seen far stranger getups than mine, in their time.

Photographer: "OK, can we have best man between the

brides? Let's have the racquet a little higher so we can see it. Lovely! I love the smile, but we know Kiichiro's an intense character, so can we try for more of a smoulder?"

Loretta: "They mean you. You've got to smoulder."

CG: "Yes, thank you, I'd got that—"

Loretta: "I don't know if you think you're smouldering, but you're not. You look like something caught in the headlights of a car."

CG: "I'm sorry, I don't get a lot of practice in smouldering. I'm a solicitor, not a model."

Loretta, to Hayley: "Look at him. God gave him those cheekbones, and he goes and ruins it with his personality."

Hayley was no help, too busy giggling. Nor was the photographer: "Try to imagine how Kiichiro felt during the Goshogawara High School showdown!"

Kriya: "Charles, you know the new limitation case you were telling me about? Can you remind me, what was the ratio?"

Frowned. I'd mentioned the case to Kriya because there was a limitation issue in her pro bono matter. Surprised she'd forgotten the point so soon.

CG: "It was on the interpretation of section 32 of the Limitation Act. The one that says where the defendant has deliberately concealed facts relevant to the claimant's right of action, limitation doesn't run until the claimant has discovered the concealment, or could with reasonable diligence have discovered it. The Supreme Court said—"

Photographer, snapping away: "That's it! Perfect."

Loretta: "Is that Kriya? She's gorgeous *and* she's a Charles whisperer! Get over here, Kriya, get in the shot!"

Was beginning to wonder if Loretta had started in on the champagne early. Kriya held back, protesting, until Hayley dragged her over and shoved her next to me, unnecessarily close.

Kriya smelled nice, of the lemongrass scent that fills the office on the days she comes in. Her bare arm brushed mine. I could feel my pulse throbbing in the base of my throat.

It was a relief when the photo was over. Kriya touched my elbow lightly, smiled, and stepped away.

Did that mean anything? Probably nothing. Just trying to show she had no hard feelings about being manhandled by my shameless cousin's fiancée.

On the other hand, it might have meant something more than that. If so, what?

Could have done with Loretta's advice. Couldn't ask then, though: Loretta had better things to be thinking about. She hugged me.

Loretta: "Thanks, Biu Gor." Not taking the piss for once.

CG: "You look amazing."

Loretta: "So do you, you big lunk." Produced a tissue from her trouser pocket and patted her eyes. "How's my mascara holding up? Good. I guess it's really waterproof. There's Ma speaking Cantonese to Kriya. I don't know why Ma does this, it's not like she can't speak English. You'd better go rescue your date."

CG: "She can speak Cantonese. Anyway, she's not really my date. She's here as a friend."

Loretta: "Are you serious? She's a polyglot on top of everything else? Charles, she's the perfect woman. You *have* to lock it down."

CG: "Most Malaysians are multilingual, it's not unusual. Shouldn't you be saying Hayley's the perfect woman?"

Loretta: "Hayley's charm point is that on the outside, she's gorgeous, accomplished, and normal. But in her heart, she's a weird little freak, like me. You know that."

Having borne witness to their many FaceTime calls over the years, I did know that. "Right."

Loretta: "We're perfect for each other, and I want you to have the same thing. You've got Kriya here for the day, you've got the guns out." Tapped my arm. "We've got an open bar, there's going to be a band, dancing. *And* you've got the flat to yourself tonight. This is your chance to seal the deal."

Looked over at Kriya. She appeared engrossed in conversation with my aunt.

CG: "Are you telling me all of this—insisting I bring a date—was simply a scheme to set me up with Kriya?"

Loretta: "No!"

CG: "Good."

Loretta: "It's both. I did want you to bring proof of your heterosexuality, so I wouldn't get in trouble with the aunties. But I also knew you'd never shoot your shot with Kriya unless you were forced. I mean, there's a reason I'm marrying the love of my life, and you're terminally single."

There were so many scathing things I wanted to say, I wasn't sure which to start with. Clearly Loretta did *not* have better things to think about than my (admittedly pathetic) love life, even though she was, as she said, in the process of marrying a stunning girl she'd wooed online with nothing more than her native wit, *Lord of the Rings* memes, and obscene images of cartoon badminton players.

CG: "Look, you—"

Loretta: "There's no need to say thank you. You go get the girl."

Gave me a push towards Kriya and turned away.

There are times I feel Loretta does not have a proper respect for me as an elder.

CHAPTER EIGHTEEN

Kriya

After the photos, Loretta drew Charles away, and Hayley joined her family, leaving me vulnerable. Loretta's mum pounced, like a lioness that had spotted a sickly wildebeest trailing behind the herd.

"So you're Charles's friend," she said. In Cantonese.

Had Charles told her I spoke Cantonese? If so, he'd done me dirty. I understood it, mostly, which is a very different thing from speaking.

The problem was, I'd never really had to practise speaking it. In Malaysia it took a Herculean effort to convince the Chinese aunties and uncles I understood Cantonese. The mental dissonance caused by me being Indian—not even Chindian—was too much for them.

Even if they did by some miracle address me in Cantonese, there was no call for me to reply in the same language. I generally answered in Malay, a language I was actually fluent in, and which, crucially, has no tones.

Unfortunately, that was not an option here. Loretta's mum gazed at me, her eyes coolly assessing. She was wearing a cheongsam in a royal blue brocade and had silvering hair in a razor-sharp bob. She was about half my size, but three times as elegant, and I didn't think I was merely imagining the air of menace around her.

"Er, yes, auntie," I said.

The word "friend" in this context carried a lot of weight, as I well knew. Tom had been my "friend" to my extended family for the entire thirteen years we'd been together, and he would have stayed my "friend" unless and until we got married.

"I work with Charles," I said. "At the same company." I couldn't remember the word for "colleague."

"So you're a lawyer?" said Loretta's mum. "That's very good. Your father and mother are from India?"

"Malaysia, auntie. But we are Indian, yes."

"What do they do?"

"My father is not working anymore, but he was a—er— *government servant.*" That was another term I didn't know in Cantonese, so I said it in English. I added, "My mother looked after me."

Auntie's expression suggested she was not impressed. A pearl necklace was draped around the collar of her cheongsam, and she had sparkling bracelets on both wrists. I was no expert, but I had a feeling they were real diamonds.

Was Charles a Crazy Rich Asian? I'd known he was well-off, but there was "my dad had a good job and we could afford overseas holidays" kind of money, and then there was "our family travels to our overseas holidays by private jet" kind of money. I made a mental note to check Charles's LinkedIn profile to see if it said which school he'd gone to.

"Working for the government, that's very decent." Auntie made it sound like an insult. She raked me with a look, from top to toe. "You're a big girl, aren't you? Charles's friend, the old one, she was very small-sized."

That stung, but there was also something funny about it— the flash of the claws. As though this auntie could say anything worse to me than pretty much everyone around me had already said, multiple times in multiple languages, before I'd turned sixteen.

The most annoying thing I could do was make it clear I didn't care what she thought.

"Yes," I said peaceably.

Auntie's gimlet stare drilled into me. "His mother and I, we were starting to think maybe Charles is not interested in getting married."

I recognised this sideways language. My relatives spoke in a similar way about the LGBT people they knew. They didn't have any of the vocabulary. Though given Auntie's own daughter was gay, her refusal to learn had a stench of wilful ignorance to it.

"Nowadays many people don't like to get married," I agreed. "Auntie must be happy about Loretta getting married. Hayley is very pretty."

Auntie's face twitched. "Yes, she's very pretty. I don't know why she wants to marry Loretta. A pretty girl like her, she could marry any man. Even Loretta, even though she's so fat, she could find a husband if she tried."

I couldn't tell if this was a deliberate jab—Loretta was notably smaller than me—but she couldn't hurt me anyway. I'd already decided Auntie's good opinion wasn't one I valued.

"I told Loretta she just needs to look harder to find a husband. But she didn't want to try," said Auntie. Her mouth pulled into a disconsolate moue. "That's how it is these days. Children don't want to listen. You can say everything, but they don't care about their parents."

I thought of the absurd rigmarole that had led to me being here, at this wedding of two strangers, purely because Loretta wanted to please her mother. When I spoke, my voice was gentle—not for Auntie's sake, but because I was thinking of Loretta and Charles.

"I don't think that's true," I said. "Loretta's so happy you came. It's great you are accepting. Even if parents and children don't agree, it's not that they don't love each other. Being together is important."

At least, that was what I tried to say. Given the longest conversation I'd previously had in Cantonese had been about how many sar kok liew I wanted to purchase, and whether I wanted a second bag for them or not, I wasn't sure how much of my intended message I'd succeeded in conveying.

"Hmm," said Auntie, which didn't tell me much. She looked around the room.

Charles and Loretta were whispering together. Auntie's husband was talking to Hayley and her parents. Auntie raised an imperious hand and flagged down one of the bridesmaids, a white woman in a suit, with an undercut.

"Em, can you take a photo of me and Charles's friend on my phone?" said Auntie, in perfect English. "I must send it to his mother. She wants to see what does Kriya look like."

Once my image had been captured (it felt like my soul had gone with it), I was graciously dismissed, with another wave of that beringed hand. Charles came up to me, looking worried.

"Sorry, Loretta wanted to speak to me about—uh, about wedding stuff. Was it all right, with her mum?"

"I might take a while to recover," I said. "I have to say, Loretta is incredibly well adjusted, all things considered."

"That bad?" Charles grimaced. "What did my aunt say?"

"Nothing that terrible," I said. "I now know your last girlfriend was much thinner than me, though."

Charles looked horrified. "I'm so sorry. That's obviously not—I don't—I mean, it's completely unacceptable. I'll talk to her."

"Honestly, don't worry about it. I've experienced worse," I said. "It's not like she's my first Asian auntie. But you should know she does think I'm your girlfriend, and she's sending a picture of me to your mum."

Charles waved this away. "I'll handle things with my mum.

She's the easy one. That's what Loretta says—she got the good dad and the nightmare mum, and I got the good mum."

I noticed the fact he didn't mention his dad. Either absent or nightmare, then. Probably both, but perhaps he was sensitive about it.

"We should be making our way down," said Charles. "Loretta says you can leave your stuff here, if you want. She's passed me a spare keycard, so we can get back in if you need anything."

"Great," I said. "I'll hang on to my clutch, but the tote can stay here. Shall we go?"

The wedding ceremony took place in a pretty Georgian room, with a pink, seafoam green, and lilac ceiling, ornate ivory plaster moulding, and a grand crystal chandelier. The celebrant stood by a table at the front of the room, heaped with pink and white roses and dark greenery.

The brides were each escorted down the aisle by both parents. A girl in a rockabilly dress, with impressive full sleeve tattoos, did a reading from the Song of Solomon. Charles read Wendy Cope's "The Orange," gravely and without affectation. When he was done, Hayley and Loretta got up and hugged him.

Charles was red-eyed. He patted Loretta's back a few times before letting her go. I swallowed down a lump in my throat.

The brides read vows they had written themselves—except for the quotes from *The Duke of Badminton*, which were as overwrought as Charles had led me to expect, and made everyone laugh. Then the couple proceeded out to a rousing Japanese rock anthem, with half the room cheering and singing along.

I was about to join the flow of people streaming out of the room when Charles appeared at my elbow.

"Hey," I said. "Good job with the reading."

Charles ducked his head. "Thanks. Do you know where you're going?"

I gestured at the door. "We've been promised drinks and canapés if we head that way."

"I've got to stay with Loretta and Hayley," said Charles. "They're going to do the tea ceremony now, just with family. It shouldn't take long. Will you be all right on your own?"

I smiled. "Yeah. Don't worry about me. I'm having fun."

"Great," said Charles. "That's good. I, uh, I'll see you later, then."

He was standing close enough that I could smell his cologne—a woody, peppery scent, rising off warm skin. I wondered what it was.

"Looking forward to it," I said inanely.

Charles blushed. For some reason my cheeks were hot, too.

"All right," he said, and then he was gone.

I followed the other guests out of the room, pressing my hand absently against the side of my face. The room had been on the chilly side, and my fingers were cool on my cheek.

I wasn't upset to be by myself. I didn't know anyone there, but there was plenty to keep me entertained. In my satin cocktail dress, I fit right in with half the guests—at least in terms of what I was wearing. The crowd was predominantly white and East Asian.

But I'd expected that. It was the other half of the attendees I hadn't expected. They had hair—and wigs—in every colour of the rainbow, as well as piercings, tattoos, quirky glasses, and mobility aids, and they were dressed in everything from badminton gear to giant sparkly ballgowns paired with elaborate headdresses to full kimono, complete with obi and geta. It was as though a carnival had crashed a reception at Buckingham Palace.

People were laughing and squealing and grabbing each other to pose for photographs in their costumes. A mysterious towering figure shrouded in black, with a ghostly white mask, silently offered me chocolate coins.

I accepted two and watched him? her? turn to another guest, a red-haired woman in a floral dress. She smiled and shook her head, but she looked a little sorry when the masked figure wandered off without saying anything. Like me, she didn't seem to know anyone else there.

I said, "Do you think they're on stilts under the costume, or do you think they're really that tall?"

"I was wondering that," said Redhead. She had an American accent. "I've been trying to remember where I've seen that character before. I'm sure it's from a movie." She laughed. "This wedding is *so* Hayley. Everything about it is totally her."

"You're a friend of Hayley's?"

"Oh yeah. Me and Hayley go way back. We met in first grade. When she said she was moving to England for a girl, I thought, you know, when else am I going to get to fly over to London for a wedding? My partner's English, but this is my first time visiting." Redhead smiled at me. "How do you know Hayley and Loretta?"

"I'm here with Charles," I said. "He's the best man."

"Oh, Loretta's cousin Charles?"

I nodded. "I only met Loretta and Hayley today, for the first time."

Redhead pulled a face. "Oh my God! In at the deep end. I'm going to see my partner's family for the first time too."

I was about to explain that I wasn't with Charles in that sense, and there was nothing inherently intimidating about being introduced to his family. Apart from the fact I'd been expected to speak Cantonese to his frightening aunt.

But Redhead went on, "We're headed to Norwich tomorrow to visit his parents."

"Oh, Norwich is lovely. My ex was from there." But talking about Tom felt like pressing a bruise. I said, "Is London living up to expectations?"

It was amazing, said Redhead. "We've been saying, maybe we should move here. My partner was living in London when we met, so he knows it well."

"You guys met online?"

Redhead nodded. "We did the long-distance thing for a while at first, before he moved over. How did you meet Charles?"

"We work at the same firm," I said. "We actually share an office."

"Oh wow," said Redhead. "My partner works at the same company as me too. But he joined after we got together. It can be a lot, right?"

"Oh, Charles and I are just friends." It was the first time I'd said it out loud: that we were friends. It was comforting to feel it was true.

Redhead turned pink. "Oh, sorry. I just assumed."

"It's fine. You're not the only one," I said lightly. "What's it like, working with your partner? It must be challenging to navigate. Have you guys been together for long?"

"A year and half," said Redhead. "But we've only been in the same country for, like, a year. I worried about it when he first got hired, but we're in different departments, so that definitely helps. And getting the job enabled him to move over. We're making it work so far."

"That's great." I looked at her wistfully. She had such a glow of optimism, of new love. Would I ever feel that way again about someone?

Redhead glanced around and brightened. "Oh, hey, there he is. Babe!" She dived into the crowd and extracted a tall, lean white man in a slightly dishevelled suit.

"Come and say hello to—" She cut herself off, turning to me. "Oh, I don't think I got your name! I'm Alexis. And you are . . . ?"

I didn't answer. For a moment I couldn't speak.

Redhead's boyfriend had a mop of curly brown hair—it grew

with unnatural rapidity, and I knew its exact texture, what it felt like as it slipped through the fingers. The last time I'd seen him was on a video call, six months ago. He'd seemed off, distracted, but I'd assumed it was tiredness, or stress, or that I'd caught him at a bad time. Though all the times I spoke to him seemed to be bad times, since he moved.

When people show you what they are, believe them, my friends had told me, when we got stuck into overanalysing Tom's behaviour. But I didn't want to believe what he was showing me. He'd had to tell me, in so many words. That probably hadn't been any nicer for him than it had been for me.

On the other hand, I hadn't been cheating on him. All that time, while we were living together, while he was applying for the big job in the States, while I was encouraging him and making sure I only cried in the shower, because I didn't want my fears to hold him back from his dreams. All that time.

"Kriya," said Tom. He was white to the lips.

I turned, pushing blindly through the crowd, ignoring Redhead's wide eyes and the exclamations of concern springing up in my wake. I didn't know where I was going. All I knew was that I needed to be alone.

CHAPTER NINETEEN

Charles

Emerging from the tea ceremony, £500 poorer, when I saw Kriya. She burst out of the room where people were having canapés, darted across the lobby, and vanished through the revolving door, out of the hotel.

Loretta came out after me. "What's up?" She hadn't seen Kriya.

CG: "I have to nip out for a second. You carry on."

Paused in the portico when I got out, looking around. Couldn't spot Kriya, though she'd only had a few seconds' head start. Couldn't have got far. But which way would she have gone—towards the main road, or away?

Attendant in a grey suit said: "Can I help you, sir?"

CG: "I'm looking for my—" Got stuck on how to refer to Kriya. Date? Most accurate, but misleading. Friend? Felt presumptuous. Colleague? Baffling. "I'm looking for someone. A woman in a green dress? She would've just come out."

The attendant pulled a sympathetic face and jerked his head towards the main road. So Kriya had scarpered, I thought. But as I went in that direction, I saw what had been hidden from me when I was in the portico. There was an alcove in the side of the building, with discreet wooden doors leading to a lift. Kriya was leaning against the wall in the alcove, crying.

Not in itself a shock. Thought that was what was going on. The violence of her distress was what was shocking. She didn't even clock me.

What would I want, if I were her? To be ignored, left to it, given the chance to pull myself together.

But was that true? Wouldn't want to see just anyone. But if it were Kriya, it might be all right if she came and said the right thing to me.

No point arguing with myself. I wasn't about to return to the hotel to knock back champagne with the cosplayers while Kriya was out here, upset.

CG: "What's wrong? Did something happen?"

Kriya started. Looked up and saw me. Shook her head.

She was struggling to speak. Opened my mouth to say, *It's all right, don't worry about it, let's get you inside,* when I heard someone shout:

"Kriya!"

Guy had come out of the hotel. Looked like a wedding guest—in a suit, face vaguely familiar. Kriya couldn't see him from where she was standing, but she stiffened at the sound of his voice.

Kriya: "It's Tom." Panicky, like a cornered animal, the whites of her eyes showing. "I can't let him see me, I'm a mess. What do I do?"

Kriya was shielded for now, but the guy—Tom—would see her if he came this way, and there were only two directions to choose from. He'd definitely spot her if she tried to leg it.

Could see him addressing the attendant. Attendant looked torn, couldn't help glancing in our direction. Tom caught the look and started over.

CG: "He's coming this way." Could I step out and misdirect

him? What would I even say? *Nothing to see here, guv, move along now*—

Kriya, in a strange, urgent voice: "Charles, can I kiss you?"

My head whipped around. "What?"

She put her arms around me and pressed her lips to mine.

Kriya's lips were soft, slightly tacky from her lipstick. Her hair grazed my face, ticklish.

It wasn't a real kiss, or a real embrace. Kriya wasn't doing anything with her mouth other than resting it against mine. She was holding her body away from me, the way one does when colleagues from overseas offices insist on hugs. Or worse, air kisses.

But Kriya wasn't one of those colleagues, none of whom I'd wanted that close to me. I didn't mind it with Kriya.

"Didn't mind it" was understating it. My body didn't know the kiss wasn't real, and it was extremely excited about this development. And the smell of Kriya's hair, and her breath on my face, and the flutter of her eyelashes against her cheek.

Despite the distance between us, I could feel her trembling, very slightly. Cooled me down a bit. I patted her on the back, gingerly.

Kriya laughed against my mouth. Sounded more like a sob than I would have liked, but when she pulled away she was smiling, though tremulously.

She whispered: "Is he still there?"

I could hear footsteps retreating away from us. Sneaked a look out of the alcove. Tom was disappearing through the revolving door. The attendant stood by, stone-faced.

CG: "He's going back into the hotel."

Kriya: "Thank God." She collapsed against the wooden doors. "I'm sorry for lunging at you. I couldn't face talking to him. It was the only thing I could think of."

Nodded, mute.

Kriya looked at me, concerned. "Are you all right? I'm really sorry."

CG: "There's no need to apologise. It's fine. I understand why you did it."

Good idea, really. Don't know why it didn't occur to me.

Realised I was staring at Kriya's mouth. Adjusted my gaze, fixing it on a point two inches above her left shoulder.

CG: "Who was that guy?"

Kriya: "My ex-boyfriend. He's dating Hayley's childhood best friend. Turns out he was dating her for about a year before he broke up with me."

CG: "Shit."

Kriya dug around in the tiny bag she was carrying and took out a tissue, dabbing her eyes with it. "I just found out. I was chatting to the new girlfriend and she didn't realise who I was. I didn't realise who *she* was, until I saw Tom." Wiped her eyes. "I feel so stupid. I should have seen it coming. He moved to America last year. We talked about me coming along, but he said, let's see how it works out first. Guess he wanted to try out his new life before committing."

Her voice broke. She crumpled the tissue in her hand. "Sorry. You don't want to hear all this."

Didn't know what to say. So I said what I was thinking:

"Those shoes must be uncomfortable to stand around in."

Kriya blinked. Looked down at her feet. "They're fine. They're pretty comfortable, for heels."

Her toenails were red. Was it creepy to stare at her feet? I've got feet, too. My feet aren't as good, though. Tore my gaze away, to be safe.

CG: "But you could probably do with a break. Do you want to go get a coffee and sit down somewhere?"

Kriya hesitated, glancing at the hotel.

CG: "Not in there. There's a good café around the corner."

Kriya gave herself a little shake. "You should be at the wedding. Loretta and her family will be wondering where you are."

CG: "You're forgetting Loretta's family have met me. They'll assume I've holed up in a room to check my emails. That's what I used to do at all the family gatherings—without the emails. It wasn't Chinese New Year unless I was off in a corner, hiding from everyone else."

Kriya laughed. I felt like a superhero.

CG: "It's only a couple of minutes away. We'll have a coffee and come back. No one will notice."

Loretta would probably approve. Stealing Kriya away was definitely what she'd think I should be doing.

After a pause, Kriya nodded.

I turned, but Kriya said: "Wait first." She produced a packet of wipes from her bag. "Hold still."

She reached out and smoothed a wet wipe across my mouth.

Froze. Poor old body sat up and begged like a dog.

Kriya was close enough that there was a real risk she might hear my heart trying to hammer its way out of my chest. Her touch was firm as she stroked my lips once, twice. A third time.

Was going to stroke out myself if this went on for much longer. Shied away.

Kriya: "I think I got it all." Showed me the wipe, smeared with a plummy red. "Thought you wouldn't want to be seen with lipstick all over your mouth." She grinned.

CG: "Yes. No. Of course."

Heart pounding as though I'd been sprinting. Stupid heart.

Café was quiet. We sat on a banquette in a narrow back room, with scuffed wooden floors, worn rugs, and tiny coffee tables with hairpin legs. Like having coffee in somebody's living room, but more uncomfortable.

Wished café had seen fit to have normal tables and chairs. It was awkward perching on one end of the banquette while Kriya perched on the other. Because it was warm and we'd dressed for the weather, we didn't even have coats to pile up between us.

Was acutely conscious of her: the warmth coming off her skin, the fragrance she was wearing.

It was that fake kiss, that was the problem. Couldn't unknow what it felt like. Body wanted it to happen again. Brain knew better, of course.

At least the coffee was good. Kriya got a cappuccino, with chocolate on top. I had a black filter coffee.

Kriya: "Sorry about all the drama." Looked rueful, but calm. "I haven't done a great job as your date."

CG: "It's not really a job. More of an imposition. If I'd known your ex was going to be here . . ."

Kriya: "How could you have known? It's for the best. I might never have found out about Tom cheating on me, otherwise. I heard he was seeing someone new, but I had no idea about the timeline." Stared down at her drink. "Alexis—the new girlfriend—she said they were dating long-distance before he even got the job in America, when he was still in London. We were living together at the time."

CG, with feeling: "What a bastard."

Kriya laughed. Wasn't a happy laugh. "Right?" She put her hand up to her face, as if to shield it. "I'm so stupid."

CG: "You weren't stupid for trusting someone you love— loved." Was the past tense correct? I wasn't sure.

Kriya shook her head. "Things weren't great for a while, even before he moved overseas. He wasn't happy. I just didn't want to see it. We met at university, we were together for thirteen years. I mean, I loved him. I told myself it was his job, he wasn't fulfilled at work. Then this US role came up and he wanted to give it a shot. I thought, who am I to hold him back, you know?

I wanted to be supportive." She fumbled in her bag for another tissue, blew her nose. "Sorry."

Found myself saying: "My dad was convicted for fraud, when I was a kid."

Kriya looked up, startled.

I was equally surprised. Never told anyone before. Don't even talk about it with people who know, like Loretta.

Kriya: "Really?"

CG: "He embezzled funds from his company. It was a family business, owned by his cousin. It was messy. He got a fine and prison time, but he ran, he left the country. My mum and I didn't know where he'd gone or what had happened to him, for years."

Kriya's eyes were huge. "Oh my God, Charles. That's terrible."

CG: "My mum got the worst of it. He'd spent her savings, racked up all this debt she hadn't known about. I was lucky, my uncle agreed to keep paying for my education until I turned eighteen. After that, I managed to cover university myself, with loans and so on. But it took my mum years to pay off my dad's debts."

Kriya: "Oh, Charles." She touched my arm.

Had to exert myself in order not to recoil. Didn't want her to get the wrong idea. It was simply that that kiss had primed my body to read too much into any touch from Kriya, however fleeting.

CG: "No matter what, my mum would never blame my dad. It drove me wild, how she'd make excuses for him. She keeps worrying about him to this day, even though he remarried and had a second family."

Kriya: "That must have been so hard on you."

Wasn't wrong, but that wasn't the point.

CG: "I didn't mean to make this about myself. I only mention it because . . . I hate how my mum defends my dad. But in a way I admire it, too. She's not ashamed of the fact she cared about him. She doesn't think it makes her stupid. And it doesn't."

Kriya's eyes were soft. "She sounds amazing."

CG: "She drives me bonkers. But yeah." Paused. "I'm sorry about not covering the drinks at the pub. You know, with the work experience lot. My dad needs a lot of help still. With the wedding and everything, money's been a bit tight. But I should have said, if you don't mind waiting, I can pay you back."

Kriya: "Oh no, don't be ridiculous. I said I'd cover it. It wasn't a problem. Have you been worrying about that all this time?"

Didn't answer. Didn't have to. Felt like she was looking right through me.

Kriya: "I'm sorry, I shouldn't have put you on the spot like that. I know what it's like to have family to support. My parents need help as well. And it's harder when they're far away, right?" She shook her head, rueful. "That's a learning for me. You shouldn't assume you know all there is to know about someone."

Kriya smiled at me—a real smile, though there was a bitter-sweet twist to it. "At least you become nicer the more I learn about you. The opposite of Tom."

Felt a glow at the compliment, though I wasn't sure how I felt about the comparison with her ex-boyfriend. Bastard or not, she'd loved him. Thirteen years together, she'd said. I couldn't imagine she was over him yet.

Not that it was any of my business. Nothing to do with me.

CG: "I could knock him over the head? Have an accident with the racquet? Though there's probably an upper limit to the amount of damage a badminton racquet can inflict. It's a pity Loretta isn't into a golf anime."

Kriya laughed. "I appreciate the thought, but no."

She downed the last of her coffee, putting the mug back on the coffee table. I stared at the shelf of fancy coffee beans across from us, so my conscience couldn't accuse me of watching her swallow.

Kriya: "We should get back to the wedding."

Had been thinking about this. "You don't have to. I can tell them you've had an emergency and had to leave."

Kriya: "Oh." She considered it. But after a moment, she shook her head. "Thanks. But I'd rather go back. Loretta and Hayley have been so hospitable. It doesn't feel right to run out on them."

CG: "They wouldn't mind."

Kriya: "Maybe, but I would. Anyway, I don't want Tom to think I've run away because I'm scared of seeing him." Raised her chin. "*I* haven't done anything to be ashamed of."

A spark glinted in her eye. Made her seem more like the Kriya of every day. It was reassuring.

CG: "If you're sure."

CHAPTER TWENTY

Kriya

I felt a little less brave, going back to the hotel, than I'd let on to Charles.

His offer to cover for me while I sloped off had been tempting. I'd thought about it for a good five seconds.

But it didn't feel right to stand him up, when he'd been so decent about everything. Looking back on it now, I couldn't believe I'd jumped on him like that. In the moment, the only thing I'd cared about was getting out of talking to Tom.

Was that all there was to it, though? There must have been a part of me that wanted Tom to see me in a clinch with another guy. *You didn't hurt me. Look, I've got someone new, too.*

Poor Charles. Honestly, he'd be in his rights to report me.

At least it had been barely a kiss. It had felt like it had lasted forever, but it had probably only been a few seconds, at most.

His lips had been a little dry, but not unpleasantly so. I could still feel the rasp of his stubble against my chin. The warmth of his breath, and his hands on my back, soothing.

I tore myself out of the memory. It wasn't going to help me in the task I'd volunteered for—being Charles's normal, pleasant, cheerful date to the wedding. If that fleeting touch had revived appetites my body had been too sad to notice in the past six months, that was something I was going to have to deal with another time. In private, with the necessary equipment, and fantasies about someone appropriate—Hyun Bin, or my first crush from primary school, Vijay, who'd grown up to be an incredibly hot ophthalmologist based in Phoenix, Arizona, or literally anybody except the guy I shared an office with.

The dead time between the ceremony and the reception was nearly over. I only had to tough out the dinner. There was dancing after, but Charles would probably be as keen as me to slip away once the cake was cut.

It was surreal rejoining the bustle and merriment of the wedding, with the guests in their fancy dress. I was on edge, seeing Tom in every white guy there, and his new girlfriend in every white woman.

Dinner was in the same room that the ceremony had taken place in, set up now with round tables bearing lavish floral centrepieces: pink and white roses, peonies, ranunculi, and hydrangeas. The effect was only slightly marred by the fact that around the base of each vase of flowers were ranged cartoony little action figures of badminton players.

I scanned the room, but I couldn't see Tom or Alexis. My shoulders loosened, the tension seeping out of them.

As we took our seats, Charles nodded at the action figures. "Those are the wedding favours."

On closer inspection, I could see tags tied around the figurines, labelled: *Take me home!*

"Cute," I said. "Which one's the character you're dressed as?"

"There are three on this table," and Charles pointed them out to me.

I picked the one of Yamaguchi Kiichiro gazing into the distance, his badminton racquet at the ready, his mouth a resolute line. There was something very Charles about it.

I didn't speak much to Charles himself, after that. He kept getting summoned away, dashing off on errands for the brides and their parents. The rest of the table was occupied by Loretta's university friends, who seemed to know Charles well.

"I'm so glad he's met you," said one, a friendly Scottish Chinese doctor. "Charles is great. I've been trying to set him up for years, but it's impossible to pin him down for dates. He's such a workaholic."

Her affectionate familiarity with Charles didn't really fit with his self-image as a friendless loser. He was clearly popular among Loretta's friends. Maybe he thought that didn't count.

While we were finishing up our portions of wedding cake, Charles came back to the table and bent down by my chair to speak to me.

"Loretta's parents are having some issues with their room, I need to sort it out for them. Once that's done, we can go. Is that all right?"

His breath was warm on my ear. I caught the Scottish doctor looking at us. She murmured something to her neighbour, who glanced at us and smiled.

Heat rose in my cheeks.

"Sure," I said. "I'm not in a rush." It was true. Knowing Charles was looking out for me made me feel safe, as though I was surrounded by a force field generated by his concern.

It felt worse when we were moved on from the dinner table to the dance floor, in the same room where we'd had drinks and nibbles earlier—where I'd encountered Tom and his new girlfriend. Charles was gone, and the people we'd shared a table with had dispersed. I was alone in the crowd.

Jpop was blaring out of the speakers: "*Kiss kiss fall in love!*" sang a sweet, high-pitched female voice. A group of guests in costume squealed and rushed onto the dance floor.

I hadn't spotted Tom or Alexis yet. Maybe they'd left. If I were Alexis, I'd be pretty damn suspicious about Tom running out of the hotel after me, calling my name.

But I didn't want to think about that. Fortunately I wasn't left to brood on it for long. Loretta lurched out of the crowd, pink-faced and high as a kite on love, excitement, and champagne.

"Kriya!" she crowed. "Where's Charles?"

I explained about her parents' room issues. "I think he's speaking to the manager."

"Poor Charles," said Loretta. "My mum's probably just being a nightmare. I'll worry about it tomorrow." She beamed at me. "I'm so happy you're here. Do you do hugs? Can I hug you?"

"Of course."

Loretta was warm and smelled of alcohol, but also of a rich fragrance that was somehow familiar, reassuring. I couldn't quite put my finger on it, but it was nice.

Her eyes were wide and serious as she drew back. "Listen, I need to talk to you. Woman to woman."

Her shift from exhilaration to sobriety was disconcerting.

"What about?" I thought of Tom and Alexis, with a nauseating dip in my stomach.

"About Charles." Loretta burped. "Sorry." She swayed towards me.

It didn't seem a wholly intentional movement. I put my hand on her elbow. "Do you want to sit down?"

"I'm good," said Loretta, resisting my attempts to steer her towards the chairs arranged against the walls. She grasped my hand. "I want you to understand about Charles."

"OK . . ." Where was this going?

"I know he can come off like a robot. 'Beep boop beep, all I do is work.'" Loretta moved her arms up and down, her elbows locked at a ninety-degree angle, in something that was apparently intended to be a robot dance move. "But what you've got to understand is, under that exoskeleton, Charles has the purest little heart that man ever had. I bully him constantly and all he does is cook dinner and take the abuse." She gulped, sniffing. "That's the kind of person he is. All he cares about is the law, his gains, and his family."

"Do you want a tissue?"

"No." Loretta rubbed her eyes. "I want you to know. Charles may seem like a weirdo, but he's a gem. He's a little . . . a little diamond, twinkling alone in the night sky. His last girlfriend dumped him because she wanted something 'more exciting.'" She did the quotes with her fingers. "You saw him today, in his Kiichiro cosplay. Is that a man who is not exciting?"

"Well—"

"No! Fuck her!" Loretta turned her gaze on me. "Now you've come along, like a beautiful goddess who also does law. And you seem like you get Charles, and you laugh at his jokes, and he really likes you. That's what I want you to know. It might seem like Charles is solid metal all the way through." She banged her chest. "But his heart is soft and squishy, like a . . . like a delicious red bean mochi. And you've got that heart in the palm of your hand. You've got to be gentle with it. OK?"

I wanted to laugh, but I also felt touched—and guilty. I'd known intellectually that accompanying Charles to a family wedding as his date would involve deceiving his relatives. That had been the whole point.

But the lie had felt less bad before I'd actually met Charles's relatives. I didn't mind what his horrible aunt thought, but Loretta was different. I wasn't here to fool her. But if she was exhorting me to be gentle with Charles's heart, some wires must have got crossed somewhere along the line.

Loretta was fun and funny and full of life, someone I could imagine being friends with. And here I was, making her think I was dating someone important to her. That I was able to affect Charles's happiness in any meaningful way, when the most I could do was have my headset on during video calls and avoid eating anything too odorous at my desk.

"Will you promise?" said Loretta.

"I think there's been some confusion—"

"Please?" Loretta gazed at me, wide-eyed. "I feel like you're the kind of person who keeps her promises."

I couldn't bring myself to lay waste to her illusions. It was her wedding day. I'd have to get Charles to explain everything to her later.

"I'll try my best," I said. That was true, at least. "He's a good guy."

"He is," said Loretta. "He deserves someone like you." She gave me another hug, glimpsed someone behind me, and shrieked, "Lexi!"

I turned around with a grim sense of inevitability.

Alexis hadn't recognised me from the back. She checked as she approached us, blanching. Tom was with her.

"Hayley's been looking everywhere for you," said Loretta to Alexis. "Let's go find her!" She glanced at Tom. "You'll let me borrow her for a second, right?"

"Er," said Tom, but Loretta was already dragging his girlfriend away.

I'd been spending the hours since returning to the wedding dreading another run-in with Tom. But now it had happened, it didn't feel that bad. It helped that Tom was frozen to the spot, looking petrified.

"Hi, Tom," I said.

He looked as though he thought I might bite his head off.

There had been a shift in power between us, I realised. I'd spent the final year of our relationship feeling cast aside, unimportant. And I'd invested so much energy into persuading myself it was fine. My feelings were my own concern, I'd told myself, not Tom's. I shouldn't trouble him with them. I needed to focus on supporting him.

Now, for the first time ever, I didn't want anything from Tom. Not his attention or affection, not even an apology. What would "sorry" do? I'd been with him from age twenty to thirty-three. I hadn't been perfect, but I'd tried my best for him. I'd done all I could to build a good life for us, together. And he hadn't even had the decency to be honest with me.

Learning what I had today had freed me from any longing I'd felt for what we used to have. I didn't need anything from him anymore.

I could have walked away. But I found I had things to say to Tom. We were off by ourselves, and it was unlikely anyone would overhear us over the music.

"Fancy seeing you here," I said.

"Kriya," said Tom.

"Sorry I ran out earlier," I said. "I needed a moment. Alexis told me how you guys got together, and I worked out what the timeline meant. I guess it was easier to dump me over text than to do it while we were living together and I was paying the rent."

Tom winced. "That's not fair."

"Is it not?" I said, genuinely curious. "Which part of it was unfair?"

He hunched. Everything about Tom was so familiar, still—the timbre of his voice, the way he ducked his head, the hair curling at the back of his neck. After so many years together, his every gesture was imprinted on me. And yet I was looking at someone I had never truly known.

"Why didn't you just break up with me when you left?" I said. "Or even better, before you started chatting to Alexis? Dragging it out didn't do anyone any favours."

Tom grimaced. "I didn't want to hurt you. I don't know if you remember, but it wasn't a good time for me, Kriya. I'm not proud of what I did—"

"Well, that's something."

Tom looked irritated. "Do you have to? I'm trying to apologise."

"Are you seriously telling me off for being angry?"

"No, I'm just . . ." He sighed. "I'm sorry."

Perhaps the apology should have felt like a victory, or vindication, or something. But I'd been right. It didn't feel like much of anything.

As I looked at him, round-shouldered and glum, my heart wrenched. Tom's unhappiness had always elicited a complex knot of guilt and responsibility in me. I'd felt I had to fix it—that if he wasn't happy, that was somehow due to my failings. As though, if I'd been happier with my direction in life, or been more present, or different in some way, that would have changed things for him. He wouldn't have been so frustrated. He would have loved his job, and living in London, and all the things about our life that had pissed him off while we were together.

But none of that had been anything I could have fixed. The grief weighing me down was less for him than for the Kriya of the past—who'd tried so hard, and loved him so much. That was all over. It felt like I should have more to show for it than I did.

"I did my best for you," I said. "I invested so much in our relationship. Everything I had."

Tom shrugged his shoulders, as if he were trying to throw off the burden of what I'd said.

"But that's what made it so hard," he said. "It always felt like I had to be grateful. I couldn't tell you I wasn't happy. You were always so busy and stressed about work. And then Lexi came along . . ."

"And you tripped and fell into her DMs," I suggested.

Tom elected not to take notice of this. "I didn't mean for it to happen. I was confused, and then I got the new job, and—everything was moving so fast. It's not that I didn't care about you."

"OK, Tom." I felt worn out and sad, suddenly done with this

conversation. It wasn't going to take us anywhere new. I didn't have a relationship with him anymore.

"I don't need to hear it," I said. And then I saw Charles.

He was standing at the entrance, looking around the room. Our eyes met. His forehead smoothed out. I smiled.

Tom glanced over his shoulder, to see what I was looking at. "You're here with someone?"

I wondered what Alexis had told him about what I was doing here with Charles, if anything. I'd told her we were just friends, but I imagined she'd had other things to discuss with Tom. And of course, he'd seen me embracing poor Charles.

"It's not really any of your business, is it?" I said.

"OK. I set myself up for that," said Tom. "I hope he does right by you, that's all."

"All right, Tom," I said tolerantly.

Charles was looking at his phone. He lowered it as I came over, but not before I'd caught sight of the screen.

"Are you checking your emails?" I said incredulously. I did a Sunday night scroll of my inbox ahead of getting back to work on Monday morning, but this was a little extreme. So far as I knew, Charles wasn't working on anything urgent enough that he'd have to have his work phone on him the weekend of his cousin's wedding where he was best man.

Charles looked shamefaced. "Bad habit." He put the phone away. "Are you all right to leave?"

"Ready when you are." I looked back at the room. Loretta had ditched Alexis: She was with Hayley, taking pictures with a group of costumed guests. It would have been polite to go say a proper goodbye, but it seemed a shame to interrupt them when they were having fun. Besides, I'd already had my moment with Loretta. "Have you settled the problem with Loretta's parents' room?"

"The hotel's giving them a voucher for afternoon tea. Seems to have done the trick," said Charles. "Who were you talking to?"

I blinked. "That was Tom. My ex."

"Oh. I'm not great at faces. Today's been good for that," said Charles reflectively. "Everyone's a different shape, because of the cosplay. Everything OK?"

"Yeah." But I could feel Charles's eyes on me. He wouldn't probe if I didn't want to talk about it, but I felt I owed him a little more than that.

"I feel like I sallied forth to slay a dragon and it turned out to be a lizard," I said. I thought of the geckos of my childhood that used to skitter out of dark corners of the house at moments best calculated to terrify the humans in occupation. "And then he escaped and left his tail behind."

"I can't say I understood any of that," said Charles, after a moment. "But I gather you had the best of it."

"Yeah," I said. "I think I did."

CHAPTER TWENTY-ONE

Charles

Didn't see Kriya for a couple of days after Loretta's wedding. She was working from home. Landlord coming to look at her boiler, or something like that.

Hard not to suspect she was avoiding me. Maybe just as well. Lay awake for ages the night after the wedding, staring at the ceiling.

Bad idea to bring Kriya to the wedding. She had that disastrous encounter with her ex. Even more disastrously, for me, there was that kiss.

Not a real kiss. I knew that. But it had been confusing.

Kriya was in such a state then, she would have done anything to escape her ex. Didn't mean she was attracted to me, or wanted to kiss me.

After a couple of hours of this, I turned on the lamp, thinking I'd go get a glass of water. Realised the patch of shadow on the ceiling I'd been staring at wasn't shadow, but a damp patch. So I went and emailed the building management company instead.

Relief to be able to get up in the morning and go to the office, tired as I was. Flat felt quiet without Loretta. She'd left with Hayley and her in-laws to fly off to Japan. Would be away for four weeks—in-laws peeling off after the first week so Hayley and Loretta could have a proper honeymoon.

Busy start to the week, getting the DLP settlement over the line. Was waiting around for instructions on Tuesday evening when the phone rang.

Thought it was the client, calling to confirm they had approval from their Board in the US to sign the settlement agreement. Put the call on speaker. It was getting on for ten p.m. anyway: no one in the pods outside to be disturbed.

But it was Shaw Boey's voice that issued from the phone. First thing he said was:

"Chinky Charlie! How are you, mate?"

Had a brief unpleasant shock, hearing the old nickname. Like being back at school.

Had forgotten people used to call me that. And that was when they were being friendly.

It was a different time. I was glad nobody else was around to hear him. Couldn't imagine Kriya would be impressed.

CG: "Hi, Shaw. How are you?" Remembered his text, over the weekend. "Sorry I didn't ring you yesterday. It's been on the to-do list, I just didn't manage to get to it."

Shaw: "That's all right. You're a busy man. You good to chat now?"

Glanced at my inbox. There was an update from the client:

CEO's in a meeting for the next hour. We should have confirmation to proceed shortly.

Suppressed a sigh.

CG: "Yes. I am waiting for a call, though, so I might have to jump off at short notice."

Shaw: "Fine. I'll cut to the chase. I don't know how much you know about it, but I set up an investment firm a few years back, Blackmount Capital. We've been doing a lot of work with a chap at your firm, Robert Anderson. Do you know him?"

Didn't recognise the name, but there are two thousand people in the London office. Looked him up on the intranet. Partner in Corporate, specialising in M&A. Went to our school, though that would have been some years before we were there.

Shaw: "We need help with an issue that's come up for one of our backers. Between you and me, Charlie, this guy's a big deal, very prominent person. He doesn't like people to know about his personal affairs, so I do a lot for him, you know, help him out. He needs a lawyer in the UK, someone who can go to court on his behalf. Robert said it wouldn't be him, wanted to refer me on to his Litigation colleagues. That made me think, hullo, I know who I need—Charlie Goh. You do litigation, yeah?"

CG: "Yes. This would be for an individual? Can you tell me about the case?"

Shaw: "There's this crank who's obsessed with my client—the guy I was telling you about, the VVIP. She's been posting about him on her blog for years, all kinds of lies and conspiracy theories. Harassment, really. He's been ignoring her, trying not to feed the flames, but she keeps escalating. Now she's threatening to publish her allegations in the paper. My client's a high-profile person, his name is very important to him. If people start believing this woman, that could be a problem for him."

CG, taking notes: "Your client's looking to bring an action to restrain publication? Against the newspaper, I presume."

Shaw: "This is a very reputable UK paper. My client doesn't have any issues with them. It's this woman who's making these trumped-up allegations. She's a freelancer, she's not on payroll. Problem is, my client's overseas, right? He's a foreigner. Whereas this woman is British, so of course the editors will believe anything she says. You know what these Brits are like. You can say anything you want about a third world country like Malaysia and they'll believe you, so long as you've got the right accent and went to the right school."

Funny Shaw saying that, given the school we both went to. That said, he's not wrong.

CG: "So you want to approach the person making the allegations?"

Shaw: "That's right. Enough is enough. My client wants to draw a line under this, get her to leave him alone."

CG: "It sounds an interesting case." Defamation not an area I had any experience in, but I'd been clicking around the intranet while Shaw spoke, looking people up. "Our Reputation Management team is led by Ellie Martin. I can put you in touch with her."

Shaw: "Yeah, Robert mentioned her. Not really a name to strike fear in the hearts of the opposition, is it? 'Ellie'?"

Didn't see the relevance.

CG: "She's ranked Tier 1 for Defamation Law in Law100."

Shaw: "Good for her. I'm all for senior women. Up against a wall, for preference."

He laughed. I didn't think it was that funny.

Shaw, clearing his throat: "Look, my client belongs to a different generation. He's the same age as our dads. He'd prefer to know a man's in charge. And I'd feel better knowing it's you, Charlie. This is highly, highly sensitive stuff. We need someone we can trust, not some expert."

CG: "This is a specialist area of law, not one I'm familiar with. You will want an expert advising. There's always a risk, with litigation, that you could be exacerbating any reputational issues."

Shaw: "We're hoping it won't come to that. We want you to run us through all the options. If we can knock it on the head with a stroppy letter, that would be ideal. Put your letterhead on it, remind her she'd have to pay your fees if we sue—that's how it works, yeah?"

CG: "Loser pays, yes. There are exceptions, such as—"

Shaw: "That's what I thought. Look, are you up for it? My

client's got deep pockets. He's willing to pay top dollar for top service, but you're going to have to do things his way."

Sounded like every client I'd ever worked with, except for the part where he was willing to fork out.

Farah had been encouraging me to take more of a lead on client relationships, bringing in new work. Getting this case in would boost my case for partnership.

Not in a rush, but it would be good to make partner. Farah was evidence you can be a partner and still be a good lawyer, despite the extra faff. I could use the money, too.

I would have to involve the Reputation Management team, whatever Shaw said about experts. But if the client wanted me to be the point of contact, well. The client gets what they want. That's the first rule of the job.

CG: "We'd be happy to help."

Shaw wanted a note of advice on their options, in the first instance.

CG: "That's fine. And who's the client?"

Shaw paused. "Do you need his name? He'd prefer to stay behind the scenes."

CG: "We will need to clear conflicts and complete our client due diligence processes before we can act." Shaw stayed silent, so I said: "You can trust we'll keep the details confidential. We routinely handle sensitive cases of this kind."

Shaw: "Can't you treat Blackmount as the client? We'll cover the fees. Think of it as us approaching you for advice on a hypothetical scenario."

Bit odd, but I've done similar things before—sought advice from overseas counsel on behalf of clients keen to maintain anonymity. If it was simply a matter of advising on the options available, in circumstances where any action was hypothetical, I couldn't see that there was an immediate risk of a conflict.

CG: "If your client does decide to take action, we'd need

to run conflicts checks on him and the counterparty. And his name would need to be on the court filings, if it goes to court."

Shaw: "We'll think about that when we get there, OK? When do you think you could get me the note? Tomorrow?"

We compromised on Friday, as early as I could manage it. It was bound to be late on Friday: I was going to have to either find someone in the Reputation Management team with the capacity to pick this up, or (more likely) bone up on defamation law myself. But you have to allow clients their illusions.

Shaw: "Great stuff. How's your dad, by the way? Keeping his nose clean? Good, good. Pass him my regards, yeah? Dad remembers him fondly."

Knew to take that with a pinch of salt. If Shaw's dad was that fond of Ba, presumably they'd have met up once in a while. Ba was always complaining that his rich friends from the old days had dropped him, Shaw's dad among them: "This Boey Kah Seng, he calls himself my friend, but does he call me anymore? I can message him a hundred times, I won't hear back. He thinks he's better than me."

No good pointing out that Shaw's dad did help Ba get out of jail back then, however unresponsive he might be these days. Boey Kah Seng bailed Ba out, when Ba's own family wouldn't lift a finger to help him. Shaw had made sure I knew that, back in the day.

Remembering Shaw's dad made me feel bad that I couldn't wait to end the call. I'd been thinking that Shaw was worse than I'd remembered. Obnoxious, in a word. Everyone at school had been like him, with a few exceptions, so I hadn't noticed it at the time.

But it wasn't his fault. Shaw didn't have any friends who weren't awful—I'd met them. Probably couldn't help himself. And he was trying to do me a favour.

CG: "Will do. Thanks, mate. Appreciate you thinking of us."

Shaw: "Any time, Charlie. I'm looking forward to working with you."

Couldn't quite bring myself to lie and say I was, too.

CG: "Yeah. Absolutely."

CHAPTER TWENTY-TWO

Kriya

Charles was looking frazzled when I got to the office, the morning of the Wednesday after Loretta's wedding. He was glaring at the screen, his hair standing up as though he'd been tugging at it. I smiled at him, but didn't say anything. Presumably he was busy, not in the mood for small talk.

I'd thought it might feel awkward, seeing Charles again after everything that had happened at the wedding. But it was weirdly normal. It was as if, having gone through the extremes of the possible relationships available to us—from work nemeses (though to be fair, I was the only one who'd characterised our relationship that way; before I'd turned up at his office, Charles had apparently thought of me as "that girl who drafted the witness statement for Mackintosh Cereals"), to romantic partners (albeit fake)—we'd learned the worst and could be comfortable with each other.

Though "comfortable" wasn't quite the right word for the flutter in my stomach when I looked at Charles's throat, rising out of his collar. His lower lip was surprisingly full. He chewed on it when he was thinking hard. I could have bitten it when I kissed him. Set my teeth in his lip, gently.

I shoved the thought to the back of my mind to join all the

other inappropriate and unacceptable feelings that lived there. I was sad and horny, that was all. My brain was looking for someone to latch on to after finally accepting the Tom I loved was never coming back to me—had, in a sense, never existed.

Charles was close at hand; he was kind and funny; he was professionally competent; and unfortunately for me, I knew for a fact he had amazing thighs. So I wanted to suck his dick.

Pretty pathetic all round. I needed to start dating again. Or at least buy a vibrator.

Charles finished up a spate of typing, clicked his mouse once, and leaned back, sighing.

He looked over at me. "Sorry, we had a new matter come in yesterday. It's been a bit of a scramble. Were you all right getting home after the wedding?"

"It was fine. How'd it go with your family? Have we put the gay conversion rumours to rest?"

Charles rolled his eyes. "Nobody's said anything to me. I suspect Loretta just wanted me to find a date for the wedding. She's very concerned about my love life."

He blushed. So did I, remembering Loretta's drunken petition on Charles's behalf: *He really likes you.*

I'd assumed Loretta's speech was the product of champagne and delusion. Watching the flush climb Charles's cheek now, I wondered, for the first time, if there might be some truth in what Loretta had said.

The idea was discomfiting. What I liked about my relationship with Charles was how nice it was, in a surprisingly uncomplicated way. If Charles really did like me, it was not going to stay uncomplicated.

Because I liked him. Enough, I suspected, that I'd be willing to ignore the complications.

"It was nice meeting Loretta," I said, to take my mind off these alarming thoughts. "Have she and Hayley gone on honeymoon now?"

Charles was telling me about their trip to Japan when my personal phone buzzed.

Amma was due to see the dentist that day about her dodgy tooth. Maybe she'd sent an update.

I had received a message, but it was from Rosalind. Despite all my efforts, I'd yet to train her out of using WhatsApp for business communications.

Sorry, I know you're desperately busy, but the new lawyer is useless and I don't know what to do. Do you have time for a call? I promise it will be quick!!!

Strange. I popped my headset on and rang Rosalind on her direct line.

Rosalind picked up on the second ring.

"Oh thank God, Kriya. This German woman is driving me mad. She keeps peppering me with questions about the compliance protocol. When I answer them, she turns around and sends me a million more questions. I sent the latest batch to this new lawyer who's taken over, but he's hopeless. You won't believe his reply—wait, I'll read out his email. 'These questions depend on the context of Sanson's operations. We believe Sanson is best placed to answer them, but please let us know if it would be helpful to have a call.' Can you believe this little shit? It would be helpful for him to go fuck himself."

"Rosalind—"

"I know you're on this big new case now, but can we find a solution? I can't work with this guy."

"Rosalind, slow down," I said. "What new lawyer is this? Who are you talking about?"

"This guy Milo. Milo Deacon."

"Milo Deacon," I echoed. I'd seen Milo around: he was a junior associate who did banking litigation. If we exchanged "hellos" when we passed in the corridor, that was as much contact as I'd ever had with him. I only remembered his name because of its association with the beverage. "Why is Milo Deacon emailing you?"

"He's taken over, because of your new case."

"Who told you I've got a new case?"

"Arthur," said Rosalind. "He emailed saying you no longer have capacity to advise on the protocol, so Milo will be helping going forward. But I have to say, Kriya, he's no replacement for you. Fine, he's cheaper, but I don't come to a firm like BRC because I think you're going to be cheap."

Rosalind's voice throbbed with feeling. It wasn't the moment to pick her up on her slip about the firm name.

"I come to you for advice because you make my life easier," she continued. "So far, this Milo is not making my life easier. I don't care if I have to pay more. You tell me, have I ever made an issue of the bills? You have targets to meet, I understand. If the work is good, it's not a problem."

"No, you're very good with bills," I said absently. "One of my prize clients."

A prize client Arthur had reassigned to an associate with all of two years' post-qualification experience, who was too busy to even pretend to be interested. And Arthur hadn't told me.

"There's been some misunderstanding," I said briskly. "I'm never too busy for Sanson, or you. I'll talk to Arthur. Let's go through these questions from your German colleague. Can you forward me the email?"

We ended the call after a productive hour and a half, Rosalind fully soothed.

"Thank you so much, Kriya. When Arthur said you weren't going to be advising anymore, I felt like a baby bird thrown out of the nest by its mother. Like you had abandoned me in the desert with these idiots."

"No problem," I said. "Let me know if there's any follow-up from Germany. I can hop on a call and we can hammer out the issues together. I'll feed back to Arthur that the cover he put in place wasn't satisfactory. Take care."

I took my headset off slowly.

"Was that Rosalind?" said Charles.

When I didn't answer, he looked away from his computer, his forehead starting to crease. "Kriya? You all right?"

"Yes," I said. "Sorry. I need to go speak to Arthur."

Thinking about challenging Arthur on why he'd pushed me out of the Sanson work made me feel sick. I knew if I didn't do it straight away, there was a real risk I wouldn't do it at all. So I charged off down the corridor before I could think better of it.

I could see how there might be good intentions behind Arthur trying to boot me out of the office I shared with Charles. It probably *would* be a bad idea to share an office with someone you were dating. I wasn't even dating Charles, and I was already finding it distracting being in the same room with him for around ten hours a day, three days a week, watching him bite his lower lip.

Taking my most important client off me without telling me, though? I couldn't see how Arthur could spin that, to me or himself, as being in my interests, or the firm's. It couldn't be about anything except retaliation for what had happened in Hong Kong.

Except there was no way Arthur would admit that. He couldn't afford to. So he'd have to make it about me, about my fitness for the job.

If Arthur was willing to lie to Rosalind, what might he start saying about me to other people? To other clients and partners?

A blonde woman was emerging from Arthur's office as I arrived at the end of the corridor. I'd seen her around the floor before, but it took me a moment to remember her name—Emily, one of the junior associates. She'd only qualified into the department a few months before Arthur and I had joined.

There was something odd about this, but I didn't have capacity to worry about it now. I filed it away to think about later.

I poked my head around the door. "Arthur, have you got a moment?"

Was I imagining it, or did Arthur look guilty?

If so, it was only for a split second. He said, perfectly naturally, "Oh, hi, Kriya. Sure. What can I do for you?"

"I just got off a call with Rosalind." This was a closed-door conversation, but I didn't really want to shut myself in with Arthur. This end of the corridor was too quiet, with no witnesses. Nobody came down here unless they wanted to talk to Arthur, or the main colour printer was broken. Our PA Victoria, who usually sat in the pod outside, worked from home on Wednesdays.

I compromised by pulling the door to, but leaving it ajar.

"Rosalind said you told her I'm too busy with a new case to advise on the protocol, and she should speak to Milo Deacon." I crossed my arms. "I'm not sure if there's been some confusion? I am not working on any new case, as far as I know."

I gave Arthur a pointed look.

"Yes," he said, unflustered. "That was when I thought Xinwei was going to confirm instructions to proceed right after we got back from Hong Kong. That's obviously been going more slowly than we'd like. I'm confident we'll get the work—they're still saying it's urgent, we'll have to move quickly once it comes through—but it's got stuck in their internal processes.

"Anyway, I've been thinking about Sanson," he went on. "The relationship needs a refresh. The way it's limited to you and Rosalind is a real risk to us. What if she moves on?"

Arthur's lack of embarrassment took the wind out of my sails. He wasn't speaking like a man who was conscious of having done anything wrong. I found myself scrabbling for the indignation that had borne me down the corridor.

"I agree we could do more to strengthen the Sanson relationship," I said. I'd been trying for years to persuade Arthur to let me introduce colleagues in other practice areas to Sanson, with limited success. "I'm happy to get others involved. But I would have appreciated a heads-up before you spoke to Rosalind."

Arthur nodded slowly. "I should have spoken to you about it." He raised his eyes to mine. "But I haven't been sure if you wanted to talk to me."

I didn't roll my eyes, but it took a conscious effort not to do it. "I would have liked you to talk to me about *this*."

"But not about anything personal?"

I didn't know what to say to that. As I hesitated, Arthur's lip curled, wry.

"I'll be honest, Kriya," he said. "These last few weeks have been challenging. I've tried to give you space, since that seemed to be what you wanted. But it hurt to find out you didn't trust me enough to be honest about your relationship with Charles. I consider you a friend. It's been tough realising that's not how you see me."

I recognised this self-pitying mood in Arthur. Since the divorce, he had a tendency to wallow. I was used to making the necessary sympathetic noises about Arthur's woes, but I'd never been identified as the source of those woes before.

Well done, Kriya. You happy-happy rushed down the corridor to scold your boss. Now he's turned it on you. What are you going to do?

"There's nothing between me and Charles," I said, then stopped.

It did sound like a lie, now. I could hear the ring of falsity in it. From the way Arthur was pursing his lips, I could see he heard it, too.

It wasn't a lie, though. The spark of chemistry, a fake kiss in the alcove of a hotel, even an entire wedding where we were pretending to be dating for one specific auntie's benefit, didn't amount to a relationship. And anyway, whatever was going on between me and Charles, it was none of Arthur's business.

"But even if there was, are you surprised I might not want to tell you?" My palms were damp, my heart hammering against my ribs, but I held Arthur's gaze. "What happened in Hong Kong did affect how I see you, Arthur. I don't think it's surprising if I don't feel as comfortable sharing certain things as I might have before."

Arthur was practically vibrating with coiled energy. He sprang to his feet and went to the window. "I apologised. I wish it had never happened."

Not *I wish I'd never done it*, I noticed. "And I appreciated the apology, but—"

"Our relationship is so important to me," said Arthur, turning away from the window. "We've been through so much together, over the years. You've seen sides of me Kelly never saw."

I did not like the way Arthur was looking at me, or the way he was comparing me to his ex-wife. If only Victoria was in the pod on the other side of the door today. I would have been much more comfortable with witnesses around.

I needed to redirect this conversation away from the personal, back towards work, and my grievance.

"And I hope we'll continue to work together for many more years," I said. "But it'll take time to rebuild that trust. What won't help is if you make decisions that affect me and my clients without consulting me."

Arthur's shoulders drooped. He sat back down, sighing. "You're right. I'm sorry. It won't happen again."

"Thank you," I said.

I was very ready to escape, but then Arthur said:

"I do think it's not a good use of your time to be drafting

emails for Rosalind. You need to be focusing on bigger-ticket work."

The abrupt reversion to normal work talk was dizzying. If I'd been less bewildered, I might have pointed out that my relationship with Rosalind *had* led to big-ticket work several times. Our old firm's New York Product Liability team had been kept busy for three years on a class action against Sanson US that Rosalind had originally referred to me.

But the reminder wouldn't have helped. Arthur had a chip on his shoulder about that case, since the work hadn't gone to him.

"I'd like you to get Emily involved in the Sanson work," said Arthur. "If you can start pushing the BAU stuff down to her, that will free you up for higher level work. I'd like you to lead on the Xinwei project, for example. That's the sort of thing we need you to be doing."

"OK," I said, mostly because I wanted to get out of his office. This was the kind of conversation I didn't mind having with Arthur, but I had no way of knowing when he might strike off again and start talking about his feelings.

Sure enough, Arthur looked up and said:

"Kriya. Are we all right?"

"Yes," I lied, and fled.

CHAPTER TWENTY-THREE

Charles

Kriya was gone long enough, talking to Arthur, that I started to worry. Maybe I should go looking for her. Check she was all right.

Kriya was well able to handle Arthur, I told myself.

But was she? Couldn't say there was equality of arms. Not only that he was a partner and she his associate. He seemed to have some sort of mental hold on her, maybe because they'd worked together for so long. And the circumstances were all in his favour. Presumably she was still on probation, so didn't have the full set of protections under employment law.

Needed to focus on the advice note I was drafting for Shaw—had to allow time for the Reputation Management team to look over the draft. But I started looking up employment law rights instead. Was reading the Practical Law note on constructive dismissal when Kriya came back.

Had already told myself I wouldn't probe. Kriya might not want to talk about it. But when I saw her face, I said:

"What happened?"

Kriya: "Nothing." Sank into her chair. "It's not a big deal. I mean, it's OK."

Waited.

Kriya: "Arthur told Rosalind I was on a new case and didn't have time for Sanson work anymore. He put Milo Deacon on it instead."

CG: "Milo? His whole team is flat out on the NAB trial."

Kriya, grimly: "I know. That's why I went to speak to Arthur."

CG: "Didn't go well?"

Kriya shook her head. "It was OK. He apologised." Paused. "He'd like me to scale it down with Rosalind, push more work down to junior fee earners. I can see what he means, to be fair. The work I do for Rosalind doesn't always need a senior associate."

CG: "Has the client complained about fees?"

Kriya: "No, Rosalind's said she's happy to pay for my time. And I view it as an investment in the relationship, you know. But Arthur's always been a bit funny about Sanson. They're our only client where I'm the main point of contact, because Rosalind doesn't get along with Arthur. But it's almost like Arthur's jealous of the relationship I have with her . . ." Her voice trailed off. Then, in a tone of dawning realisation: "He *is* jealous."

CG: "Did he say anything . . . inappropriate?"

Kriya: "No, no. I mean, yes. But not like that. He wasn't hitting on me. He was just being weird." She was frowning, working through a thought. "There was something else that pinged me as weird. When I got to his office he was talking to Emily. And this business with getting Milo to cover Sanson . . . it's very out of character for Arthur."

CG: "How so?"

Kriya: "I could never get him to talk to other associates at our old firm. He made me relay his instructions to them. I was like the Mouth of Sauron."

She pulled a face. I decided it wasn't the time to get her to explain the reference.

Kriya went on: "The junior fee earners didn't mind, but it caused some ill feeling with other senior associates. People said I was gatekeeping Arthur. When that was the last thing I wanted to do! Who wants their boss on their case all the time? It would have been a relief if he'd talked to somebody else, once in a while."

She leaned back in her chair, covering her face. "I wish he'd go back to normal. I guess I need to give him more time."

Didn't think time was going to improve matters. It didn't sound like Arthur had ever been normal.

The longer I knew Kriya, the more strongly I felt the best thing for her would be to take on work without reference to Arthur. Would help her build connections with other partners and clients. He sounded like a controlling headcase to work with, even leaving out his recent conduct.

CG: "Have you got capacity?"

Kriya raised her head.

CG: "There's this new matter that's come in, for Blackmount. They're an existing client of the firm, we've done M&A work for them, but this is a potential defamation case. A blogger's been making politically motivated allegations against an individual connected to the client. They're now threatening to publish the allegations in the press. The client has asked for advice on their options."

Kriya blinked. I supposed the change of subject was a bit abrupt. Should have worked up to it.

She said: "It sounds interesting. But I don't know anything about defamation."

CG: "Me neither. Unfortunately, the Reputation Management team is under the cosh, so we've said I'll pull a draft together and run it past them before it goes to the client. I've got a call with the partner later today."

Kriya: "What have you got in mind for me to do?"

CG: "Libel's the obvious cause of action, we'll be focusing most of our fire on that. But there is a possible breach of copyright angle. The other side's quoted extensively from the client's

documents. Ellie—she's the partner leading the RM team—
she also suggested looking into data protection. There might be
arguments we could run there."

Kriya: "So you're studying up on libel, but I can help by
learning intellectual property and data protection law?"

CG: "Right. It would be a huge help. The client wants the
note by Friday."

Kriya: "Farah's leading?"

Nodded.

Kriya thought about it. "I have got capacity. Arthur likes
me to check with him before taking on work for anyone else,
though."

Didn't say anything, but my face must have betrayed what I
thought of this. Would be one thing if Kriya was a trainee and
Arthur was her supervisor, but she's a senior associate.

Kriya: "I know. I think he gets anxious about the idea I
might not be available if he gets new work in. This is a time-
limited thing, though? It'll be over by Friday?"

CG: "The initial push will be. Presumably once they've had
a chance to consider the advice, the client will want to take
some form of action. We'll probably need to move quickly with
that."

After a long moment, Kriya said, "Count me in. Arthur will
just have to deal."

CG: "Great." Relief that Kriya was up for it. Thought of
involving her for her benefit, but it was going to be for mine,
too. "I'll send you the draft I'm working up. You'll see it's got
sections on the possible intellectual property and data protection arguments to fill out."

Kriya: "Is there anything else I can look at, to read in?"

CG: "The facts are limited at the moment, but I'll forward
you what we've got. The allegations are very sensitive, so Blackmount's asked us to treat them as the client. The details of the
parties involved have been anonymised. We're to advise on

options for taking down the existing writings and restraining future publication, making certain assumptions—I've set them out in the draft note."

Kriya: "I see. Understood."

CG: "Thanks. I appreciate it."

She smiled at me. Could feel myself blushing, like an idiot.

Kriya: "No, thank *you*."

CHAPTER
TWENTY-FOUR

Kriya

Charles's matter for Blackmount was a good one to get involved in. It was an interesting case; it took my mind off the weirdness with Arthur; and it got me meeting new people across the firm.

While Farah was technically supervising, she was away at a conference and content to leave it to Charles and me to lead. Over the next few days we had multiple calls and email exchanges with the Reputation Management, Intellectual Property, and Information Law teams.

At some point I'd meet the client as well: They had asked for a meeting to discuss next steps, after we'd delivered the note to them. Apparently the contact was an old school friend of Charles's. It was the kind of networking and profile-raising Arthur and I always talked about me doing, but Arthur had never got around to letting me do.

I was starting to see Arthur, and our working relationship, in a new light. It was something about the faces Charles made when I told him about Arthur. Maybe it wasn't a harmless idiosyncrasy when, for example, Arthur blocked me from working with other partners, even when I had the capacity to do the work. Maybe it *was* weird how possessive he was about my time. It could be said that there wasn't a big step from that to Arthur being possessive of *me*.

Usually I would have dropped him a line to let him know I was working on a new matter for a different partner. But I didn't this time. If Arthur had anything for me to do, he could let me know. In the meantime, I had plenty to get on with. The note we'd been tasked to produce could easily have taken a couple of weeks to research and write. We had three days.

I spent them in the office, since I'd worked from home earlier in the week. Charles and I had to be in constant contact, anyway. Working out of the same office made sense.

On Friday, around half an hour before the canteen was due to close at ten p.m., I stood up. The longest I'd spent away from my desk that day was during my trip to the bathroom so I could wash my hands after lunch. Lunch itself had been a sandwich at my desk.

The advice note was in good shape, but there was still some work to do before we'd be able to get it off to the client. Fortunately we'd committed to sending it to him by the end of the day—*not* "close of business," which everyone knows means the end of the working day for normal people, so six p.m. at latest. "End of day" gave us all the hours of darkness to work with: so long as the note was on the client's desk by the next morning, we were good.

"I'm heading down to the canteen," I said. My shoulders were stiff, and the back of my neck ached. I stretched, rolling my shoulders and cracking my neck. "Want me to pick something up for you?"

Charles didn't answer straight away. I looked over and he was staring at me, his mouth half-open. He looked like he knew precisely what he'd like to bite into.

He turned back to his computer, his face bright red. "Sorry, I didn't catch what you said."

I closed an open notebook on my desk and straightened

it, so as to have something to do. "I was saying, do you want anything from the canteen? I'm going to grab dinner before it closes."

"It's fine. I'll go get something myself after I send this email," said Charles. "Thanks."

"I can wait."

"No, no," said Charles, earnestly. "This will take a while. Don't let me keep you."

He was clearly desperate for me to go. I went.

He really likes you, said Loretta's voice in my head.

"Oh shut up," I said out loud, making the other tired lawyer in the lift jump. "Sorry. Talking to myself."

She looked worried, but not as worried as I knew I should be.

It had been an intense few days, but they'd been enjoyable, in a way. The work was interesting, and working so closely with Charles had been fun. I'd already known he was a good lawyer. This case had proved we were surprisingly compatible.

As colleagues. I did not need to be wondering if we were compatible in any other ways, when I shared an office with the guy. And when my boss of eight years was going through it, and I was starting to suspect I needed to reconsider my entire career.

I needed to get my head sorted. *Not* any body parts south from there, no matter how insistent they were being about their needs.

I'd been planning to get takeaway—the sooner I was back at my desk, the sooner we could hammer out the draft, and the sooner we could go home. But it was so nice being somewhere other than my office, even if it was merely the firm canteen, that I decided to eat there.

I had sausage pasta, transparently made using leftovers from the posh bangers and mash served at lunch, and scrolled idly on my phone. Zuri had messaged in the afternoon, in our uni friends WhatsApp group (currently named "Milo Dinosaurs"):

Still on for nasi lemak at Kriya's place tomorrow? @Kriya Going Chinatown later to buy ingredients, you want anything?

May Yin and Esther had confirmed. Sze Kim, Harminder, and Reuben weren't going to make it.

I'd forgotten I was hosting the cookout, but that was fine. We'd get the note out this evening, so I wasn't going to be working the next day. I'd have the morning to tidy up the flat before people started arriving.

I typed:

Thanks for buying @Zuri. I got rice and santan so don't need to bring ok. Looking forward to it!

When I got back to the office, Charles was gazing thoughtfully at his phone.

"Has there been anything else from Ellie?" I said. The Reputation Management partner had reviewed our working draft of the note earlier that day and flagged a line of recent case law that undermined one of our arguments, necessitating some hasty research and redrafting.

Charles blinked like he was stirring from a doze. "No." He put his phone down on his desk, exhaling. "I got a call from the company that manages my building. Apparently a pipe burst in the flat above mine. The ceiling of my bedroom's collapsed."

"Oh shit. Is your stuff OK?"

Charles took off his glasses, rubbing his eyes. "It's not looking good. I'll have to see what the damage is tomorrow. I've got insurance, but you'd think the management company would take responsibility. They've sorted the pipes and stopped the flooding, but they're saying I can't go back tonight. My room's not habitable."

He winced as a fresh thought struck him. "Loretta's anime things!" He put his glasses back on and grabbed his phone. "I don't know if her room's affected. They only sent me photos of my bedroom. She'd be gutted if anything happened to her collection."

Poor Charles, he really was having a mare. "Are they going to cover the cost of a hotel? You definitely shouldn't have to pay for that."

Charles was distracted, presumably texting his building manager an urgent demand to recover Loretta's anime things, whatever they were.

"Oh, I'll book a sleeping pod," he said.

My old firm had had sleeping pods, too, for when you were working late enough that a firm-funded taxi home wasn't going to cut it. I'd never used one, though colleagues said they were nice. It had always seemed to me tantamount to giving up on life. I was lucky enough to be able to afford to live in central London. I'd take the cab home even if it was four a.m. and I had to be back at my desk in a few hours' time.

"Don't do *that*," I said, on impulse. "I've got a spare bed at home. It's just a sofa bed, but you're welcome to use it."

Charles's expression froze. "Oh—no, that's, um, that's very kind, but the sleeping pods will do me fine." He went red.

"If you're sure," I said.

Just as well. What had I been thinking?

"They're very comfortable," said Charles, typing. "I need to track down the booking form on the intranet. I haven't booked one in a while . . ." His voice trailed off, his eyes on his computer screen.

"What is it?"

"They're closed for refurbishments." Charles massaged his temples. "I'll get a hotel." He started typing again, presumably looking up options.

I made a decision. "Charles, seriously. The sofa bed's in the living room, there's a door, you can shut yourself in. I'll never know you're there. It's a good bed, my family use it when they're over."

"It's fine, I'll—"

"It's ten o'clock," I said. "You could spend the next half hour finding a hotel that has availability and won't bankrupt you. Or you could take up my offer, and spend the time finishing the draft. The sooner we're done with this, the sooner we get to go home—" *and go to bed,* I was going to say, but cut myself off. Given how skittish Charles was looking, that was not going to help my argument.

"I don't want to impose," he said, but he was weakening. From the alarm that had crossed his face, I guessed he had just seen what he'd have to fork out to get a hotel room at this time of night.

"You wouldn't be imposing. You'd be doing me a favour," I said. "You might not mind spending your evening at your desk, but I want to be home with my feet up, watching my kdrama."

I thought that would clinch it. Sure enough, Charles said:

"OK. If you're sure you don't mind."

"Not at all," I said. "Come on. Let's knock this note on the head."

Bringing Charles home might have felt more illicit if we hadn't both been shattered. It was midnight by the time we left the office. The advice note was in the client's inbox, so we *had* managed "end of day."

I fell asleep in the taxi, only stirring awake as it pulled up outside the development where I lived. Charles, predictably, was still on his phone.

"Have a good one, guys," said the cabbie serenely. Goodness knew what he thought of the fact he was ferrying colleagues from the same law firm to the same block of flats, at this time of night.

It likely wasn't the first time he'd done that, to be fair. If anything marked us out, it was the fact there *wasn't* anything exciting going on. We were keeping enough of a distance from each other that he probably thought we were married.

Charles put his phone away as we got in the lift, but we didn't talk until we got to the flat.

"Nice place," he said politely, as I let us in. He took off his shoes before I could ask.

"Do you want to have a shower?" I paused to yawn, then said, "I'll get you a towel. My dad left some clothes here last time he came. I think they should fit you."

Charles mumbled something to the effect that I shouldn't bother. I waved this off:

"You don't want to be sleeping in your suit. Unless," I added, "you're one of those people who sleep naked."

"I, er, no. No, I'm not."

"That's good." I grinned. "One less thing to worry about, in case I forget you're here and walk in on you."

Charles went red.

I lost the fight over who got dibs on the bathroom, so I went first. Then, while Charles had his shower, I got the sofa bed ready.

I was fluffing the pillows when he emerged from the bathroom in a cloud of steam. He was wearing a grey cotton T-shirt and black shorts, from Appa's Reject Shop hauls. The T-shirt was too wide across the waist, but a perfect fit across the chest and arms.

Well. Some might have said it was too tight across the chest and arms—Charles was shrugging his shoulders apprehensively, as though worried he was going to rip a seam—but not me.

I found myself wishing I was wearing something sexier than the roomy batik kaftan Amma had bought from Simee Market. I was covered up from collarbone to ankle: I could have walked into any government office in Malaysia without fear of challenge.

But that was good, I reminded myself. I didn't want to be sexy. This was Charles. My colleague, but also my friend.

I'd never had a real work friend before. I'd had coworkers I was friendly *with*—lunch buddies, people I'd have a chat with when I saw them by the coffee machine. And there was Arthur, of course, but I'd never thought of him as a friend, no matter what he said about how he saw me.

There had never been anyone, male or female, that I'd have been comfortable offering my sofa bed to, as I had done that evening, without even thinking about it. How funny to think it was Kawan Baik who merited that level of trust.

He had earned it, to be fair. Charles had stood my friend through some pretty dicey situations. I should treat him as such.

I tore my eyes away from his shoulders. "There are snacks in the middle cupboard there if you get hungry. And there's fruit and yogurt in the fridge, and—what's this? Oh, leftover rasam. Help yourself to whatever. The bowls and plates and everything are here, and the mugs and glasses are here. And you can watch TV. I'll show you how to get Netflix on."

Charles raised an eyebrow. "It's quarter to one."

"You mean you don't want to have a bowl of rasam and binge *Nailed It!* right now?"

Charles smiled. "Maybe not tonight."

"Suit yourself." Perhaps I *had* been overdoing it with the hostess spiel. "Sleep well—oh, shit, what time are you planning to wake up in the morning?"

Charles blinked. "I'm usually up by seven."

I'd been starting to get stressed about the fact I'd forgotten to tell Charles about my nasi lemak party, but this diverted my attention. "Really, that early? Even at the weekend?"

"It might be a little later tomorrow," Charles conceded. "I'll definitely be up by eight thirty, though. Is that a problem?"

"No, no. But I should have mentioned, I've got some friends coming over tomorrow. We're making nasi lemak. I was worried about disturbing you, but if you're an early riser, that shouldn't be an issue. People should start turning up from around eleven at earliest. My friends aren't morning people."

"That's fine. I'll be gone by then," said Charles.

"You're welcome to join us," I said, before I could think better of it.

It wasn't that I objected to Charles's company—far from it. But his presence was likely to raise questions among Zuri and the others, who'd heard all my stories about him over the years. I could just imagine how they'd react to the news that Charles Goh—*the* Kawan Baik—had spent the night at my flat, no matter how innocent the reasons for that were.

Luckily for my reputation for virtue, Charles shook his head. "I've got to sort out my flat, anyway. I'll clear out well before eleven."

"OK," I said, and let out a jaw-cracking yawn. "Well, I'll be next door. Knock if you need anything."

"I'll be fine," said Charles. "Thanks."

CHAPTER
TWENTY-FIVE

Charles

I was uncomfortably conscious of Kriya. Hard not to be, knowing she was in bed on the other side of the wall. Whole flat smelled of her.

So did I, after my shower. Turned out her lemongrass fragrance was from her bath wash. Didn't help with how keyed up I was.

Kriya had emerged from her shower in a flowy print dress, her hair down her back. Dress was perfectly decent, only she wasn't wearing a bra. Could see her nipples outlined against the fabric.

Stopped looking after that first electric moment of realisation, but mind harder to control than eyes. It was impossible not to imagine what lay underneath her dress.

Relief when we said good night and she went off to her room. She didn't seem to have noticed anything.

Suppose she trusts me. That's a nice thought, or should be. Don't want Kriya not to trust me, of course. But equally . . .

Looked up how long it takes to get over an ex, after Loretta's wedding. Found a forum discussion that said it takes a month for every year of the relationship. Kriya was with her ex for thirteen years, and it sounded like the breakup had been relatively recent. She was probably at least half a year off from being over it. Not that it was any of my business.

Couldn't fall asleep, knackered as I was. Bed was comfortable enough, but there was a humming noise from the fridge and light shining from the display on the oven. Air on my face felt different, the way it does in an unfamiliar place.

Rolled over in case lying on my side turned out to be more sleep-inducing. Heard my phone buzz.

Reached out for it. Already broke my rule about not looking at my phone after seven p.m., when the building manager rang. Seemed late for them to be getting in touch, but they might have sent an update about Loretta's things. She spent years acquiring all those books and figures and prints, cost a bloody fortune. Can't imagine having to tell her they've been ruined.

Message was from Loretta herself:

Are you awake? Do you have time for a call?

It was past nine a.m. in Tokyo. On the early side for Loretta to be getting up while on holiday, but maybe she was jet lagged. Must be serious if she was asking to speak at this time of night.

Switched on the lamp on the side table by the sofa, put on my glasses, and rang her.

Loretta: "Charles! You're up late."

Looked remarkably tragic for somebody on honeymoon. I was starting to get worried when Hayley popped up in the background and waved, beaming: "Hi, Charles!"

CG: "I just got out of the office. What's up?"

Loretta: "I've been meaning to talk to you, but it's been crazy busy. We've been spending all our time with Hayley's parents, or I would've rung before. They left for Kyoto this morning." She took a deep breath. "Charles, I've got to confess. I did something terrible."

Thought of Loretta's collection. "Did you buy something expensive?" If Loretta had bankrupted herself buying action figures in Japan and needed a loan, she'd have to join the queue.

Loretta: "No—I mean, yes, but that's not what I meant. I meant, at the wedding."

CG: "What was it?"

Loretta: "I want you to bear in mind that it was the day of my wedding. I was drunk. So, so drunk. And I didn't say anything that wasn't true. But you and Kriya were being so cute together, with your lawyer banter, and I felt like there was a real energy there, you know . . ."

CG, with sense of foreboding: "What did you do?"

Loretta: "Hayley, you sensed the energy, too, right?"

Hayley: "Don't drag me into this. I told you to keep your mouth shut and let love bloom in peace."

Loretta: "I only wanted to help! I—wait. Where are you?"

CG: "What?"

Loretta: "That's not the flat, is it? What's that above your head?"

Glanced up. There was a framed painting on the wall, done on cloth, of purple and white flowers amid green blades of leaves. At the bottom right-hand corner of the painting was the word "MALAYSIA."

CG: "They're meant to be orchids, I think. I'm at Kriya's place."

Loretta: "*What?*"

CG: "She offered me her spare bed, because the flat—" Remembered uncertain status of Loretta's anime things. "I need to tell you about the flat. But you go first."

Loretta: "Go first? What do you mean?"

CG: "Tell me whatever it was you rang me to talk about."

Loretta: "Oh, that. Don't worry about *that*." She was transformed, bloody radiating good cheer. "Tell me about Kriya's place. She invited you over, you said?"

CG, severely: "It's nothing to get excited about. I'm in the lounge. Our flat got flooded. A pipe burst in the floor of the flat upstairs and the ceiling of my bedroom gave way. It happened today, while I was at work. I haven't been back yet, so I don't know what the damage is." Hesitated, but best for her to know. "They haven't said what's happened to your room. I don't know what state your anime shit is going to be in."

Loretta: "That's fine! Don't stress out about it. It's an excuse to buy more stuff while we're here. We're going to Ikebukuro today. We can stock up. I should go. You'll want to go to sleep, or something." Waggled her eyebrows.

CG: "Wait, Loretta—"

Loretta: "We mustn't cramp your style. Are you wearing something nice?" Peered at me. "Babe, what's sexy for guys to wear?"

Hayley, off-screen: "Women's lingerie!"

Loretta: "True, but Charles isn't going to go for that." To me: "At least you're not wearing your stripy pyjamas. Those make you look five years old."

CG: "But what were you saying earlier, about being drunk at the wedding? What did you do?"

Loretta: "I said don't worry about it. I'll tell you when I get back. It's no big deal. Have fun!" Winked meaningfully.

Hayley: "Bye, Charles!"

Call ended. Sat there gaping at my phone.

Loretta rejected the call when I tried ringing her back. She messaged:

Go to sleep, or whatever. It's fine! I'll tell you some other time
We're going out now

She added an emoji of winged dollar bills in flight.

I texted: *What were you on about? Did you say something to Kriya?*

But Loretta didn't answer, even though I could see from the double blue tick that she'd read my messages.

Turned off the lamp and flung myself back on the bed.

First thing I did when I woke up was grope for my phone. But there was nothing from Loretta. I wasn't going to find out what terrible thing she'd done at the wedding until she was back in the country, probably.

Almost certainly something to do with Kriya. The lack of denials in response to my question was damning.

Rubbed my temples. It was eight a.m. Could have done with another hour of sleep. But I had promised Kriya to clear out before her party. Best to get on with it.

Rolled out of bed, located my shirt, underwear, and trousers, and put them on. Folded Kriya's dad's clothes and put them on the coffee table Kriya had pushed into a corner to make space for the sofa bed. Then I stripped the bed and had a go at collapsing it so I could put the sofa cushions back on.

Wouldn't collapse. I was struggling with it, trying to be quiet, when there was a knock at the door.

Kriya put her head round the door. "You all right?"

CG: "Sorry. Did I wake you?"

Kriya: "Yes, but it's OK, I wanted to get up to tidy anyway. Don't worry about the sofa, it's a bit stiff. I'll sort it out later. Can I come in?"

CG: "Of course. It's your flat."

She was in the flowy dress she'd worn to bed the night before. And presumably still not wearing a bra.

Strangely intimate, seeing her like this. Was consciously keeping my eyes averted, but somehow I'd managed to absorb a complete impression of early-morning Kriya, regardless. Soft, bright-eyed, stray curls escaping from her ponytail to frame her face. Her skin would be warm from sleep if I touched her.

Kriya was getting a mug out of a cupboard. Said: "Do you want coffee?"

Obviously I wasn't going to touch her. *Get a grip, Charles.*

CG: "Yes. Thanks."

Would have thought it would feel awkward, sitting there at Kriya's small dining table while she pottered around the kitchen. But it didn't. It was comfortable. Even as wound up as I was, it was easy being with Kriya.

She glanced over her shoulder, grinning. "Hope you don't mind using competitor merch." Showed me the mug she'd put my coffee in, with the name "Brown, Rosenburg and Cushway" on it.

CG: "I've got a Swithin Watkins mug at home. And a tumbler. They gave them out when they were phasing out paper cups at the coffee machines."

Kriya: "I'll need to get a Swithin Watkins mug." Smile faded. "If I last that long."

Didn't pretend not to know what she was talking about.

CG: "There's no reason you'd need to leave the firm. I know you haven't wanted to make a formal report about Arthur, but you have accrued evidence of a concerning pattern, if nothing else. With what's happened with Rosalind, and his objecting to you sharing an office with me—there's external evidence of both those things. It wouldn't simply be your word against his."

Kriya: "Yeah." Didn't sound convinced.

She handed me a mug of coffee, her fingers brushing mine. Like getting an electric shock.

Observed my body's reaction with resignation. At least Kriya didn't seem to notice.

She said: "But even if I make a report, and they get rid of Arthur, where does that leave me? I've worked with Arthur since I qualified. Even before then—he was my supervisor when I was a trainee. I can't imagine my work life without him." She pulled a face. "That sounds pathetic, right?"

CG: "No."

What I was thinking was that Arthur had really done a number on her. Hadn't realised he'd been around when she was doing her training. She wouldn't have been older than twenty-two or twenty-three. No wonder she couldn't envisage a career without him.

Kriya: "It's fine. All of my friends hate Arthur. And I haven't even told them about what happened in Hong Kong." She sighed.

CG: "Why not?"

Kriya: "Oh well, you know, it's kind of a heavy topic, right? We're all so busy, we don't get to meet up that often. When we are hanging out, I'd rather not waste the time moaning about my job . . . You know, Charles, you could never be a therapist. It is one hundred percent obvious from your face when you think someone is talking bullshit."

CG: "I didn't mean—"

Kriya: "That wasn't a criticism! It's not a bad quality in a litigator. OK, I didn't tell my friends because they already hate Arthur. They're not lawyers. They don't get what it's like, that relationship with your supervising partner. Arthur's been my mentor, he's taught me how it all works. You work with Farah, you know what it's like."

CG: "Farah's not like Arthur."

Kriya: "No. Fair enough. I wasn't suggesting she'd cross boundaries, like Arthur—"

CG: "Farah expects me to do the job. It's a high-pressure job, it requires long hours. It's hard to get away from that, in a client-facing role. But Farah doesn't think she owns me or my time."

Kriya winced. "I was wrong. You'd make a great therapist. You might have to work on your bedside manner, though."

CG, after a moment: "I'm sorry. It's not my place to comment."

Kriya shook her head. "That's not what I meant. I like your honesty."

Her foot knocked against my leg as she sat down at the table. Her proximity made me feel light-headed.

CG: "Loretta says that about my bedside manner, too. And Farah. It causes issues with clients."

Kriya shrugged. "I'm not a client. I like that I always know where I stand with you."

Felt a pang of guilt. Kriya didn't really know where she stood with me. If she did, she'd know an inconvenient part of my brain was wondering what it would feel like to kneel down and press my face against her thigh.

Bet it'd feel incredible. I needed to stop thinking about it.

She said: "I know Arthur hasn't been at his best lately. But he's been decent to me, over the years. I wouldn't be where I am now without him. I get some crap from him as well, don't get me wrong. But he's been a good boss a lot of the time. That's as real as the crap. And if I report him, either it goes badly for me, or it goes badly for him. It could ruin his career. His personal life is already in a shambles. I don't know if I can bring myself to do that."

If Arthur continued behaving as erratically as he was now, Kriya might not have a choice. Seemed to me he was on a course to force her hand. At some point, it was going to be him or her.

But I didn't need to say that. Kriya wasn't stupid. On some level, she must know she was heading for a collision.

Kriya: "I'm going to get dressed. Have you got everything you need?" She jumped up and started taking things out of the cupboard. "I've got oats, muesli, Koko Krunch . . . There's bread in the freezer if you'd like toast. Butter's in the fridge. Or would you like peanut butter?"

Was going to say, automatically, that it was fine, but realised I was actually pretty hungry. Had forgotten to have dinner the night before. "Muesli's good. I'll help myself. Thanks."

Was working my way through the bowl of muesli when there was a loud rapping at the door. Glanced around for Kriya, but the bathroom door was shut. Could hear the buzzing of an electric toothbrush through it.

A voice called through the front door:

"Hello? Kriya?"

Went to the door and looked through the peephole. Two women outside, both some variety of Asian and laden down with shopping bags. One was wearing big spectacles and yellow dungarees. The other was wearing a baby.

Opened the door. "Can I help you?"

They gaped at me.

The one with the baby said: "Oh my gosh, sorry! We thought this was Flat 57."

CG: "It is Flat 57. Are you looking for Kriya?"

Kriya emerged from the bathroom, in jeans and a silky green top. She was putting earrings on—pretty dangly gold ones, with green stones.

Kriya: "Eh, what are you guys doing here? I thought we said brunch?"

Yellow dungarees: "Yeah, we said brunch. Nine a.m. Baby has to be back in his cot for his nap by eleven, or May Yin won't get to sleep tonight." She pointed at me. "Who's this guy?"

CHAPTER TWENTY-SIX

Kriya

I t turned out there were damn a lot of messages in the group chat that I hadn't read. Everyone had agreed they'd show up before nine a.m. to help make the nasi lemak, so May Yin could eat and get back home in good time for the baby's nap. Only Esther had overslept: she was on the Tube and would be turning up around ten a.m., in time to eat but not to cook.

"When did you send these?" I said, scrolling through my WhatsApp backlog.

Zuri was unpacking the bags of groceries, laying out ingredients for our early brunch on the kitchen counter, while May Yin fed her baby.

"Don't know," said Zuri. "Last night. Why weren't you checking your phone? What were you doing—?"

She cut herself off. She and May Yin looked from me to Charles, wide-eyed.

"I was *working*," I said. "We had a late night." I realised how that must sound. "*At the office.*" I cleared my throat. "Charles is having issues with his flat, so I offered him my sofa bed."

At least the sofa bed was still out, evidence of our chastity.

"Let me put this away," I said. "I'll put the yoga mat down. Then Ethan can have a play on the floor."

Charles had been hanging back, looking like he was wishing he was well out of it. But he came and helped me with the sofa bed.

"I'm Zurina," said Zuri to Charles. "I didn't catch your name?"

"This is Charles," I said. To Charles, I said, across the expanse of sofa cushions: "Zuri and May Yin and I went to uni together. We met organising Malaysia Night. Zuri's a book publicist. May Yin's at Deloitte, but she's on leave right now. Oh, she's in tax, you have something in common there. Charles did a seat in Tax Law when he was a trainee," I added to the girls.

"Charles," said May Yin slowly, but it was Zuri who said: "Wait. This is *Kawan Baik*?"

I could practically hear the whirring in Zuri and May Yin's heads. Charles looked polite and uncomprehending.

"Charles works at the same firm as me," I said. "We share an office."

"You didn't tell us Kawan Baik looks like *that*," said May Yin.

Thankfully Zuri shushed her. I said hastily, "Do you have to get back to your place straight away, Charles? You might as well stay for brunch. You like nasi lemak, right?"

Charles muttered something about not wanting to intrude, but he might as well have saved his energy. There was no way the girls were going to let him go until they'd got to the bottom of what was going on.

"Come and help us cook," said Zuri. "May Yin was going to do the chopping, but technically she shouldn't be cooking when she's got the baby in the carrier."

"Are you from Malaysia?" said May Yin. "Oh, Hong Kong."

"Eh, have you tried this place on Brick Lane?" said Zuri. "It's like a Hong Kong style diner. It's really cute."

I considered intervening, but Charles was already measuring out rice into the rice cooker while Zuri gave instructions. I tidied away all the choking hazards I could identify in the living room and put down the yoga mat for May Yin's baby, then said:

"Sorry, guys, I've got to do my laundry, or I won't have anything to wear next week. You all know where everything is? Do you want me to get out the air fryer for the chicken?"

"No need. It's in that cupboard over there, right?" said Zuri. "Go, go. It's all under control."

Inevitably, they'd drifted onto the topic of Malaysian politics by the time I came back. Charles was looking a little watery-eyed from the sambal—the pungent smell of chillies and belacan frying in oil pervaded the flat. But otherwise he seemed to be bearing up well under the full force of my friends' personalities.

"Is Ethan OK with that?" I said, raising my voice over the sizzle of the wok.

May Yin's baby was on his stomach on the yoga mat, trying to roll over, with limited success. I pushed the windows open as far as they'd go, for his benefit.

May Yin said, "He's a Malaysian baby, he must get used to sambal. We're talking about the *Hornbill Gazette* lady's *Guardian* article. Have you read it? It's very detailed. Supposedly it's going to be a series."

"Oh, I've seen it going round on social media," I said. I added to Charles, "This is a write-up of our big corruption scandal. Our Prime Minister stole billions of dollars of Malaysian public funds. I haven't had a chance to read it yet."

"I cannot tahan," said Zuri, who was making the sambal. She gave the red slurry in the wok a vengeful stir. "Every time I try reading it, I get a stomachache."

"Do you think it'll make a difference to the election?" I said. I came over to slice up some cucumber. The chicken was marinating, and Charles had been set to work peeling hard-boiled eggs.

"No lah," said Zuri. "Most it will do is give Jamaludin a

stomachache also. But it won't kick him out of office. The rural Malays are not going to be reading the *Guardian*."

"Have you seen the YouTube videos by this guy, Stephen what's his name?" said May Yin. "This Iban guy, he's an activist."

"Oh, the whistleblower? Stephen Jembu."

"I haven't heard of him," I said, but I wasn't really paying attention. Should I bring my laundry out onto the balcony? I didn't want to go into work smelling of belacan.

"He's the one who gave the evidence to the *Hornbill Gazette*, for the article," said Zuri. "They tried to get rid of him, but he got away. Living in Switzerland now. He can't go back to Malaysia, if not they'll catch him."

May Yin frowned. "You didn't read the article also, how come you know so much?"

"My friend knows his boyfriend." Zuri raised my spatula and waved it at me and Charles. "Eh, the boyfriend is a lawyer, you know."

"Oh, is Stephen Jembu gay?" said May Yin, interested. "I've been watching his videos, they're pretty good. Explaining what happened, who stole what, where did the money go. They're in Malay, but with subtitles, Chinese and English. He put out a call for a Tamil translator actually."

Zuri said, "Kriya, you should do it!"

"So long as he keeps it to Standard One level, maybe I can manage," I said.

I would bring my laundry outside, I decided. The sun had come out, so that would help the clothes dry faster, too.

I'd hauled the drying rack out onto the balcony and was coming back in when Charles said to me:

"I'm going to head off. Thanks for letting me stay the night."

"Oh, don't you want to wait till the nasi lemak is ready? It's almost done, right, Zuri?"

Zuri nodded. "We just need to fry the peanuts and ikan bilis. Chicken done already."

Charles shook his head. "Thanks, but I should see what state the flat is in, and get my things. And see if I can rescue Loretta's collection."

"But have they fixed it? Will you be able to stay there?"

Charles glanced down at his phone. "The building management company hasn't replied to anything since yesterday. I think they're probably offline till Monday. It's fine, I'll get a hotel."

My friends had made no pretence of not listening in on the conversation.

"What's wrong with your flat?" said Zuri. When she heard the story, she said, "I've got a spare bedroom. You could stay with me."

It wasn't a terrible idea. Zuri's estranged father was a bigwig in Bank Negara. She lived in a palatial flat in Wimbledon. She would have hosted the nasi lemak party, if not for the fact Wimbledon was a pain for everyone else to get to.

"That's probably more comfortable than my sofa bed," I said.

Charles looked alarmed. "Thank you, that's very kind, but I really couldn't—"

"I'm serious," said Zuri. "Any *good friend* of Kriya's is a good friend of mine." May Yin choked on her green tea.

I ignored them.

"You're welcome to come back here," I said to Charles. "I'm going to be out most of the day tomorrow anyway. I'm volunteering at a legal advice clinic for asylum seekers. You should be able to get in touch with the building management company on Monday, right? You should at least get them to confirm they'll cover a hotel before you pay for one."

Charles slanted a look at Zuri, who was grinning like a shark.

"If you don't mind me staying over the weekend . . ." he said, turning back to me. He'd clearly figured out that Zuri was not going to let him out of the flat unless he agreed to stay with one of us, and he'd identified me as the lesser of two evils. Wise man. "I'll be out of your hair by Monday."

"Of course. So you'll be coming back?"

"We'll save a plate of nasi lemak for you," said Zuri sweetly.

Esther turned up as Charles was leaving. He was so intent on escape he only gave her a perfunctory nod before he fled.

Esther handed me a bottle of red wine. "Sorry I'm late."

"Shouldn't I be the one getting the wine?" said May Yin. "We scheduled this at nine is because of me!"

"We scheduled this at nine is because of Ethan," Esther corrected her. "He's too young for a bottle of Pinot. Who was that guy?" She jerked her head towards the door through which Charles had disappeared.

"Yes," said Zuri. "Who *was* that guy, Kriya?"

The focus of collective attention swung round to me before I could invent another household chore to take me out of the room.

"Is it Kawan Baik?" said May Yin. "It's Kawan Baik, right? Kawan Baik's name is Charles."

"The question is, why is Kawan Baik staying at your place?" said Zuri.

Esther's eyes went round. "That was Kawan Baik? Wait, did you rumpy-pumpy with Kawan Baik?"

"What?" said the rest of us.

"I just learned this word today," said Esther, with pride. "'Rumpy-pumpy.' It means 'have sex.'"

"Oh, that's a very interesting term," said May Yin, seriously.

"Right?"

"OK, to be clear, I did not rumpy-pumpy with Kawan Baik," I said. "You all heard what. His flat got flooded, so I let him stay over. On the *sofa bed*."

"That's not an explanation," said Zuri. "The girl who sits next to me in the office and is always having personal calls at her desk, if she got flooded out, I'd wish her all the best. I wouldn't say, 'Come back home with me.'"

May Yin said, "Why don't you rumpy-pumpy with him?"

The quorum promptly descended into chaos.

"May Yin! Is that the kind of language they use at cell group?" shrieked Esther.

"Don't shout, don't shout," said Zuri, wiping her eyes. "What about Ethan's ears?"

"I don't mean, as the first step," said May Yin, injured. "I meant it metaphorically. He's cute what. And he can cook. And he seems nice."

"Upgrade on Tom, on all points," Zuri agreed.

I sighed, settling on the sofa. "I haven't even told you about Tom yet."

It caused another uproar when I told them about my encounter with Tom at Loretta's wedding.

"I always hated that guy!" said Esther.

"But why were you going to the wedding with Charles in the first place?" said Zuri.

"I told you. Because his cousin is gay, the relatives thought he might be gay. He had to bring a woman along to show he's not gay."

"What nonsense," said Zuri disdainfully.

"Sounds like an excuse to ask you out," Esther agreed.

"No lah," I said. "Why wouldn't he just ask me out, if he's interested?"

But the answer presented itself to me even as I spoke. Charles knew pretty much all my problems in the past month had been caused by Arthur coming on to me. Charles wouldn't want to do anything to put me under further pressure.

What was it he'd said to Loretta, when they'd been arguing about him bringing me as a date to her wedding? *Bad enough the boss is chasing her.*

Zuri and the others didn't know about Arthur, of course. I didn't feel ready to talk about that yet.

Zuri said, "What's stopping *you* from asking him out?"

"He's my colleague," I said. "I share an office with him. It's not a good idea. What if it goes wrong? It'd be so awkward."

Esther said, "You're always asking, what if it goes wrong. What if it goes right? You're thinking of the worst-case scenario, but there's a best-case scenario too. The one where you live happily ever after with this rich hot guy who can cook and is nice."

"Or at least where you get to rumpy-pumpy him a couple of times," said May Yin.

"*May Yin!*"

"What's gotten into you?" I said.

Right on cue, the baby started crying. May Yin gathered him up into her arms.

"Ethan is so cute," she said mournfully. "But he's really disrupted my sex life."

I jumped on this with relief. I'd had quite enough of talking about *my* completely imaginary sex life.

"Next time, drop Ethan off for a couple of hours and you can have some private time with hubby," I said. "OK, who's ready for some nasi lemak?"

CHAPTER TWENTY-SEVEN

Charles

I t was with a degree of relief that I left Kriya with her ter-
rifying friends to go to my own flat. Now knew what it felt
like to be a lowly staff member at Jurassic Park, cleaning up the
raptor enclosure while being eyed up by the inmates.

The moment Kriya had turned her back to do her laundry,
the scariest friend, in the yellow dungarees—Zurina—had
said:

"Can I ask, are you and Kriya seeing each other?"

CG: "Er, no."

Zurina: "Hmm."

The innocent-looking one with the baby (May Yin) piped
up. "Can I ask something too?"

Zurina: "I haven't finished." To me: "Are you interested in
her?"

CG: "Er—"

Kriya must be right that I've got a terrible poker face. May
Yin patted my arm and said:

"Don't worry. You don't need to answer. Is it my turn yet?"

Zurina: "I mean, if you're going to sabotage my turn . . ."

May Yin: "Is something going on at work with Kriya's boss?"

Zurina: "Forget my question. I want to know this too."

Wasn't sure what to say. If Kriya hadn't told her friends about Arthur's conduct, it hardly seemed my place to.

CG: "Why do you ask?"

May Yin: "I don't know. It feels like something's going on. She hasn't talked about her boss in a while."

Zurina: "Yeah, usually she'll mention him. It's suspicious."

May Yin: "We should ask you, since you're in the same industry. Kriya's always saying we don't understand about her boss, because we're not lawyers. Is it normal, how the boss treats her? She's almost like the second wife like that."

Zurina: "Without the benefits of being bini kedua!"

CG: "I have limited visibility of their relationship."

Hesitated, with two hopeful pairs of eyes on me. Three, counting the baby, but he was probably just hoping to have another go at grabbing my spectacles.

CG: "But from what I've seen, I wouldn't say it's normal, no. It seems fairly dysfunctional."

Zurina, to May Yin: "I told you."

May Yin: "I know! I also told her what. We all told her." She sighed. "The problem with Kriya is she's so used to looking after other people. But if you ask her to stand up for herself, she doesn't want."

Zurina: "It's because of her parents. They're nice, but they're a bit useless. It's like they're the children and she has to look after them."

Thought of Ma and Ba.

CG: "That happens in some families."

Rice cooker clicked to "keep warm" mode as the rice finished cooking. Zurina opened it and made an approving noise. Said:

"Well, he has my blessing to go out with Kriya." Looked up at me. "Just please don't be a manchild like Tom. She earned most of the money, she did all the cooking, she did all the housework."

May Yin: "Last time I went to see the fortune teller, I

asked him to put a curse on Tom. He said they don't really do that."

Zurina, cheerfully: "You're going to put Charles off."

CG: "I'm not—I don't think she's interested."

Zurina and May Yin exchanged a look.

Zurina: "I'd give it a shot, if I were you." Gave me a look over the top of her spectacle frames.

Thought about that all the way home. The way Zurina had said, *Any good friend of Kriya's is a good friend of mine.*

Stuck with me, for some reason. Not sure Kriya sees me as a friend, much less a good friend. It's not how I feel about her.

Not that I see her merely as a colleague. But "friend" isn't the word for it.

My flat felt especially empty when I let myself in, like somewhere abandoned by its occupants in a hurry.

My bedroom was a disaster zone. Worse than I'd imagined. There was a load of ceiling on my bed and a big hole, crisscrossed with beams, where the ceiling should have been. Carpet squelched underfoot.

I'd thought I might be able to sleep in Loretta's room, if it wasn't affected. Building management company had said there shouldn't be any further flooding. But having seen my room, I wasn't confident it would be safe to stay in the flat.

Opened my wardrobe, prepared for anything. To my surprise, most of my clothes had escaped damage, as well as the suitcase I kept in there.

Removed clothes and suitcase to the living room and packed one into the other. Loretta's room was OK when I checked it, though the wall adjoining my room needed looking at. Emailed a reminder to myself to raise it with the building management company on Monday.

Reflected a moment, then sent another reminder to buy a suitcase, so I could pack up Loretta's anime shit. Just in case. Would probably need two bags.

Stomach rumbled while I was locking up. Was glad that I had somewhere to go, and someone who was saving a plate of nasi lemak for me.

Kriya's friends had left by the time I arrived at her place. The kitchen was clean—no sign of our labours earlier. Kriya was muttering to herself over piles of paper, spread out on the coffee table.

Kriya: "I've been catching up on life admin. Your nasi lemak's in the oven, but it might be cold by now. You can microwave it if you'd like it hot, but the chicken you should probably air-fry. Or you could pop it under the grill—"

CG: "I'm sure it's fine. Thanks."

Kriya seemed busy, so I shoved my bag in a corner and tried to be inconspicuous. Not easy, given the size of the place. One bedroom, tiny hall with a bathroom off it, and the open plan lounge-cum-kitchen I'd slept in the night before. While Kriya was in the lounge, there was nowhere for me to go, to give her space.

Did my best anyway. After finishing my nasi lemak, I checked my work inbox. Wasn't expecting anything to have come in, given we'd sent off the advice note late last night, but there was an email from Shaw:

Thanks. Reading advice now. I'll give you a call tomorrow.

Felt somehow typical of Shaw. Though I'd never worked with him before, I could have predicted he'd have no respect for work/life balance. Of course, I don't have a personal life to disrespect, but he wasn't to know that.

Knocked through my emails, then went for a run. Partly because it was a nice day out, but mostly because I needed the exercise. I was getting edgy, spending all that time with Kriya in her flat.

A discreet wank would have been more to the point, but that was out of the question for now. Could have tossed one off in the bathroom, I suppose, but didn't feel right.

Kriya had tidied away the papers on the coffee table when I got back. She stared at me.

Looked down at myself, wondering if I'd stepped in something, or got splattered with mud.

Kriya: "Those shorts are very . . . tight."

CG: "Compression shorts. They help recovery. Well, they're said to. I haven't actually looked at the research."

Kriya: "Learn something new every day. What do you want to have for dinner?"

We had hard-boiled eggs, fried so they were crispy on the outside, in the sambal Kriya's friends had made earlier, along with the leftover rice cooked in coconut milk, and other leftovers scrounged from Kriya's fridge: the rasam and some wilting bok choy, stir-fried with garlic.

Best day's eating I'd had in a while. Food at Loretta's wedding was good, too, but Western food never quite hit the spot in the same way.

That said, Western cuisine had its virtues. After dinner, Kriya said: "I'm going to open the bottle of wine Esther brought over. Do you want some?"

We ended up drinking it on the sofa, with some kdrama playing on the TV.

Felt relaxed and fuzzy and weirdly at home, as though I belonged there. Dangerously easy to imagine living there for real, waking up with Kriya every day.

Kriya: "I forgot to ask, how was your flat?"

CG: "Not great. Loretta's things are all right, but I'll have to move out till they've fixed the place. They said repairs should take a couple of weeks."

Kriya made a face. "Aren't you broke?"

CG: "Yeah." Two weeks at a London hotel would have been a significant expense at any time—one I could afford, usually, but that I would notice. Right now, when I was cleaned out from sending money to Ba . . . "I'll have to put it on my credit card, if the building management company doesn't agree to cover it."

Kriya: "If they don't pay, why don't you just stay here?"

She wouldn't have offered if she knew how comfortable I was after all of one day. She'd have to pry me out with a crowbar if she let me stay for two whole weeks.

CG: "It's not so bad. I'll only have to hang on till we get paid at the end of the month."

Kriya sat up. "Seriously, Charles. I'd rather you take my sofa than give some depressing Travelodge all that money. It's only for two weeks."

A strand of hair fell over her face. She was so exercised she didn't seem to notice it.

Wanted to reach out to tuck it behind her ear. I could almost feel the warmth of her skin, the springy texture of her hair against my fingers. Looked away, clutching the stem of my wine glass.

CG: "It might take longer, you never know with repairs. We'll see on Monday. Hopefully they'll stump up. They've been pretty good historically. I've lived there a long time."

Kriya: "Do you own the flat?"

Nodded. "I started out renting it with another trainee in my intake, when we both started at Swithin Watkins. He dropped out and went off to Australia—he's a scuba diving instructor now—but I kept the place. Then the landlord wanted to sell up and offered me the flat, so I went for it. It's in Kentish Town, easy commute to the office."

Kriya: "Yeah, Thameslink, right? It's a nice area."

CG: "I should probably think about selling, once they've sorted the repairs and Loretta moves out. I don't really need the space."

Hate the idea of selling. After Ba left, Ma and I had to move all the time. It's been nice, being able to stay in one place. I'm used to the flat now.

But I don't need a second bedroom. If I downsized to a studio, that would free up some money.

For what, though? Ba's next emergency? He's never going to be done having those.

Kriya: "Where are Loretta and Hayley moving to?"

Told her about the plan. Loretta and Hayley staying with me when they get back from Japan, but only till they've completed on the flat in Peckham they've offered on.

CG: "Do you own this place, or . . . ?"

Kriya: "No, I'm renting. Tom and I wanted to buy a place together, but he wasn't that happy at his job. He wanted to wait till he got a better role, something he could see himself doing long-term." Her lips twisted. "Guess he's got that now."

She took a swig of her wine.

I'd had a few too many swigs myself. Knew I shouldn't ask. Nonetheless found myself saying: "Do you miss him?"

Kriya didn't seem offended. She thought about it. Finally: "No. It's funny. He was so important to me for so long. But you know, I worked so hard to make him happy. When it didn't work, it felt like there was something wrong with me. So not feeling that anymore, it's a huge relief. Like a weight off my back."

She gazed pensively at the TV. On the screen a preternaturally beautiful couple were walking through Seoul in the rain, shielding under the same umbrella. "No. I don't miss Tom.

"I miss some things," Kriya added. "I miss being with someone. Having someone to watch shows with. Someone to cook for—it's so pointless cooking for yourself only. And I miss the sex."

Luckily I was already flushed from the alcohol. Kriya glanced at me and smiled, as though she saw my embarrassment anyway. Somehow I didn't mind.

After a couple of episodes, she stretched her arms over her head, sighing.

Kriya: "I should get out and let you sleep. Hold on, I'll help you get the sofa bed out." Paused. "Charles?"

Had been watching her, mouth dry. Took me a moment to register the silence. Kriya was waiting for a response.

CG: "I, uh, yes. Thanks. I mean, it's OK, I can do it myself."

Kriya eyeing me, speculative. She'd noticed me looking at her.

I'd give it a shot, if I were you. Zurina was her best friend. She should know. What was the worst that could happen?

Knew the answer to that. Worst wouldn't be getting rejected, though that would sting. Worst would be if Kriya felt she'd been wrong to trust me.

Felt sick at the thought. I couldn't risk it—

Kriya: "Did Zuri they all tell you, we've got a nickname for you?"

Blinked. "What, really?"

Kriya: "Kawan Baik. It means 'good friend.'"

CG: "Oh. Is that why Zurina said that about any good friend of yours being a good friend of hers?"

Kriya: "Yeah, she was being a troll. We've been friends since age seven, you can't impress somebody like that." Shook her head. "I hope they weren't too much for you."

CG: "They seemed nice." Decided not to mention May Yin's attempt to get a fortune teller to curse Kriya's ex-boyfriend.

Kriya: "It was kind of a joke, calling you my good friend. Because we kept running into each other after I bombed my training contract interview at Swithin Watkins. You probably don't remember, but that was the first time we met, you know."

CG: "When you fell on the steps."

Kriya stared at me. "Wait, you remember that?"

CG: "It wasn't my finest moment. I should have been more helpful."

Kriya's eyes softened. "You did help. You told me I was at the wrong building."

CG: "Loretta and I have a name for you, too."

Kriya: "Serious?"

CG: "It's, um, 'Hot Lawyer Who Hates You.' 'You,' as in me. Loretta came up with it."

Kriya started laughing. "Yeah, I would've guessed that. Did I really come off like I hated you?"

CG: "As I said, it was Loretta's idea. She thought it likely, on the evidence. I wouldn't have felt confident drawing any firm conclusions. Assessing people's feelings isn't one of my skills."

Kriya: "I think you do fine. I don't hate you, for the record."

Said, stupidly: "OK. That's good."

Was acutely aware there wasn't much distance between us. Kriya had switched off the ceiling lights when she turned on the TV. The only light was from a floor lamp next to the sofa, and the glow of the TV screen. We were talking in hushed voices, as though we might be overheard.

Kriya was looking at me as if I were a puzzle she wanted to solve. "It's a flattering nickname, apart from the 'hates you' part."

CG: "I agreed with the basic premise. It was hard to argue."

Kriya drew closer. I could see every one of the ridiculous curling lashes shading her eyes. Her lips looked very soft.

She said, smiling: "Is it?"

A long moment passed.

Kriya: "Charles, I'm going to need you to make the first move here, because—"

I kissed her. Touch of her lips on mine went right through me, a full-body shock. Discovered I'd been waiting for this since Kriya kissed me outside the hotel at Loretta's wedding. Wanting it to happen again.

Kriya's lips were as soft as they'd looked. Wanted to burrow into her, her warmth and softness and smell. I put my hand on the back of her head, stroking her hair, then the back of her neck. Followed the curve of her spine down the slope of her back, before cupping the lush rise of her arse.

She bit my bottom lip gently. Licked it, soothing the sting. Then she pulled away.

It was cold everywhere where she wasn't pressed against me. Wanted her back. I was so hard it hurt.

Kriya: "I'm sorry about, you know, that time."

CG, blurrily: "What time?"

Kriya: "When I kissed you at the wedding. I was thinking later, I was lucky you didn't report me."

CG: "I didn't mind."

Only thing I minded was that she'd stopped kissing me. Drew her back down.

Had my hand up her top, having managed to get her bra off, and she was tracing my cock through my jeans lazily, when she pulled away again. This time she said:

"Do you want to move this to the bedroom?"

CG: "Yeah."

Kriya took off her top. *Great* development. She said: "I should warn you, I'm not sure I've got condoms. It's been a while since I've done this." Without much hope: "You didn't happen to bring any with you?"

To have done that would have required an optimism wholly foreign to my personality. I shook my head. "It's also been a while. For me."

Kriya: "I'll have a look. We might have to be creative." She grinned. "I've got some ideas for things we can do."

CG: "Great." Fully ready to do anything Kriya had in mind. I had a feeling this was about to be one of the nicest things that had ever happened to me.

CHAPTER
TWENTY-EIGHT

Kriya

Charles wasn't there when I woke up. It felt like mid-morning: Sunshine was glowing through the gaps in the blinds. I heard movement in the living room and got up, pulling on a T-shirt and shorts.

Charles was hunched on the sofa, scrolling on his phone. That was normal enough—except it didn't look like his personal phone.

"Are you checking your emails?" I said.

Charles started and looked up. "Er—yes. The client said he'd ring today, but we've set up a meeting on Monday morning instead. It would be good if you're able to join. He's keen to crack on."

"No kidding." I went to sit next to him on the sofa. Charles scooted up, making space for me. "Is there a reason for the urgency?"

"They've got wind that the accuser's going to be publishing a second article this week. She's reached out to ask them to comment on the piece. The client wants to send her a letter, saying we'll sue if she publishes. We've got instructions to prepare an application for an injunction to restrain publication as well. We'll have to move pretty quickly with that if the letter doesn't do the job."

It sounded like we had another busy week ahead of us. "The letter shouldn't take too long to put together. We've laid out all the arguments in the note."

Charles nodded. "That's what I was thinking."

"I don't think I've got any meetings Monday morning. You'll lead it, right? Do I need to do any prep?"

"It's mostly so the client can bring in ID. We'll need to clear conflicts. I should probably email the CDD team so they can kick it off first thing in the morning." Charles looked sideways at me, apologetic. "Sorry. This probably wasn't what you wanted to wake up to. I ran out and got milk from Tesco, I could make you a coffee—"

I leaned over and kissed him. Charles made a little surprised noise. Then he put his arms around me and kissed me back.

"That would be nice," I said, when we came up for air. "I need to get ready. I've got to head out for my clinic soon."

"OK." Charles looked dazed. He blinked, sat up, and said, "Yes. Coffee. I'll do that."

The coffee was good. I'd been sceptical about my friends' claims about Charles's cooking skills—I'd only seen him make rice and boil some eggs, which hardly seemed MasterChef worthy to me—but he could certainly make coffee. We drank it at my small dining table, our knees touching.

As I was leaving, I said, "You know where everything is, right? I should be back around four. Don't spend the whole day working."

"I won't," said Charles. We kissed again: this time, a chaste press of the lips, as though we'd been together for years.

Were we together? I should probably ask.

At some point. I didn't feel the need to have that conversation yet. For now, it felt enough to enjoy this, whatever it was.

It was probably a terrible idea to be doing it with the guy I shared an office with. But it didn't feel like a terrible idea. It felt right.

Charles took my advice. When I got back from a day of filling out forms and writing letters and trying to advise people in impossible situations, Charles was in the kitchen. There were bags on the floor, full of groceries he was busy putting away.

"I went to Chinatown," he said. "Thought I could make dinner. Do you like noodles?"

"I love noodles. Sounds perfect." I put down my bag, shrugged off my blazer, and got stuck in, helping him empty the shopping bags.

Charles put a bag of frozen tiger prawns in a bowl of water to defrost, then turned to me, wiping his hands. "Good day?"

"Yeah." I told him about the clinic: It had been set up by a former City lawyer who'd got the idea of getting her mates working in the City to come along to give free legal advice to asylum seekers and refugees. I'd first got involved as a trainee at my old firm. "It's more tiring than the work we do, in a way. It's more personal. But it's rewarding."

"That makes sense," said Charles, but I wasn't sure he was paying much attention to the words. He was watching my mouth.

I glanced around the kitchen: the prawns thawing in the sink, vegetables waiting on the counter to be cut. "It's nice of you to do this."

"I wanted to do something for you," said Charles.

I smiled at him, touched. "Aw, Charles."

"Kriya," he said, his voice low, and kissed me.

The kiss was hungry, as if Charles had been thinking about this all day. Waiting for me.

I pressed myself against him, humming encouragingly, but after a moment Charles pulled away.

"I also bought condoms," he said.

"Fantastic. We love a man who can share the mental load."

Charles's eyebrows drew together. "What?"

"Don't worry about it," I said. "We can talk about it another time."

I drew him in, and he came very willingly.

CHAPTER TWENTY-NINE

Charles

Shared an Uber to the office with Kriya on Monday morning. Original plan was to walk in together—it was only a half an hour walk, Kriya said—but we'd got a bit distracted. Then my phone had buzzed with the news that Farah wanted a pre-brief before our meeting with Shaw at ten a.m. I'd ended up booking a cab on my phone with one hand and buttoning up my trousers with the other, while Kriya pulled her dress back down and fixed her makeup.

She said in the car: "Is it the old school friend we're meeting? The client contact."

CG: "'Friend' is overstating it a bit. But yeah, we were at school together. Our dads are mates." Lowered my voice, glancing at the driver. He was listening to a podcast in Urdu. "Shaw runs an investment firm we've done some work for, but he's not the client in this instance. It's one of his investors, an individual. Shaw's bringing the paperwork we'll need to register him as a client."

Kriya, frowning: "Is the investor going to be there?"

CG: "Just Shaw."

Kriya: "Seems an odd way of doing things." It seemed as

though she had more to say, but she looked at the driver and fell silent.

She didn't know the half of it. Shaw had been talking about getting a letter out to the blogger today, even though I'd explained over email that we'd need to clear conflicts and complete the client due diligence process first. The CDD team hadn't yet responded to the email I'd sent them on Sunday, and I was worried the process was going to be complicated. Shaw hadn't said so in so many words, but it sounded like the client was a politically exposed person.

There were other things I was worried about. Like Kriya. Was she my girlfriend now?

Hadn't asked before. It hadn't seemed necessary, over the weekend.

Now, with her at the other end of the backseat of the taxi, was not the place or time. I should have raised it this morning and clarified the point.

Instead, had used the time to eat her out. Seemed a good move at the time. Starting to reconsider that.

CG: "We can discuss it later."

At least we weren't late. The cab drew up outside Swithin Watkins at 9:20 a.m. Farah wanted to speak at half past. We should have had ample time to get our heads together before the client showed up.

But as we were getting out of the Uber, I saw Shaw, walking towards us.

Shaw: "Hey, Chinky Charlie! Long time no see!"

Kriya's jaw dropped.

CG: "Hello, Shaw." We shook hands. "We weren't expecting to see you so early. Are we not meeting at ten?"

Hadn't seen Shaw in years, but he looked exactly the same as he used to, except in a suit instead of school uniform. Short, chubby, baby-faced guy, with spectacles.

Looking at the two of us, you would have thought Shaw was

the one who'd got bullied at school. But you would have been failing to take into account the power of Shaw's personality. Everyone had liked him. Even the masters, for all the trouble he gave them.

Shaw: "I had a nine a.m. down the road. Thought I'd come round and see if you'd give me a coffee and somewhere to sit down."

He smiled at Kriya. Not in a nice way.

Well. Not in a way I liked. Wolfish.

Kriya smiled back at him. Couldn't tell if this was automatic politeness to a client, or if she'd taken to Shaw. Women said to admire confidence in men. One thing about Shaw, he's never lacked for confidence.

He lowered his eyes. Kriya was wearing a purple dress that crossed over at the top, making a V at her neckline. No denying her breasts looked fantastic in it, but you're not supposed to visibly take notice of that sort of thing in a professional setting.

Shaw not bothering to hide the fact he'd noticed.

Could hear the touch of frost in my voice when I said:

"This is my colleague, Kriya Rajasekar. She's kindly stepped in to assist on the matter."

Shaw shook her hand. "Shaw Boey, Blackmount Capital. Appreciate your help on the case."

The smile dropped off Kriya's face.

CG: "We've got a meeting in about five minutes, but we'll be with you by ten. I'll see if I can get you into the meeting room we've booked, so you don't have to move." To Kriya: "Can you tell Farah? I'll join you two after I've got Shaw settled."

There was something going on with Kriya, but I didn't know what it was, and I couldn't ask in front of Shaw. Wished I could touch her, but I couldn't do that either.

After a moment she nodded. Said: "Good to meet you, Mr. Boey," and turned away from us, heading through the revolving door.

CHAPTER THIRTY

Kriya

Charles led the meeting with Shaw Boey. We'd briefed Farah—that is, we'd told her what we knew about the facts of the case, which wasn't much. But she took a backseat during the meeting with the client, as she'd been away.

Shaw explained his instructions. We had a trainee take copies of the identification documents he'd brought for the true client, one Jamaludin Abdul Rashid, who was the beneficial owner of multiple companies named in the *Guardian* article that was the subject of the complaint.

Charles explained that we would not be complaining of it that day, since completing client due diligence for a person of Jamaludin's status was not straightforward. We'd asked the team to treat it as top priority, but we were in their hands as to when we'd be able to confirm we could act.

Then we saw Shaw off and went back to our office.

When we were back at our desks, Charles said, "Maybe we should get started on drafting the letter. The client will want it sent out the moment we're good to go."

I'd been very quiet throughout the meeting. I turned in my chair and kicked the door shut. "You think we'll get cleared to act?"

Charles blinked. What he'd suggested—starting work before conflicts were officially cleared—wasn't strictly according to protocol, but I'd done it before. It was easy to fall into the habit of viewing the client due diligence checks as a mere formality, if you were reasonably confident there wasn't a conflict that would preclude the firm acting. And of course, this new client was linked to Blackmount Capital, which had already been through all the checks to get registered as a client of the firm.

"Have you read the article they want to sue for?" I said.

Charles's forehead furrowed. "Not yet. Shaw only confirmed the blogger's name today." He sat down at his desk, flipping through his notes. "Helen Daley?"

"We were talking about her *Guardian* article at the weekend, when my friends came over," I said. "I'll send you the link."

I only had to type the first two words of the title before the link to the article popped up in the search bar of my browser. I'd read the piece a few months ago, while having lunch at work.

The biggest scandal you've never heard of . . . except all of urban Malaysia had heard of it, even my terminally offline parents. The theft of billions of ringgit of taxpayer money, the barefaced shamelessness of the people who'd done it, and the lengths they'd gone to to conceal their crimes had shocked even Malaysians, inured as we were to the misbehaviour of our public officials.

I leaned back in my chair, running my hands through my hair. How had this become my life? My boss had gone nuts, I was in a situationship with my work nemesis turned office roommate, and to top it all off, I'd spent the morning with Shaw Boey looking down my dress.

"Charles, do you know who Shaw Boey *is*?"

Charles had just started reading the link, from the look of it. It wouldn't teach him about Shaw Boey's role in the scandal—he and his investment firm weren't named. Maybe he was due to appear in the next article in the series, and that was why he was so keen to get an injunction to restrain publication.

It wasn't like no one had written about the scandal before, but its being featured in the *Guardian* gave it a new level of notoriety. The faint hope of those to whom this was all old news was that the article might incite someone who had the power to do something to take action. They said the US Department of Justice was launching an investigation, and the Swiss and Singaporean authorities were taking an interest, too.

If I were Shaw Boey, I might be feeling that London was a little too close to Switzerland for comfort. But then again, he had billions of ringgit to hide behind. It wasn't surprising that he wasn't concerned.

"He's the Malaysian Prime Minister's fixer," I said. "His right-hand man. He's the guy who set up the whole fraudulent scheme." I shook my head, incredulous. "I thought when you were talking about 'Shaw,' it was a surname. Like George Bernard Shaw."

"No, Boey's the surname," said Charles absently. He was still reading. "His full name's Boey Heng Shaw."

"Yeah! I know!" I hadn't recognised Blackmount Capital as the name of his investment firm, but if I'd seen Shaw Boey's name in any of the documents, I would have known something was up. But all the emails I'd seen had come from some Blackmount staff member, too low down the chain to have made it into the reportage of the scandal.

"I should have guessed," I said. "A blogger making politically motivated allegations. Helen Daley's had a blog about Malaysian politics for years, it's called the *Hornbill Gazette*. I suppose their story is she's in the opposition party's pay, or something like that. And this poor man she's harassing is Jamaludin, of all people. The Prime Minister of Malaysia."

I couldn't act for the PM. I'd acted for plenty of companies

that didn't have much to be proud of except for their annual profits. It was part of the job—you worked for whoever could afford
the firm's fees. After all, we merely advised. It was up to the
client to decide what to do with our advice—even if what they
decided to do wasn't ethical, or possibly wasn't even lawful.
The whole reason we got paid was to help people navigate the
grey area where what was lawful and what wasn't was unclear.

But there had to be a line somewhere. A point at which it
was no longer possible to disclaim responsibility for what the
client did, because we were only the lawyers. I'd hit mine.

Charles sat back. "I don't understand. How does this affect
you?" He gestured at his screen, meaning, presumably, the
wholesale theft of the wealth that rightly belonged to my friends
and family back home.

I stared at him. "Did you read the article?"

"Yes, but—"

"That's state money being funnelled through Blackmount
Capital and all those other companies," I said. "That means it
belongs to the people of Malaysia, not Jamaludin and his wife
and his stepson and all their cronies. Who's going to have to
pay off the debts they've run up? Malaysians, that's who. If
the country wasn't run by these self-interested jokers, maybe I
wouldn't have had to leave. I could be home right now with my
parents, instead of knowing I'll only get to see them once a year
every year until they die."

"I didn't mean—"

But I was too angry to stop, all the old bitterness rising up
in me. "I left because I was sick of being cheated by people like
Jamaludin and bloody Shaw Boey. You don't know what it feels
like to have your future stolen like that. To have your home
taken over by people who're going to destroy everything good
about it, and you're powerless to stop it."

"Kriya," said Charles, his lips twisting. "I'm from Hong
Kong. You think I don't know?"

I shut up. After a moment, I said, "I'm sorry."

"It was a stupid thing for me to say," said Charles. "I only meant it wasn't clear to me if you had any direct involvement. But you've got a conflict. Is that fair to say?"

"Yes. If you want to put it that way." I certainly wouldn't be able to act in the client's best interests. I probably wouldn't kill Jamaludin and his wife if I had the opportunity, but if I could slip something in their drink to give them explosive diarrhoea, I would.

Charles took a deep breath. "All right."

I could tell he didn't quite know what to do. It wasn't the kind of work dilemma one ran into every day. There wasn't going to be a firm policy on what to do if you objected to the firm taking on work for the corrupt PM of your country.

"I need to talk to Farah," he decided. "If you're recusing yourself, we might want to get another associate on board."

That wasn't what I had in mind. "We shouldn't be acting for them at all. It's a reputational risk for the firm. You saw what the article said."

Charles hesitated. "We do already act for Blackmount. And there's nothing to indicate this instruction is for the purposes of fraud. If there is a money laundering risk, that should come up in the checks."

"They won't be trying to launder money through us," I said. Jamaludin and his crew would have made sure their money laundering was conducted through other, more amenable routes, with fewer hoops to jump through. And they wouldn't have left obvious tracks for our CDD team to find. "That's not the point of approaching a firm like Swithin Watkins. The point is to intimidate Helen Daley and anyone else who wants to report on their activities. They don't have to win. The cost of defending the claim is deterrent enough, for an independent journalist. I mean, this is basically a SLAPP, isn't it? A lawsuit designed to silence criticism."

"The client's within his rights to pursue the claim," said Charles. "We advised to that effect. That's what our note says. You helped draft it."

"That was before I knew who I was advising!" I crossed my arms. "Charles, do you really feel all right being part of this? If we act for these guys, we're conferring legitimacy on them. People will think Helen Daley must be a crank, if these big London law firms and banks and consultants are on Jamaludin's side."

"I understand the concern," said Charles. "I'm not saying I don't share it. But ultimately, it's not for us to decide whether the firm takes him on. If there's reliable evidence of what's alleged in Helen Daley's article, presumably it'll come to be considered by the CDD team and the partnership. You are satisfied the allegations are credible?"

"Everyone in Malaysia knows what's going on," I said.

But all the reporting I personally had seen had been in blog and Facebook posts, and Malaysian online news outlets. All of these sources could well be dismissed as unreliable. In a country like Malaysia, where the mainstream media was subject to political control, it wasn't easy to get reporting on the allegations in sources that a Westerner would consider to be authoritative. That was part of the reason why everyone was so excited about the *Guardian* series.

"Zuri said she knows the boyfriend of the guy who was Helen Daley's source," I said. "Maybe she could put me in touch with him. He might be able to share proof." A better idea came to me. "Or he could put me in touch with Helen Daley. If she blogged about being under threat of litigation, that might put them off actually suing. And it might make the case less attractive to the firm."

The silence that followed made me realise that was not an idea I should have spoken out loud, at least to this audience. Charles was so shocked, it took him a moment to recover enough to speak.

"You can't disclose client confidential information," said Charles. "You'd be breaching privilege."

It was as though I'd suggested we go out and find some baby seals to club for sport.

I said, "Charles, Jamaludin has had people *murdered*. Shaw Boey was probably in on it too."

Charles's eyebrows drew together. "What do you mean by that? They've been convicted?"

"If you knew anything about how things work in Malaysia," I said, "you wouldn't be asking."

"Even if he was a convicted murderer, he'd still be entitled to privilege," said Charles. "It's a fundamental right. The system only works if we, as lawyers, protect the process."

"Does the system work?" I said. "If it means people like Shaw Boey and his masters can suppress reporting of their crimes, because they've got the money to throw around, that doesn't say much for the system, does it? Everyone says English libel laws are a problem for free speech."

"All right, but the answer isn't to subvert the rule of law—"

"Oh, come on. Let's not pretend this is about the rule of law. It's about the fact Blackmount is going to pay full rates, no discount."

Charles's lips flattened into a thin line. "Whatever your feelings about the client, you have a duty of confidentiality. You could be struck off. And you'd be implicating the firm."

And me, he didn't say. But he didn't have to. I knew it was true. And I knew Charles was right, according to the rules we'd both been trained to follow.

But the rules, the whole system, had been designed to benefit and protect people like Shaw Boey and Jamaludin. The wealthy, the powerful, the unscrupulous. There had to be times when the rules didn't apply.

"We're not acting for them yet," I said. "This is the window of time when I could make a difference. Anyway, the fact they approached us for advice isn't in itself privileged."

Charles ignored this as the sophistry that, to be fair, it was.

"I should be clear," he said. "If you are serious about this, I would need to report you." He looked miserable. "I don't need to remind you that you're in a vulnerable position."

"Trust me," I said. "I know."

There was no reason to feel disappointed. Why should Charles back me up on this? It was unreasonable of me to expect that of him. Just because he could cook and made me laugh and we were, as it turned out, incredibly sexually compatible, it didn't mean we had anything meaningful in common.

"I know this is . . . difficult," Charles said carefully. "But don't rush into doing anything you might regret. You've had a lot to take in. It's worth sitting on it."

I looked at him, the worried crease in his forehead, and felt a pang. I could see he wanted to do the right thing. So did I. If only we could have agreed on what that was.

"You should talk to someone," added Charles. "You could talk to Farah."

"I guess," I said. "Yeah."

I did feel in need of advice, from someone I could trust with my concerns—someone senior, with a lifetime's worth of experience navigating thorny cases. Someone who understood me. I didn't know Farah well enough, and she didn't know me. But there was someone I could ask.

I didn't tell Charles I was going to speak to Arthur. He would have thought it was a bad idea.

I could see his point of view. Arthur had hit on me on a business trip. He'd pressured me to give up my office. He'd tried to take my biggest client off me. And he'd been weird about it the whole time.

But Charles hadn't seen the years when Arthur had been kind and reliable: all the opportunities he'd sent my way, all the times he'd stepped in to help disentangle legal dilemmas and client dramas. I'd trained under him. I'd relied on his professional judgment for the best part of a decade. Surely, I thought, he'd come through for me now.

More fool me. When I got to Arthur's office, there was someone in there with him—a blonde woman, sitting with her back to me.

According to Outlook, his diary was free for the next half an hour, but after that, he was booked up for the rest of the day. I hesitated, wondering whether to knock on the door and find out how much longer this meeting was going to run, and if I'd have a chance to have a word before his next meeting.

Then Arthur reached out and took the woman's hand.

She moved, her profile coming into view, and I saw it was Emily, the junior associate I'd run into on the way out of Arthur's office the other day. She flinched away from him, her body language screaming discomfort, but she stopped short of pulling her hand away. Or maybe she was trying, and he wasn't letting her.

I opened the door without knocking.

"Sorry, Arthur. Emily, have you got a moment? It's urgent."

Emily's head whipped around. She looked like a rabbit caught in headlights, her eyes huge.

Arthur rose to his feet, flustered. "Oh, I—we were talking about Sanson. I was telling Emily I'd like her to pick up more of the work. As we discussed."

"Great. Yeah. I can brief you about Sanson some other time," I said to Emily. I jerked my head towards the corridor. "Come on. I'll tell you about the case."

I marched her along the corridor until we were out of sight of Arthur's office, then ducked into one of the refreshment areas—the coffee machine was broken, so we'd be safe from interruption.

"Are you OK?" I said.

Emily came to life. "I—yes. I'm fine." Her eyes darted nervously to the entrance to the refreshment area. "What—um—did you say you were going to tell me about the case?"

"There is no case," I said. "It was an excuse. Did Arthur do anything? Or say anything to you?"

"No, I—he was just, kind of, stroking my hand." Emily shuddered. "And talking about his ex-wife."

"Oh my God," I said, with feeling. I got the sense the encounter was only just starting to sink in for Emily: she was rubbing her own hand, absently. I wasn't sure if she knew she was doing it. She looked very young to me in that moment—and Arthur was eighteen years older than me.

"You might want to take a moment," I said. "Go for a walk or something, get out of the building for a bit. I'm going to talk to Arthur."

The door to Arthur's office was ajar. He was at his desk, though it didn't look like he was working. He was gazing off into the distance, his shoulders slumped. I went in and shut the door behind me.

"What was that with Emily?" I said.

Arthur started. He looked relieved when he saw me. That was going to change very shortly.

"With Emily? I was telling her about Sanson, like I said. Sorry, I should have asked you to join us. I happened to have a gap in my diary, so—"

"Arthur, I should not have to tell you that you cannot stroke the hands of junior associates," I said. "I don't know what you think you were doing, but you made Emily very uncomfortable."

Arthur's face was a picture. I'd never spoken to him like this before. Probably no one ever had.

"Did Emily say she was uncomfortable?" he said.

"Anyone with eyes could see it," I said. "You need to get ahold of yourself. You're going to get in trouble if you keep behaving like this."

I expected Arthur to take offence, to snap that it was none of my business. I was almost looking forward to it, I was so angry. At Arthur, for every insane thing he'd done since I'd agreed to follow him to Swithin Watkins. But also at myself, for putting up with him for all these years—because I had to admit the insanity had started long before the move.

I was braced for a fight. Part of me wanted it.

But instead, Arthur's expression went from taken aback to tolerant, even fond.

"All right. I see what's happening here," he said. "I appreciate the concern, but my relationship with other fee earners is none of your business." He was being firm but kind, like a teacher. "Look, I know we've had some challenges lately. Change isn't easy. The move has been destabilising, I've felt it too. Clients haven't moved as quickly as we'd like. You're probably not as busy as you want to be. But I want you to know, you don't need to worry about being replaced."

I stared at him, baffled. Did Arthur think I was *jealous* because he'd started pawing up other associates?

"I'm not worried about being replaced," I said. "I'm worried about you being inappropriate with junior members of staff. Having been put in that position, I know how difficult it can be. I thought how you behaved in Hong Kong was a one-off, that's the only reason I haven't said anything. But—"

"You haven't said anything?" said Arthur. "That's not strictly true, is it? Charles, for example, he hasn't heard anything about what you say happened in Hong Kong?"

I paused, disconcerted. "That's not—"

"You made it clear you don't want my advice on your personal life," said Arthur. "So I backed off. I'd appreciate it if you would give me the same respect. As for Hong Kong, I apolo-

gised. I haven't raised it again. We're both grown-ups. Surely
we can move on."

"Arthur," I said, "you were pressuring me for sex as my *boss*.
I only accepted your apology because I thought you understood
that was wrong, and you weren't going to do anything like it
again. That's clearly not the case, so—"

Arthur shook his head.

"Look, I'll discuss this with you when you're ready to talk
sensibly," he said, with maddening calm. "But not when you're
this emotional. We need to draw a line under this, until you're
able to have a productive conversation."

He rose to his feet, making to shepherd me to the door.

"I am not emotional!" I said.

I was, of course, seething with emotion. But so was bloody
Arthur. He was one of the most high-strung people I knew,
emotions coming out of his fucking ears.

No white man in a position of power was ever over-
emotional, though. His feelings, like his laundry, his social
calendar, and the care of his children, were always someone
else's problem.

I said, "I haven't wanted to make trouble. I moved here so
I could keep building my career, working with you. But if you
can't even acknowledge your behaviour for what it is, you won't
be able to commit to not repeating it. And if that's the case, I'm
going to have to take action."

Arthur went still. "What are you trying to say?"

His voice had dropped a register. It was the sort of tone in
which intimacies are whispered—or threats.

I stepped back. Arthur followed me.

"I don't know what you're planning," he said. "But you
should know I'm not going to be blackmailed, or lied about.
I've taken enough shit these past few years."

His voice was rising, his face flushed. And—I noticed for
the first time—he'd put himself between me and the door.

"Arthur . . ."

"I think you're forgetting the terms of our relationship," he said. A fleck of saliva landed on my cheek. "You moved here to build your career? You wouldn't have a career without me. If you want to keep it, I'd suggest you remember that."

I wiped his spit off my cheek, meeting his eyes. "Maybe I don't."

Arthur raised an eyebrow. "What's that?"

It was the condescension that did it, even more than that stray drop of saliva.

"I'm resigning," I said. "You can take this as my week's notice. I'll put it in writing to HR."

Arthur looked like he'd stepped on a worm only to have it turn around and swear at him. I could have laughed, furious and scared as I was.

"You can't—" He pulled himself together. "You're going to regret this."

"I don't think I will."

I knew I'd said enough, that I should keep my mouth shut. But it felt like I might as well get out everything I had to say to Arthur while I was here. It wasn't like we were going to be staying in touch in future.

"But you might," I said.

I was realising, for the first time, that Arthur needed me more than I needed him. That was all I meant.

But Arthur took two strides towards me and grabbed my arm, shaking me like a misbehaving child.

He ground out, "You are *not* going to threaten me."

I tried to jerk my arm out of his grip, but his hold didn't slacken.

"Arthur," I said, trying for a warning tone. My voice only wobbled a little.

If he didn't let me go, I was going to stamp on his foot. I was wearing Ferragamo dupes from Next, with a low block heel, but if I stamped hard enough I was pretty sure I could make him feel it.

Before I could do it, the door swung open, slamming into Arthur's shoulder. He yelped and staggered, releasing me.

"Oh. Sorry," said Charles, in the doorway. "I was looking for Kriya. Is everything all right?" He looked Arthur up and down, with an air of faint distaste.

I was familiar with that expression on Charles—the expression of someone who's stepped in something nasty and is annoyed about his upcoming trip to the dry cleaners. But I'd never seen him wield it on purpose before.

It was, in fact, the first time I had seen Charles menace someone. It was incredibly attractive.

"Er—" said Arthur. He collected himself, throwing back his shoulders and pushing out his chest. "Kriya and I were just talking."

"Yes," I said. "And now we are done talking." I held Arthur's gaze until he dropped his eyes.

"Great," said Charles. He looked at me and his eyes went soft. "Shall we go?"

CHAPTER THIRTY-ONE

Kriya

The walk back to our office was quiet. I waited till Charles and I were safe in the room to say:

"Thanks for coming to look for me."

"It felt like you were gone a long time," said Charles.

I glanced at the time on my computer screen. The exchange with Arthur had taken all of thirty minutes.

In that half an hour, I'd taken a wrecking ball to my relationship with my boss and my career. Everything I had spent my entire adult life building up was gone.

You're well and truly buggered now, Kriya, I thought.

But I didn't feel it. I felt free.

"Your timing was impeccable," I said. "I was trying to decide whether I should step on Arthur's foot, or kick him in the balls."

Charles wasn't in a mood to see the funny side. "Are you OK?"

I touched my arm gingerly. It felt tender where Arthur had grabbed it. "Just a bruise. Nothing serious."

Charles's face darkened. He jumped to his feet, moving to the window, then came back to his desk, looking over at me. "This is intolerable. I know you haven't wanted to escalate, but something has to be done about him." He was bouncing on the soles of his feet, as though he was on the verge of bolting.

I wasn't sure it was HR he was going to bolt to. I wouldn't have taken bets on Arthur's chances if Charles met him in the corridor in this temper.

"I've resigned," I said. "I told Arthur just now."

That stopped Charles in his tracks. He sat down with a thump. "What?"

I told him about what had happened, from the moment I saw Emily in Arthur's office. I didn't go into why I'd been heading to Arthur's office in the first place. Charles could probably guess, but he didn't ask, which was a greater kindness than I deserved.

"So you don't need to do anything," I concluded. "I'm going to email HR to give notice in writing. And I'm going to ask for a meeting, so I can tell them about Arthur. I'll need to talk to Emily, confirm if she's OK with me mentioning what happened with her. If she doesn't want to get involved, I'll stick to my story. Hopefully that's bad enough for them to take it seriously."

"I should think so," said Charles.

He looked so fierce it made me smile, but only for a moment. I didn't regret anything I'd said to Arthur, but it was coming home to me how wrong I had been about him. How little he resembled the person I'd thought him, and how much I was losing, in finally accepting that.

Mostly, I felt incredibly stupid. First Tom, now Arthur. I was used to thinking of myself as reasonably intelligent. How had I wasted so many years of my life on these terrible men?

"You're right," I said. "The situation isn't sustainable. So long as I thought I was the only one having issues with Arthur, it was harder to make that call. But clearly it's a wider problem." I leaned back in my chair, sighing. "I thought I knew Arthur so well. I can't believe it took me so long to see him for who he is."

Charles did not chime in with my self-recriminations—

which showed extraordinary restraint on his part, all things considered. "Have you told anyone else about resigning?"

"Just Arthur. I didn't know I was going to give notice until I said it."

"If you haven't given notice in writing yet, it doesn't have to be final," said Charles. "Arthur's not the only partner at the firm. I'm sure Farah would have your back, if you told her about everything that's happened. She's in a Board meeting for the rest of the day, but you might be able to catch her in the evening, or tomorrow."

"That's a good idea." Partners divided into two categories: the surprisingly human ones, and all the others. Farah was one of the former, a rare breed. "I'll see if I can catch up with her before I speak to HR about Arthur. It would be helpful to have Farah on side, and it might encourage Emily to raise a complaint about him too. But as for giving notice," I said, "that's been a long time coming. I'm not going to resile now."

The practicalities of the situation were beginning to obtrude. I had a lot of feelings about how stupid I had been and for how long—but I'd have to deal with those another time. I needed to crack on.

In theory I had a week left at the firm, starting now. The fact I was on probation worked both ways: the firm only had to let me know a week in advance of firing me, but I didn't owe them any more than a week's warning of my departure.

But I didn't know if I was going to be allowed to work out my notice period. If I were Arthur, I'd want to get in with my version of events first—discredit me, before I could discredit him.

It was a good thing I'd never had the chance to confide in him about my dilemma regarding the instruction from Shaw Boey. It would have been the perfect excuse for him: He could have said that I was contemplating gross misconduct and needed to be escorted off the premises, out of reach of client confidential information, as soon as possible.

The only person who *did* know I'd been contemplating gross misconduct was staring at me now from across the room, looking tragic, as though someone had run over his cat.

"Are you going to be all right?" said Charles.

"I'll be fine." I'd been saving up for a deposit on my own place, back when I'd thought I was going to buy with Tom, so technically I had enough money to cover my costs and keep Amma and Appa housed for a while. It wasn't like I was in a rush to buy a home now.

I'd never wanted to be in a position where I had to dip into my savings. When I was a kid, Amma and Appa had lived hand to mouth, despite Appa's government servant's salary. Every unexpected expense had been a crisis, a potential disaster. Now, in their old age, they didn't have a nest egg: they had me.

But I didn't regret my decision to resign. I'd figure things out.

"At least it means I won't have to work on the Jamaludin matter." I grinned at Charles, weary. "Silver linings. It's your problem now."

"I've been thinking about the concerns you raised," said Charles. "I'm going to speak to Farah. There may be enough in what you've told me, and the *Guardian* piece itself, to convince the firm this isn't a matter they want to take on." He paused. "I wouldn't do anything on impulse. It may be resolved if we wait and trust in the process."

After a moment, I nodded. It was safer for Charles—for both of us—if I didn't tell him what I was planning. Let him think that, since I was leaving the firm, I was washing my hands of the affair. It was technically no longer any of my business whether Swithin Watkins chose to represent the corrupt Prime Minister of my country or not. In a week's time, I'd have nothing to do with Swithin Watkins.

"I need to send this email to HR," I said. "Is it all right if I name you as a witness?"

"Please do."

I emailed HR, giving formal notice of my resignation, cc'ing Arthur and Farah. Then I rang the HR contact for the Litigation department and asked for a meeting: "I have serious concerns to report about sexual misconduct by a partner."

By the time I rang off, I had a calendar invite in my inbox for a meeting with the head of HR in a couple of hours' time. Whatever Arthur's next move was, I'd have a chance to tell my story.

There wasn't much else to deal with in my inbox—if you ignored the emails from Blackmount Capital addresses, and I had no intention of doing anything else. I found myself thinking that it was not a bad time to quit. I had hardly anything to hand over—a small pro bono case, and Rosalind's protocol.

The thought of Rosalind gave me a pang. I should tell her.

I'd pinged Rosalind an email asking when she'd have time for a call, when Charles cleared his throat.

"I forgot to mention," he said. "I rang the building management company about my flat. They're going to start work on the repairs tomorrow. It took some arguing, but they've agreed to cover a hotel till the repairs are done. I'm going to book somewhere, starting this evening, but could I come by your flat to pick up my things?"

"Of course," I said. "That's great!"

I only meant it was good the building management company was taking responsibility, but maybe I'd sounded too enthusiastic at the idea of him getting out of my flat. His face fell.

I was about to reassure him, when it struck me that if Charles wasn't going to be in my flat that evening, I'd be able to ring Zuri and ask her to put me in touch with Helen Daley's source.

I could message her even if Charles was around, of course, but it was a lot to explain over text message. Also, if I was going to be breaching client confidentiality—which I hadn't quite made up my mind to do yet—I for sure was not going to leave a written record of it.

My phone buzzed before I could say anything to Charles. It was Rosalind.

Saw your email. Can you talk now?

"I've got to make a call," I said.

Charles said, "I've got a Teams meeting in five minutes, but I can go find a meeting room."

"No, you stay. I'm going to go for a walk. Get some fresh air," I said. After an unprepossessing start, the day had turned beautiful, sunshine streaming through the window behind Charles.

Silhouetted against the light, Charles looked like a sexy guardian angel of drama-plagued lawyers. Defender of legal professional privilege, surprise cosplayer, skilled noodle chef, and the sweetest guy I knew.

"We should go for dinner later," I said. "If you think you'll be able to log off before eight."

Charles brightened. "That would be great."

Outside, the skies above the City were a pure cloudless blue. I crossed the road, heading for the church at the end of the street. There was a tiny churchyard that filled up with City workers at lunchtime on sunny days, but if you went round the back of the church, where the tombstones were, it was much quieter. There were a couple of benches there, at least one of which was usually unoccupied.

I tried Rosalind on her work number first, for propriety's sake, but the call went to voicemail. I rang her personal number.

Rosalind picked up straight away. "Kriya! Are you in the office? Is there anyone around you?"

Her voice was full of suppressed excitement.

"No," I said. "I'm outdoors, but I'm good to speak. Rosalind—"

"I'll let you tell me what you wanted to talk about," said Rosalind. "But first, I wanted to let you know. I'm moving to Hong Kong to take up a role as the Regional Head of Compliance and Regulatory Affairs for ASPAC. It was announced internally today."

This was a promotion—one she'd worked hard and schemed ruthlessly for.

"Rosalind, that's fantastic! Congratulations. It's so well deserved."

"Thank you." Rosalind sounded delighted. Besides the professional recognition the promotion represented, she'd been talking about moving closer to her family in Indonesia for years. "Now, what did you want to discuss?"

"My news isn't quite so happy," I said. "I've resigned. I'm due to leave Swithin Watkins next week. I'm sorry it's such short notice."

I was prepared for Rosalind to interrogate me about the reasons for my departure. I was planning to be discreet, but not so dignified as to deny it if she guessed it had something to do with Arthur.

But you could always rely on Rosalind to be surprising.

She said, "Oh, have you got a job somewhere else?"

"Er, no, but—"

"But then this is perfect timing. It must be fate," said Rosalind. "Listen, Kriya, I know I'm forever asking you to do crazy things, but you know there's always a method to my madness. I have an offer to make you. I want you to listen and think about it seriously. Will you promise me you'll do that?"

There was no one on the benches behind the church that day. I sat down on the one that didn't have a broad streak of fresh bird shit on it.

"OK," I said. "Tell me more."

CHAPTER THIRTY-TWO

Charles

Kriya came back from her walk as my call was wrapping up. She put a coffee cup on my desk.

Kriya: "I went by the nice coffee place. Black Americano, right?"

CG: "Yeah. Thanks. Is everything all right?"

She was probably sick of me asking. But there was something different about her. Like something had happened.

Kriya sat down at her desk. "Rosalind's offered me a job."

Blinked. But it wasn't surprising, in a way. Well-timed. "At Sanson?"

Kriya nodded. "It would be based out of their Hong Kong office. She's moving out there on promotion."

That *was* a surprise. Didn't know how I felt about it. "You'd be joining their in-house legal team, I assume."

Kriya: "Yeah. Sanson's manufacturing is all out of ASPAC, mostly China. Hong Kong is a major hub for them. Rosalind's got a brief to raise compliance standards across the region. They've got a new GC there, too, he's got headcount to expand the Legal team. Rosalind knows him, they used to work together when she was at Sanson France. She says he's very nice."

CG: "Are you going to take the job?"

Kriya: "Well, it's not a done deal. I'd be reporting to the GC, so he's got to approve it. Rosalind's asked me to send her my CV. And the GC wants to meet me. In Hong Kong. He's one of those old school guys who don't believe in Teams meetings, I guess. They've said they'll cover travel expenses."

She blew out a sigh. Looked overwhelmed.

No wonder. I felt overwhelmed and I wasn't even the person all of this was happening to.

CG: "Are you going to go?"

Kriya: "Why not, right? It's a free trip. And I'll be at loose ends from next week."

Hong Kong was a long way away. Probably didn't say much of me, as a son and a brother, that I'd never felt the distance so much before.

CG: "It's a big decision, moving to another country."

Always had the thought at the back of my head that I might go back. Never been able to bring myself to commit to it before, though I knew Ma would like me to live closer by. But then, I'd be closer to Ba as well, with all the complications that entailed.

Not that I managed to avoid his complications, despite living so far away. He wasn't a reason for avoiding going back. I'd just never had a good enough reason to subject myself to the necessary faff—leaving the firm, finding a new job, selling or renting out the flat, sorting out accommodation over there.

Kriya: "Yeah. But I'm not from here, that makes a difference. I kind of chose to stay for Tom, originally. And the job. Now I don't have either. And in Hong Kong, I'd be closer to my parents."

She shook herself, glancing at her computer screen. "I'll have to think about it another time. Got to go see HR now." She grimaced. "Wish me luck."

CG: "Are you all right going by yourself? Would you like company?"

Kriya looked surprised, as though she hadn't considered before that she didn't need to do it on her own. "Are you offering?"

I had a client meeting in ten minutes, but I could move it. Good for clients to learn they can't have it their own way all the time. "Yes."

Kriya: "That would be helpful. Yeah. Thanks, Charles."

Kriya left the office after the meeting with HR. It was four p.m., but nobody was likely to object. She looked exhausted, and it wasn't like it mattered anymore if she met her billable hour targets.

HR meeting went all right. I didn't say much: only spoke when called upon, to corroborate Kriya's account. Emily had agreed to speak to HR as well about her experience.

The HR people seemed to take it seriously. Apart from anything else, Arthur hadn't been at the firm long enough to establish himself. Presumably he wouldn't be that difficult to get rid of. If anything, they seemed more concerned about Kriya's departure—devoted a good ten minutes to telling her she shouldn't feel she had to leave the firm. They couldn't promise any outcomes until they'd completed their investigation, but if there was anything they could do to make the firm a safe environment, etc., etc.

Kriya had nodded, smiled a little, and maintained her desire to resign. Seemed more distracted than anything else. As though she was already mentally in a future where she was gone, and none of this was her concern any longer.

We met for dinner, as Kriya had proposed, at a restaurant near her flat, after I got out of the office. But she was as abstracted at dinner. Had the sense she regretted suggesting it.

To be fair, she had a lot to think about. Like moving to Hong Kong for a job with her favourite client.

The weekend felt very far away now. Was deeply regretting not asking Kriya what she thought was going on between us, while it was happening. If she'd said all the sex and self-revealing conversations didn't mean anything—that they were nothing more than a fevered one-off, a brief break from reality—it would have hurt, but at least I would have known where I stood.

If she'd said, conversely, *What do you mean what does it all mean, aren't we together now?* then that would have been a place to start from. I'd have a right to ask her now what was going to happen to us. I'd have a right to assume there *was* an us.

As it was, I didn't know how to raise it. Seemed trivial, next to everything else Kriya had to think about.

We didn't talk about Arthur, or what we meant to each other (if anything), or whether Kriya thought I was a gutless loser, happy to represent any fraudulent scoundrel so long as they were willing to pay up. Dinner conversation focused on lighter topics:

"I'll need to dig up that list of food recommendations you gave me, if I go to Hong Kong," Kriya said.

CG: "Where is the Sanson office?"

When she told me, I started listing more places she could go to, but Kriya stopped me: "Email them to me. Actually, can you WhatsApp me? I'll give you my number."

Weird that I'd been inside her, but this was the first time I was getting her personal number. Felt close to Kriya, but I wasn't, not really. Barely knew her.

Kriya leaned across the table to save her number on my phone. I caught a whiff of her hair. Brought back the morning with painful vividness: waking up with her scent in my nostrils, her warmth next to me.

Actually felt faint with desire. Never happened to me before.

Walked back to Kriya's flat with her, so I could pick up my things. I was planning to take the Tube to the hotel I'd booked.

Kriya: "Travelodge?"

CG: "Premier Inn. None of the rooms have windows, but the pictures on the website look fine."

Kriya made a face. "At least you get natural light in the office." Paused. "I'm going to work from home for the rest of the week, so I might not see you in the office again. I'll just come in next Monday to drop my laptop off with IT."

CG: "Right."

Hadn't been emotionally prepared for this. Hadn't been emotionally prepared for anything that had happened in the past four days, up to and including Kriya inviting me to stay at her flat.

She didn't say why she wanted to work from home. Well, why wouldn't she? No one was going to pull her up on her office attendance, any more than they were going to be tracking her billable hours. Presumably she didn't feel like running into Arthur again.

Quite fancied the prospect myself. Correct to report Arthur through the appropriate channels and demand action from the firm, of course, instead of, e.g., knocking his teeth in. But I personally would have found knocking his teeth in infinitely more satisfying.

Strange being back in Kriya's flat. The door to her bedroom stood ajar. Avoided looking into it.

Just that morning, I'd had Kriya pinned to her bed, moaning underneath me. Heat rose in my face at the memory.

Kriya didn't seem troubled by any memories of the kind. She was brisk and friendly. "You've got all your stuff? You can text me if you realise you've left anything behind."

She saw me to the door. Had the air of a hostess wrapping up a party at the end of a long night, cordial but relieved. "Good night, Charles." Smiled at me, absently. "Thanks for everything. You've been such a trouper."

Not the note I wanted to be ending the evening on. Wanted to kiss her. Wasn't sure it'd be welcome.

Took my courage in my hands and said: "Maybe we could have dinner again, whenever you're free? I had a good time at the weekend."

Sounded appallingly feeble. What I really meant was, *I think I'm in love with you. I can't bear to let you go.*

But I couldn't say that now, with Kriya looking like she was wishing she were shot of me. It was too much. If only she'd give me the time to work up to it.

Pathetic as it was, what I said worked, to a degree. Kriya came back from wherever she'd gone to in her head. Her eyes softened.

Kriya: "Oh, Charles. You're so lovely. It's just, there's so much going on right now. And if this thing with Sanson works out, you know, I might end up in Hong Kong. After what happened with Tom . . . I don't know. It's complicated."

CG: "Yeah. No. Of course."

Kriya: "Look, why don't I—" Her phone buzzed. She glanced at it, stiffening, then said: "Sorry. I don't want to rush you, but I've got someone coming over."

She wouldn't meet my eyes. Seemed embarrassed.

I was struck by a sudden, horrible suspicion that it was a date she was waiting for. Why else would she be embarrassed about them seeing me, or vice versa? She'd let me meet her friends.

I was being ridiculous. Why would Kriya meet a date at her flat? Unless it was someone she was already seeing. It hadn't seemed like she was seeing anyone else, when—at the weekend. Her friends hadn't mentioned it. They wouldn't have encouraged me to ask her out, would they, if she was dating other people?

Not that Kriya and I were dating. Shouldn't have fallen into bed with her. Seemed a great idea at the time, but look at me now. If I'd courted her properly, or at least confirmed some crucial details up front—like, did she want to be my girlfriend for real, instead of simply pretending for Arthur's and my family's benefit—I wouldn't be in this position.

Kriya *was* hiding something. I knew her well enough, after sharing an office with her for six weeks, to tell that. But it didn't matter if it was a date coming to see her. Whatever it was she didn't want me to know, it wasn't any of my business.

CG: "Sure. Sorry. Have a good evening."

Kriya: "Good night, Charles."

Hotel was fine. You didn't notice the lack of windows. Who needs a window in central London, anyway? Only going to look out on the walls of other buildings, or a row of dustbins, or some grim road, with pigeons fighting over a discarded box of chips.

Had left my laptop in the office, because there wasn't anything urgent on. If we were taking on the case for Shaw, we'd have to crack on, but I wasn't confident that was going to happen. I'd emailed Farah and the CDD team about the concerns Kriya had raised. Farah had responded:

Let's talk tmrw.

No point trying to do anything on the matter until I'd spoken to her.

Not exactly an attractive case, suing a freelance journalist. Agreed with Kriya there. At least there's generally equality of arms in the commercial litigation I do.

Thought of the student I'd spoken to at Cittie of Yorke: Razia, with her dissertation on human rights. She wouldn't be too impressed.

Still, I couldn't see that it was an inappropriate instruction. Nothing to indicate the instruction itself was to advance a fraudulent scheme. Optics were bad, of course. But if one chose one's clients based on optics, no one accused of murder would have legal representation. Must be right that it's for the courts to decide.

Kriya hadn't mentioned her mad idea of approaching the other side again. Hopefully she'd thought better of it once she'd had a chance to reflect.

Ended up lying on the bed, flipping through channels on the TV. Wasn't really what I wanted to be doing with my evening. My first choice would have been making progress on some work. Should have brought my laptop with me.

Well, no. My *first* choice would have been spending the evening with Kriya at her place. But that wasn't an option.

Loretta and Ma and all the rest of them can have a go at me for working too much. But work is better than people. You know where you are with it.

Phone rang. Personal phone—the one I don't look at in the evening.

For a moment, I thought it might be Kriya. But what would she be ringing for? *I changed my mind, Charles. A hook-up with you is exactly what I want, given everything else going on in my life.*

That wasn't what I wanted from her, or not the only thing.

Would have taken it, though. I'd take any scraps she was willing to throw me.

Wasn't Kriya ringing, obviously.

CG: "Hi, Ma."

Early in Hong Kong, but Ma can never lie in. Goes and does hei gung in a park at eight a.m. with a lot of other aunties and uncles. She hasn't learned to levitate yet, but the exercise is good for her.

Ma: "Where are you?"

CG: "Where are you? I can only see hair."

Slight exaggeration: I could see a bit of forehead as well as Ma's hairline and perm. Most of the image consisted of ceiling. Ma can never figure out how to position her phone so the camera captures her face.

Ma: "That's not your flat, is it? Are you travelling?"

Hadn't told Ma about the flat. Ma gets worried about things—bad for her—and when she's worried, she gives me advice—annoys me.

CG: "I'm at a hotel. The building management company's having works done to the flat. Should be done in a couple of weeks. They're paying for the hotel."

Ma, impressed: "For two weeks? That's very good. You should give the building manager a present."

CG: "I'll think about it." Never seen the building manager in person. Could be a robot for all I know. "What's up?"

Ma looked shifty. "I saw Ah Yi and Yi Cheung yesterday."

Could see what was coming. Heart sank. I wasn't up for this, not after the evening I'd had.

Should have thought harder about the potential consequences of bringing Kriya along as my date for the wedding, so the relatives would believe I had a girlfriend. Namely, that they would think she was my girlfriend.

But I couldn't have guessed how painful that misunderstanding would be. A week ago, I wouldn't have believed Kriya would kiss me, or sleep with me, or do any of the things we'd done over the weekend.

CG: "How are they?"

Ma: "Very tired, but they said Loretta's party was nice. It was at an expensive hotel, they said. How much did you give? Loretta wouldn't tell them."

CG: "Enough."

Ma might have nagged me for the amount another day, but that wasn't the line of inquiry she'd rung me to pursue.

She said: "Ah Yi and Yi Cheung said you brought a friend? Ah Yi told me her name, what was it . . ."

CG: "Kriya. She's my coworker."

Ma: "Oh? They said she's your friend. Indian girl?"

CG: "She's from Malaysia."

Ma: "Is that why she speaks Cantonese? Ah Yi said. She showed me the photo. Very pretty girl. She's at your firm, you said? A lawyer? She must be clever."

CG: "Yes. But she's quit now."

Ma: "Oh, what's she going to do?"

CG: "She's thinking of going in-house. Working at a company, in industry, instead of a law firm. She's interviewing with a company in Hong Kong, actually."

Mistake to mention that.

Ma: "She's coming to Hong Kong? I told you, it's a good place to work. The tax is lower. And you're closer to family. When you get older, you'll realise that's important. The parents are in Malaysia? The flight is not too long, I think. Four hours?"

I'd been doing well, but when I opened my mouth to answer, the words got stuck in my throat.

Had known I wanted Kriya. Just hadn't realised how much I wanted of her. It was as though her rejecting me had unlocked some door in my head, behind which all these fantasies had been lurking.

Now they poured out, images I hadn't even known I'd been harbouring. Introducing Kriya to Ma. Going on holiday with her. Putting my arm around her on the sofa, arguing about what to watch on Netflix. Pouring her tea at a dim sum restaurant.

Didn't even know if she liked dim sum. Hardly knew anything about her, really. Except that her ex had broken her heart and her boss was mental and she liked cooking and she had excellent drafting skills and when I made her laugh it felt like I could do anything.

Ma: "Charles? Hello? Can you hear me?"

CG: "Yeah. I'm here. Look, Ma, about Kriya, don't get too excited. It's nothing—"

Nothing serious, I was going to say. *Nothing real.*

Ma said: "Do you like her?"

Stared at the TV. Some kind of reality show playing, about

people going on dates. Some guy with unfortunate hair was on the screen, saying: "She's hot, she's sexy, she's fun. I felt there was a real connection there."

Cut to the woman: "Yeah. No." She grimaced.

CG: "Yes. I like her. But it doesn't matter. It's not going anywhere."

Ma: "Why not?"

Because she doesn't like me back. Not enough.

CG: "Never mind. There's no point talking about it. How's your leg?" Turned off the TV.

CHAPTER THIRTY-THREE

Kriya

Z uri was never too busy to talk, so long as you rang her during the working day. She was still at the office when I got home at four thirty and rang her—the first time in recorded history I'd ever logged off earlier than her.

She said, "Yeah, I can talk. Let me go find a quiet corner."

Once she was settled in a suitably quiet corner, I said, "Eh, you know the Helen Daley piece in the *Guardian*? You said you know somebody who knows the source, right? The YouTuber May Yin was telling us about."

"It's his boyfriend my friend knows," said Zuri. "Why?"

"I've got a work issue." I paused, staring out of the window of my living room.

Charles was basically right about confidentiality and privilege. But I was also right that it was fucked up that, with sufficient money, any criminal could make the legal system into a tool to hammer any critic into silence. This had to be the right thing to do.

"I can't say much," I said. "It's all super sensitive. But my firm's been approached to act in relation to the article, let's put it that way. I've been thinking whether there's anything I can do about it."

My parents would take the view that I'd done more than enough in announcing my resignation. Leave it to the firm to decide whether they wanted to get involved in Jamaludin's business, Amma and Appa would say. Even if I could do anything to affect that decision, what difference would it make to the likes of the Prime Minister and his right-hand man? They'd just go and find another law firm to act. They were bound to find one willing to hold its nose and take their money. Getting Swithin Watkins to decline representation was, at most, an inconvenience—a pebble in their shoe.

But it was the most I might ever be able to do. It wasn't explosive diarrhoea, much less a criminal conviction for multiple counts of fraud, money laundering, conspiracy to murder, and all the rest of it. But it was better than nothing.

"I'm assuming it's not Helen Daley who's approached your firm," said Zuri. "They're willing to get involved in this kind of thing? Isn't it bad for their reputation?"

"If you offer enough money, people stop worrying so much about their reputation."

Zuri snorted. "True. Four billion dollars is probably enough, right."

"I need evidence," I said. "You know what lawyers are like, it's the documents that matter. I was thinking, they probably had to be super careful about what they said in the article, right? The underlying proof must go even further."

"I'll ask my friend," said Zuri. "I don't know the guy myself. I'll let you know."

I figured she meant in a couple of weeks' time, if that. I put my phone down and went for a bath. I had a bath about once every two years, but this day, I felt, merited a long soak and a glass of wine.

When I got out, warm and pruney, my phone was ringing.

"He says he'll come meet you," said Zuri, without precursor. "The boyfriend."

"*What?* What did you tell him?"

"Just what you told me," said Zuri. "OK lah, maybe I elaborated a bit. I might have implied Jamaludin approached your firm. I got a little carried away." She laughed.

I didn't. Zuri stopped laughing.

"Are you serious?" she said.

"I can't say anything!"

"That's *crazy*," said Zuri. "OK, OK, I won't ask. Maybe the guy's heard something. He wants to meet today. Says he's free from seven thirty. Can you do it?"

I hesitated. Charles had said he should be able to get out of the office around seven, to meet for dinner.

This was important enough that I should probably cancel on dinner. But I might not be seeing much more of Charles, if it all went ahead with Sanson. Rosalind had indicated they'd want me to start as soon as possible, assuming the GC liked me ("he will definitely like you, he is not an idiot").

I didn't want to think about how that made me feel. Maybe it would be better to avoid Charles till I knew whether I'd be staying in the country or not. But after everything that had happened between us, I couldn't decide to do that—at least, not till I'd had a chance to say goodbye.

"Would nine o'clock be OK?" I said.

"Yeah," said Zuri. "Only thing is, right, he says it needs to be somewhere private. He didn't come right out and say it, but I think he's worried about being followed. Is it OK if I bring him to your place? He works close by only, the office is across the river."

"Oh, you're coming?"

"Are you kidding?" said Zuri. "Of course I'm coming. This is the most exciting thing that has happened in my entire life."

I might have been a little distracted at dinner with Charles that evening, but he didn't say anything to show he'd noticed. Zuri turned up shortly after he had left my flat with his suitcase.

She had a Chinese guy in tow. He was in a slightly rumpled suit and looked completely ordinary.

There was something weird going on with Zuri, though. It took me a moment to realise what it was. She was starstruck.

"This is Ket Hau," she said. "Ket Hau, Kriya." To me, she said, "Eh, turns out I follow Ket Hau's sister-in-law on Instagram!"

I blinked. "Is she the mutual friend? The one who introduced you?"

"No lah. I don't know her," said Zuri. "She's an influencer. She runs that brand, Virtu, damn expensive one. It's nice," she added, glancing at Ket Hau. "But I can't afford the clothes. I can only admire from afar."

"Yeah, me too," said Ket Hau. We shook hands.

"Thanks for letting me come here," he said. "I was telling Zuri, I'm trying to be careful at the moment. Everyone is jumpy, with the election coming up, and the *Guardian* series being published. Stephen's had a couple of incidents. Might be nothing, but after he was kidnapped that time, he's a little paranoid."

"Yeah, fair enough," I said, resolving internally to catch up on Stephen Jembu's YouTube explainers. "Do you want a drink? Coffee? Tea? Milo?"

"No," said Ket Hau, then: "Oh, if you have Milo . . ."

Once we were sat down with our hot drinks, he said: "I should explain why I was so keen to meet. You see, we knew they'd be trying to suppress publication of the series. Helen's been waiting for the legal letter. So when Zuri got in touch, I thought, here we go."

"I don't know how much I can tell you," I said. "Zuri said you're a lawyer, is that right? So you'll know I have professional duties. We haven't cleared conflicts yet, or confirmed we'll be acting. But it's a bit complicated, because one of the parties involved is an existing client of the firm.

"I resigned today, actually," I added, and felt Zuri start next to me. "But I don't want the firm to represent these people. I mean, I know they'll just go off and find some other lawyers who are willing to take their money, but . . ."

"If you can make life difficult for them, why not, right?" Ket Hau grinned. "If a firm like Swithin Watkins turns away a client like that, that might filter out into the market. Make other people more cautious about signing on. It makes sense to me."

He was a reassuring sort of person. I felt the knot of tension in my chest start to unwind.

"Why don't you tell me what you can," he said. "And I'll see how I can help."

CHAPTER THIRTY-FOUR

Charles

S haw rang Tuesday afternoon. He tried my personal phone first. Then my office phone started ringing.

Didn't pick up. Farah had popped by my office first thing in the morning to talk about the Shaw instruction.

Explained Kriya's concerns, though I didn't identify them as hers. Focused on the reputational risk to the firm of taking the matter on.

Farah got the point: "This needs to go to the risk management committee. The CDD team should escalate it, since the prospective client is a politically exposed person. But can you drop them a line and check they will do it? Who's the relationship partner for Blackmount, can you remind me?"

CG: "Robert Anderson."

Farah pursed her lips. "He'll put up a fight, if we say we're not going to act. All right, leave it with me."

CG: "If the client chases, I'll put him off, shall I?"

Farah: "That's right. Tell him it's going through our processes, if you must. But it's probably best to avoid engaging until we've got a better sense of where it's going to fall out."

So I let my office phone ring until it stopped.

Then my personal phone buzzed. Shaw had sent a WhatsApp message. Notification read:

Call me when you've got a moment

Put my phone aside without tapping into the message, so Shaw wouldn't know I'd read it.

Felt unnatural ignoring a client, but I was following instructions, after all. Irrelevant that I wasn't particularly keen on talking to Shaw. Hadn't enjoyed it the last time. And if I'd known it was going to upset Kriya . . .

Nothing I could do about it. She'd seemed all right at dinner the night before, not angry at me or anything like that.

But if that was the last time I was going to see her—which didn't, at the moment, seem out of the question—I could wish our disagreement about the case hadn't been hanging over it.

Stop thinking about Kriya. Path to nowhere.

Shaw got me the next day, Wednesday morning. Was waiting to hear from chambers about trial dates when my work mobile rang. No caller ID. Picked up, assuming it was the clerk coming back to me.

Shaw: "Morning, Charlie. I tried to catch you yesterday, but I didn't get through. Did you see my message?"

CG, clearing throat: "I haven't been checking my phone, sorry. It's been busy."

Shaw: "No worries. I'm at Swithin Watkins now, came by to talk to Rob about a deal we're doing. We're wrapping up now, but I wanted to grab you while I'm here. You free to talk? It's to do with this case you're picking up for my client. We've got a little problem on our hands."

Shaw's tone was light, but I felt a sense of foreboding.

CG: "We're still in the process of doing our checks, so we aren't cleared to act yet. It's probably best if we avoid discussing the case till we've completed the processes to register Mr. Jamaludin—"

Shaw: "Call him 'the boss,' that's what I do. He doesn't

appreciate having his name bandied around. Look, mate, you do what you have to, we understand that. But I need to talk to you. Won't take two minutes. Hold on."

Could hear Shaw conferring with someone else, before his voice came back on the line.

Shaw: "Rob says he'll walk me down to your office."

Looked around my office. One does less on paper now than twelve years ago when I started as a trainee. But I was still surrounded by stacks of files with clients' names on them, papers crammed with confidential information, notes on my noticeboard with sensitive internal data.

What was Robert Anderson thinking? Hardly correct practice to agree to walk a client through the working areas of the firm. But then again, Shaw was hard to say no to.

CG: "There's no need for that. I'll come and meet you. Are you on fourteenth floor?"

Shaw: "I'm outside the building. We went for a coffee. You good to come out now?"

It was only Shaw waiting on the pavement outside the firm when I got out.

Shaw: "I sent Rob back to his desk to get on with things. Blackmount's bid two hundred million for a major fashion brand"—told me the name. "All very hush hush till the deal's announced, but I know you won't say anything. We want to get it through ASAP, so Rob won't be sleeping for the next few weeks." Laughed. "But he's all right. He made equity partner last year on the strength of our fees. Got to make him work for it, eh?"

He glanced around. "Mind if we walk? Trying to keep my steps up." Held up his wrist to show me his fitness tracker.

Patek Philippe on his other wrist. I recognised it because Ba got me a fake for my twenty-first birthday. He was proud of it: "This dealer, he sources the best fakes for the foreigners to buy. I got this one for $5,000. If it was real, it would cost over $1 million."

Had to stop wearing the watch: it kept losing time. A year after Ba gave it to me, I took it out of a drawer and found the fake leather coming off the strap in flakes. Didn't tell him.

Shaw's watch probably cost over a hundred grand pound sterling. No fakes for him.

Shaw: "We could go along the river. It's not too far from here, is it?"

We walked along the curve of Victoria Embankment, dodging City workers and the occasional tourist. Bikes whizzed past us. Cars, taxis, and vans queued on the far side of the cycle lane, inching along as the traffic lights changed.

Shaw wanted to be by the water, but there were construction hoardings up along the river. We stayed on our side of the road, looking for a gap.

It was muggy, the sky greyish white. Shaw took off his jacket and slung it over his arm.

I kept mine on. Felt the need for protection, somehow.

CG: "You said there's a problem with the case?"

Shaw: "I'd say so, yeah. I had a surprise call late last night. Got rung up by the old bat herself, Helen Daley."

My face went rigid. Could feel Shaw's eyes on me.

Shaw: "She said she's received a tip-off, heard I'm instructing a major London law firm to sue her. Wanted to give me the chance to comment before posting about it on her blog."

Could only hope the fact I'm bad at emotions was helping me now: often other people can't seem to tell what I'm feeling, any more than I can guess what they're feeling.

Couldn't fault them. I can't always guess what I'm feeling myself. On this occasion, though, I knew. Main thing I felt was guilt, that I hadn't tried harder to reassure Kriya. There must have been something I could have said, so she wouldn't have felt she needed to do this.

CG: "What did you say?"

Shaw: "I told her she'd hear from my lawyers. Then I hung up and blocked her."

CG: "That seems sensible."

Shaw: "What I can't work out is, how'd she get my number? I'm not one for the limelight. I stay behind the scenes. That's where I'm most useful to the boss. So I'm asking myself, who put Helen Daley on to me?" Gave me a sidelong look. "You got any ideas, Charlie?"

CG: "You don't have any mutual contacts?"

Shaw: "That's what I'm wondering." Eyed me in a pointed way.

Did he think I'd done it? Would be better than it being pinned on Kriya. Should I say it was me?

But did this leak have anything to do with Kriya? She'd talked about it, but that didn't mean she'd done it. Besides, I couldn't imagine she'd agreed to pass Shaw's number to Helen Daley, so Daley could ring Shaw and give her away.

Shaw: "There must be something we can do. Can we sue whoever leaked the number? It must be some kind of, what d'you call it, a data protection crime?"

CG: "We'd have to think about what the cause of action would be." That's the formula Farah uses when she means *You haven't got a case*. "Though we'd have to know who it was, in order to mount a claim."

Shaw: "That's what I'm saying. There's got to be a leak somewhere. *I* didn't give the bloody woman my number."

We'd come to the end of the hoardings. The brown waters of the Thames could be seen past the low wall on the other side of the road. We crossed the road.

Shaw came to a stop by the wall along the river. We were opposite the Oxo Tower, its grey tower rising up from the brick façade. The sun had emerged, shining down through chinks in the clouds, sparking light off the waves.

Was sweating in my jacket. Shaw unbuttoned his cuffs and pushed up his sleeves.

Shaw: "That Indian girl you were with on Monday. She's Malaysian, yeah?"

CG: "I believe so." Said it quite naturally, as though I didn't know for certain.

Shaw: "You didn't mention her before."

CG: "She stepped in to help get the advice note over the line. There wasn't much spare capacity in the team, and she volunteered."

Would have said something about Kriya's cross-border experience in the ordinary course of things, to make it sound less like she was a warm body we'd chucked at our resource problem.

But this wasn't an ordinary conversation. Whatever it was Shaw was driving at, I didn't want Kriya to have any part in it.

Shaw: "She hasn't been with the firm for long. I looked her up online."

CG: "No, she was a recent hire, from Brown, Rosenburg and Cushway." That much he already knew, if he'd seen her LinkedIn profile.

Shaw was smiling. Familiar feeling: He was in on the joke, and I wasn't. Because I was the joke. "You'd vouch for her?"

CG: "Yes. She's an excellent lawyer."

Shaw: "You're wondering why I'm asking all these questions."

Wasn't the only thing I was wondering. Was chiefly ruminating on what a psychiatric assessment would make of Shaw.

Shaw: "I pride myself on my judgment of character. It's never let me down. And I trust you, Charlie. But this Kriya . . . I'm not so sure about her involvement. You know, she might think she knows more than she does."

CG: "She's leaving the firm, so she won't be involved in this matter going forward."

Shaw raised his eyebrows. "Oh, is it? Now, see, this is why we came to you." Clapped me on the shoulder. Seemed genuinely pleased. "You anticipate what we want, and you make it happen."

CG: "Kriya resigned for unrelated reasons."

Shaw: "Sure, sure. Just make sure nothing like this happens again, eh? You want people who are objective on the case. We don't want any risk of bias, you understand me?"

He took a pack of cigarettes out of his pocket, offering me one. I declined.

Shaw lit up. "I'll be honest with you, I wasn't sure about Swithin Watkins. Rob was pushing us to go with you guys, but there are other firms with better credentials, for what we were looking for. When I remembered you work there, that's what swung it for me. Relationships matter to me. They're what it's all about—working with people you know and trust. I can trust you, right, Charlie?"

CG: "We always hope to be a trusted advisor to our clients."

Knew it sounded priggish.

Shaw chortled. "That's the Charlie Goh I know! You know, Ba used to say to me, 'Why can't you be like Goh Boon Ean's boy? His father and mother don't have to worry about him. He knows how to behave himself. None of this partying or fooling around with girls.' Drove me crazy. Just because you never had fun and couldn't get girls, I had to suffer." He grinned toothily. "But who's paying whose fees now?"

He blew a stream of smoke in my face.

I didn't react. Sort of stupid thing they used to do at school. Showing you what they thought of you.

Shaw: "Funny how things work. My dad's so strict, always keeps to the straight and narrow. You want to ask him to bribe somebody, forget about it. Even if it's something small, to avoid a saman or what. And he got a son like me. Meanwhile, your dad's a wide boy, and he gets you." He snorted. "But opposites attract, right? I think you and me could be good friends. We could help each other. Like my dad helped your dad when he got in trouble. Remember that?"

Wasn't sure why he was asking. Shaw used to bring it up whenever he spoke to me at school—which, to be fair, hadn't been that often.

Remembered, suddenly, how much I'd dreaded running into him, when it was all going down with Ba. Lived in terror of Shaw telling everyone Ba was a criminal, giving them yet another reason to despise me, on top of me being small, swotty, weird, and foreign.

Shaw never did tell anyone, so far as I knew. But he'd held that secret over me until we left school.

Hadn't thought about that in years. To be fair, there had been so much going on in those days, it was hardly surprising if I'd forgotten one of the many things that used to upset and terrify me then.

CG: "I remember. It was good of your dad."

Shaw: "We got in touch with your dad, you know. He's not doing so well, is he? He told us about this latest business venture of his. It's hard on a man at his stage in life, a failure like that. He was very happy when we offered him the job."

CG: "What job?"

Shaw: "We haven't decided on the title yet, but we'll figure something out. It won't come with too much responsibility, don't worry. Your dad will want to take it easy, at his age. But we'll make sure it's a good package. He'll be able to put the kids through uni, take his pension when he retires. Won't have to worry about the future."

He surveyed me, smiling faintly. "You can't keep him going forever. You've got your own life to worry about. You'll want to get married, have a family, buy a house. How are you going to do that if you're throwing all your money at your dad's debts?"

CG: "Who told you my dad's in debt?"

Shaw: "He did. You know, Charlie, we're not that different, at the end of the day. We're Chinese, we know family is the most important thing. And we both take our jobs seriously, yeah? My job is to make my boss's life easy. This Helen Daley, she's making it complicated."

He shook his head. "I'll tell you something, between friends. It wasn't easy, getting lawyers on board. We approached another firm at first, but they passed. That's not the kind of thing my boss expects. He expects the best, and he's not used to being told no. I've put my name on the line for Swithin Watkins. I told him, this is the right firm for us. I'm keen for us to have a good relationship. You want that too, right?"

CG: "We hope to maintain good relationships with all our clients."

Shaw grabbed my shoulder, shaking it gently, then let it go. "That's right. If this Daley woman comes to you with her allegations, you'll know what to do, yeah? And if anybody else brings anything to your attention, you let us know. There's a lot of troublemakers out there—so-called whistleblowers, activists, all these busybodies. But you don't worry about them. Remember who pays the bills, and we'll be able to work together. All right?"

CG: "Was there anything else? I've got a meeting I need to get back for."

Shaw pushed off the wall. "I'll walk with you. I'm headed that way anyway."

Didn't feel I could refuse his company.

As we were approaching the entrance to the firm, Shaw said: "I'm sure you've been to Tuscany."

CG: "No."

Bone of contention with both Loretta and Farah, that I never go on holiday. Don't see the point, unless I'm going to see Ma.

Need to do that some time. Haven't been back to Hong

Kong in a while. Maybe after I've paid off Ba's debt and built my savings back up.

Maybe if Kriya ends up there . . . ? But she would have said if she wanted to see me in Hong Kong, wouldn't she? She knows I've got family out there.

Shaw: "I've got a villa outside Siena. Two pools, stunning views. I'm not there much, so my friends are always welcome to use it. You should go some time."

Made the noise I make when Farah or Loretta suggests I take some of the ten weeks' worth of annual leave I've accrued. It sounds a bit like "yes," but means "no."

Shaw: "You could bring Kriya. Better not to have her on our case, but that's business. It doesn't need to interfere with pleasure."

CG: "I'm sorry?"

Shaw: "You're sleeping with her, no? Come on, Charlie, do you think I'm stupid or what? Why else would you be getting out of an Uber with her on a Monday morning?"

CG: "I don't think it's appropriate to—"

Shaw: "It's all right. No reason you shouldn't have your fun. She's a bit of a porker, but great tits. Just remember to be careful, yeah? No pillow talk about work." He slapped me on the back. Seemed to think he was being friendly. "You know, I never pegged you as a curry chaser. Got a thing for Indian girls, is it?"

Hard to remember, later, what happened then.

Makes it sound like a red mist rose before my eyes. It wasn't that. What it was—will sound ridiculous—but in that moment, it was like I was back at school, having the shit kicked out of me by fucking Stafford-Paterson. Third cousin to an earl, favourite of the masters, and unsurpassed slimy little creep.

Difference was, this time, I wasn't half the size of the other guy. In the intervening years, I'd learned how to punch. So I did it.

There was a dull thud as my fist connected with his cheek,

crunching against bone. Shaw staggered back. His foot slipped over the curb. He wobbled, then crashed backwards down onto the road.

A cyclist swerved to avoid him. "Watch where you're going! Fucking hell!"

Woke me up. I grabbed Shaw and pulled him back onto the pavement before he could get run over.

Shaw shoved me away. "What the *fuck*, Charles?"

First time he'd ever called me Charles.

Opened my mouth to apologise, but I wasn't sorry. Wished I'd done it earlier, if anything. If I'd given him a black eye the moment I got out of the taxi on Monday morning, it would've given him something better to think about than ogling Kriya.

So I didn't say anything.

Shaw: "What's your problem?"

But before he could really get going, a group of people emerged from Swithin Watkins. Farah was among them.

Farah: "Oh, Charles! There you are. I've got a call in ten minutes, but are you free after two? I'll come speak to you then."

Then she saw Shaw.

CG: "Shaw was around and wanted to talk about the case. I explained it's best if he doesn't tell me too much, until we're cleared to act."

Farah: "Quite. These processes do take time, I'm afraid. I'm sure Charles will have explained that. We'll be in touch when we—" She cut herself off, squinting at Shaw. "Oh dear, are you all right? What's that mark on your cheek?"

Shaw: "It's nothing. I had an accident this morning. Got a knock on the face." Looked daggers at me. "I've got to go."

He left without saying goodbye. Farah had been drawn back to her group, was too busy sending off her visitors to notice.

Had a feeling I might have solved the firm's dilemma about whether to represent Shaw Boey's associate. Couldn't imagine he'd want "the boss" to instruct us, after this.

I needed to confess what I'd done to Farah. And possibly to the Solicitors Regulation Authority. Almost certainly a breach of the Code of Conduct to punch a client in the face.

But first, there was someone else I needed to talk to.

CHAPTER
THIRTY-FIVE

Charles

nbox was teeming with unread emails when I got back to my desk. Instead of catching up on them, I grabbed my personal phone.

Nipped downstairs and out the back entrance to the alley where I talk to Ma when she insists on calling me during the working day. Stepped over an abandoned coffee cup, the cardboard dissolving in a pool of cold latte, and scrolled down the contacts list on my phone.

Hadn't rung the number in a while. Wasn't sure he'd pick up. But he did.

Ba: "Wai. Son?"

Didn't blame him for being surprised. Couldn't recall the last time we'd spoken on the phone.

CG: "Hello, Ba. Can you talk?"

Ba: "What do you want to talk about?" Sounded apprehensive.

Probably thought I was about to tell him I wasn't going to come up with the outstanding £25,000, so he'd have to pay off his debts himself. In other words, he might have to face a single consequence of his behaviour, for once in his life.

Unfair of me. Ba faced consequences before, e.g., when he went to jail.

This was why I avoided talking to him. Didn't like who I was when I had to interact with Ba.

CG: "Have you spoken to Boey Kah Seng recently? Shaw Boey's dad."

Ba, perking up: "Ah, you heard? Not Boey Kah Seng, but the son contacted me. Polite boy. He's a big deal now, but he still knows how to respect his father's old friend. You know, whether you agree or not, this Shaw Boey knows how to get ahead. Most people only wish. They don't do. This boy, he does things."

CG: "When you say he 'does things,' you mean the allegations that he's embezzled billions from a sovereign wealth fund?"

Ba: "Most people, it's not that they don't want to do like him. They just don't have the guts."

I disagreed, but didn't want to be arguing about this. Had a bigger fight to pick.

Until my bizarre conversation with Shaw, I'd accepted that it fundamentally wasn't my job to decide whether or not Helen Daley's *Guardian* article was accurate. That was for a court to determine, based on the evidence adduced by each side.

But in light of the past hour or so, I was compelled to conclude that what Ms. Daley had reported was basically true. Clearly there was sufficient proof of the allegations out there as to cause Shaw concern.

It would have been more effective if he'd offered to bribe Farah and the entire risk management committee. But perhaps he viewed the £200 million Blackmount deal we were advising on in that light. Robert Anderson certainly wouldn't be happy to alienate the man who'd given him that instruction.

That was a fight for Farah to have. In the meantime, I had to sort myself out.

CG: "Did Shaw offer you a job?"

Ba: "Yes, at Boey Kah Seng's company. Haven't confirmed the package yet. Once they confirmed, I was going to tell the family." Sighed. "Back then, Boey Kah Seng and I were equals. I was better off, my salary was good. His father only gave him a small allowance. I used to pay when we went out for dinner. Now I'm supposed to call him 'boss.' Well, we don't all have the same luck, in this world."

CG: "If they come back to you, you've got to tell them you can't accept the job, Ba. They were only offering it to you as a bribe. My firm's acting for Shaw Boey's company and there are some irregularities he wants us to ignore. That's the reason he approached you."

Ba: "Who told you that?" Before I could answer, he went on: "Just because I've had some bad luck, you think nobody wants me to work with them? You don't know, your father has a lot of experience in business. People used to fight to get a meeting with me."

CG: "Well, what's the job description? What are your duties going to be?"

Ba: "That's not confirmed yet. We will discuss all that."

CG: "Ba, it's not normal to be approached for a job where you haven't even been told what you're going to do. They've promised you a lot of money, I assume. Doesn't that seem suspicious to you?"

Ba: "You don't know how things work here. In Asia, it's about who you know, not just what you know. Boey Kah Seng is my old friend from back then, so he knows I can add value to his company. But my own son doesn't think anyone would want to give me a job!"

CG: "That's not what I'm saying."

Did not, in fact, think that a man in his sixties with a fraud conviction, who hadn't been in regular employment for years, would be viewed as a catch by most employers. But I wasn't about to say so. May have problems with my bedside manner, but I'm not *that* tactless.

I said: "The problem is with this particular job offer. Shaw Boey made it because he wants a hold on me, and by extension, the firm. He wants to make it so, if I become aware of information to his disadvantage, I won't feel able to act on it as I should."

Ba: "So what?"

CG: "What?"

Ba: "You young people, you only think about yourself. You're lucky. You don't know what it's like to have people chase you for money while you have children to feed."

Could have pointed out I had an intimate knowledge of what it was like to be chased for money, thanks to him. But I could hear Ma's voice in my head: "Your father is getting older. Old people are very sensitive. If you scold him, you may feel good, but then what will happen? He will get angry, maybe he will stop talking to you. He has other children, but you only have one father."

It wasn't her argument I found persuasive, so much as the subtext: *You're strong. He's weak.*

Ba needed looking after. Had always been true. He wasn't good at it himself.

CG: "It's not just about me. You can't trust Shaw Boey. He's going to get in trouble. He's probably got the money to wriggle out of it, but if you get caught up in it, you won't."

Ba wasn't listening. "I told your mother she gave you too much face. She never listened. Now, see, it's made you selfish. You don't care about your own father, your own siblings. Don't you want us to have a comfortable life?"

Had been the subject of Ba's diatribes before, but it hadn't happened in a while. Had forgotten how confusing it was, as well as unpleasant. Like being bashed over the head by a screaming toddler, except the toddler was in his sixties.

CG: "I do. Of course I do. That's why I sent you twenty-five grand."

Ba: "Compared to what we need, that's nothing. Now I have a chance to help the family, and you're trying to tell me not to take it. We are in this situation, even one million would be just enough to pay off our debt, and you want to lecture me—"

CG: "Wait, one million?" Chill ran down my back. "Are you saying you're in debt for a hundred thousand pounds? Ma said it was fifty."

Ba, grandly: "Better not tell your mother. She's had enough stress in her life." As though he weren't the chief source of Ma's stress. "You already know I'm in a bad situation. Whether it's five hundred thousand or one million, what difference does it make?"

CG: "Of course it makes a difference. Coming up with a hundred thousand pounds is a much bigger deal than coming up with fifty thousand."

Ba: "Who's asking you to come up with anything? I didn't ask you to give me money. Once I have this job, I'll be able to help myself. I won't have to put up with you ordering me around. You are the son and you are acting as though you are the father! You're telling me I must suffer, because if I work for Boey Kah Seng, it will make problems at your job. What's the point of being a lawyer, if not to help your family?"

CG: "The point of being a lawyer is being a good one. It's meaningless if you decide the rules governing the profession can be ignored for self-interest."

Ba: "Nonsense. Who matters more than your family? What are you following all these rules for?"

CG: "For myself."

And for society, I might have added, but Ba wasn't about to listen to an account of how my work contributed to the rule of law. He was too busy working himself up into a tantrum.

Ba: "You think you're a big man, because you sent me some

money. You think I don't know it's pocket change to you? With your salary, you should be saving, investing. It's not like you have a wife or children. Where has all your money gone?"

Could have said: on living in one of the most expensive cities in the world, financially supporting Ma since it wasn't like she had a pension or had been able to save any of the money she'd worked so hard to earn over the years, and also, *bailing Ba out of all his previous emergencies.*

But Ba didn't give me the chance to reel it off. He said: "If you're going to be like this, I don't need your help. Ha! You think I have no pride? You expect your father to kowtow to you, is it? Even if you offered me one million, I wouldn't take it. Don't bother sending me the rest of the money. I will handle it myself."

Opened my mouth to reason with him. Shut it.

What was I going to say? *Don't be angry, Ba. I'll go and kill myself raising another £75,000 for you, so you can berate me the next time I try to warn you off yet another terrible decision.*

I could do what I'd been doing all along: take the drubbing, and keep giving Ba whatever he needed, when he needed it. It was what I was supposed to do. According to my parents.

But if this conversation with Ba had shown anything, it was that his judgment wasn't to be relied on. I couldn't stop Ba from working with Shaw Boey and his family, if Shaw gave him the job—which seemed unlikely, after what I'd done this morning. I couldn't save Ba from his choices.

But I could opt out of being involved.

CG: "All right."

Shocked silence on the line.

Ba: "What?"

Almost laughed, he sounded so taken aback.

CG: "I won't send you the rest of the money."

Ba: "What are you talking about? Because I am lecturing you, you want to throw a tantrum? Don't you know it's my responsibility as your father to teach you? Who are you to threaten me?"

Wouldn't have said I had any respect for Ba left to lose. Little had I known.

CG: "I've got to go, Ba. I've got work to do."

Ba, voice rising: "If you hang up now, I will no longer have a son!"

Gave me pause. *You only have one father,* Ma had said.

But it wasn't true that I had all the power and Ba none. Maybe if someone, anyone, had expected more of Ba before now, he might have learned his lesson earlier in life.

As it was, nothing would change so long as everyone behaved as though he wasn't capable of change. It was a self-fulfilling prophecy. I'd had enough of going along with it.

CG: "I hope you'll see things differently when you've had a chance to think about it. We can speak another time, if you want. But I've got to go. Bye, Ba."

Ended the call. Half expected my phone to start buzzing as I slipped it into my pocket, Ba ringing me back. But he didn't.

As I walked up the stairs, back to my office, I was working through what needed to be done.

Farah had said she'd be free to speak after two. Where should I start? Needed to tell her about Ba being offered this job, in case it affected my involvement in the Jamaludin case. But I could explain there was a low risk of the case going ahead, on account of me punching the client in the face.

Wasn't sure why Shaw hadn't told Farah what I'd done, when we saw her outside the building earlier. Suppose it was a bit embarrassing for him, really. "Weedy little Charlie Goh knocked me over." And if he'd told her, questions would naturally arise as to why I'd done it.

It was funny, in retrospect, me grandstanding to Ba about my ethical duties as a lawyer. There was a real possibility I might not be a lawyer after I spoke to Farah.

Did you get struck off for assaulting clients, or was it merely a matter of a fine and telling off? The Solicitors Disciplinary Tribunal probably published their rulings. Should take a look.

On an ordinary day, I might have felt distressed at the prospect of losing my job because of Shaw Boey. But it hadn't been an ordinary day. Hadn't been an ordinary week. More than anything else, I felt a great sense of calm.

Wasn't simply the relief of no longer being on the hook for £25,000. It was the thought of not having to live through Ba's crises anymore. Not having to be dragged into every drama he concocted.

He'd probably change his mind about disowning me, once he simmered down. I might not hear from him directly, but no doubt Ma or Iza or even one of the kids would be in touch, in due course. Life would be too simple if Ba never spoke to me again.

But I'd realised, now, that I could decide not to speak to him. I could simply decline to be involved.

Hadn't realised how wound up I'd been over the money until the tension evaporated. Felt years younger.

Back at my desk, I went through my inbox, triaging. Was typing out an email to a client explaining she wouldn't be getting a full analysis of their legal position by close of play, given that would require a review of the 384 documents she'd granted me access to that morning, when Farah appeared.

Farah: "My call wrapped up early. I've been wanting to speak to you. Is now all right?" She shut the door behind her and came to stand by my desk. "I heard the news."

CG: "You have?" Thought Shaw must have followed up and told her about our altercation, after all. "Has Shaw decided to go elsewhere?"

Farah blinked. "What?"

CG: "I thought you meant Shaw told you about what happened this morning. When I punched him."

Farah: "You did *what?*"

Gave her the executive summary of the morning's encounter with Shaw. "I was thinking I might need to declare an interest, if my dad gets a job with Shaw's dad's company. Do you know if there's a form I need to fill out?"

Farah, frowning: "It sounds very concerning, what he said to you. I think we need to look into the existing relationship with Blackmount, even leaving aside the new instruction. Apart from anything else, if our fees are being paid out of the proceeds of fraud, they may well be recoverable by the defrauded party."

CG: "I was thinking that."

Farah: "But I must say, Charles, I don't see what there was in the conversation to provoke your reaction."

CG: "Oh, that happened later. Shaw, er, used inappropriate language. About a colleague."

Found myself looking over at Kriya's desk. Farah looked too.

Farah: "I see. I was thinking it was out of character for you, but that explains it."

What did that mean?

Farah: "We'll have to see what Shaw decides to do, if anything. He might choose to raise it, but I can't imagine he'll want to go into the details of what was said. As for the bigger picture, if he decides to take his business elsewhere, that would make life simpler, in a way."

She seemed remarkably unperturbed.

CG: "Do you think I should report it?"

Farah: "We may need to make reports if money laundering is at issue, but I wouldn't worry about the, ah, exchange between the two of you. At the moment, it's your word against Shaw's. He told me it was an accident, this morning. And I'm sure you won't do anything like it again."

CG: "No. But—"

Farah: "It was actually Kriya I wanted to talk to you about.

I heard she's resigned, and she's leaving at the end of the week. Can you tell me what happened?"

CG: "Is that all you've heard?"

Farah, after a pause: "Does it have anything to do with Arthur?"

CG, carefully: "Kriya spoke to HR. I was present at the meeting, to corroborate the details I witnessed. But I don't think it's my story to tell."

A shadow passed over Farah's face. "I see. This is very upsetting." She glanced over at Kriya's desk again. "She's working from home today, is she?"

Started to say, "For the rest of the week," but the words wouldn't come.

Didn't understand what was happening at first. Then it hit me. There was a real risk I was about to *cry*.

Farah realised around the same time as me. Saw her face change.

Jumped to my feet and turned to the window, blinking. Could see the corresponding floor of the office building across the road, occupied by a mid-size national firm. It was close enough you could see the computer screen of the guy in the office opposite. He spent a surprising amount of time watching video game play-throughs on YouTube.

He wasn't there today. Must be working from home.

Somehow it made me feel even lonelier.

CG: "I might never see her again."

Didn't mean to say it out loud.

Farah: "Oh, Charles."

CHAPTER THIRTY-SIX

From: kethau.yap@gmail.com
To: charles.goh@swithinwatkins.com
Subject: Potential legal action against Helen Daley

Dear Charles

Kriya Rajasekar suggested I contact you in the first instance. I'm writing in connection with an approach Swithin Watkins may have received from Shaw Boey, to act in a potential claim against the journalist Helen Daley, in respect of a series of articles she is publishing in the *Guardian* (the first can be read here).

I am not aware of whether you will have been instructed on behalf of Mr. Boey, a company connected to him, or one of his associates. However, before your firm agrees to act in this matter, you may wish to consider the attached materials, which provide extensive documentary evidence for the misconduct described in Ms. Daley's article.

You may also be aware that Ms. Daley has posted about the threat of legal action on her blog here. This has gained significant attention in Malaysia.

Please feel free to contact me if you have any questions, or would like to discuss further.

Kind regards,

Ket Yap

CHAPTER THIRTY-SEVEN

THREE WEEKS LATER

Kriya

I tried to argue with Zuri when she said she'd see me off at the airport: "No need lah. It's two hours out of your day."

"Not like I have anything else to do what," she said. "We can chit-chat."

Which was what we did, at first. Zuri told me about the acar she'd made the other day and her adventures on dating apps. I told her about the kdrama I was watching and Amma's campaign to get me to lose weight by drinking a cup of bunga telang tea every day.

Zuri grimaced. "Are you going to be OK living with her for weeks? How long has it been since you spent that much time under the same roof with your parents?"

"I was eighteen the last time," I admitted. "It'll be fine. I'll run away and visit friends in KL if it gets too much. It's only until I figure out what's happening on the job front anyway."

I was planning to stay with my parents in Ipoh for a few weeks after the Sanson interview in Hong Kong—since I was between jobs, there was no reason I had to stay in London.

I had a feeling Sanson would make an offer, and I would

take it ("You are destined for this role," Rosalind had said, with her usual predilection for understatement). But I'd reached out to a recruiter who specialised in placing English-qualified lawyers in the region anyway. I figured there was no harm in keeping my options open.

"I might have to fly back to Hong Kong for more interviews, for all you know," I said.

Zuri glanced around. The carriage was fairly quiet—the nearest person was sat two empty seats away, a beefy guy wearing headphones, from which the strains of a Taylor Swift song could faintly be heard. She lowered her voice. "Have you heard back from Ket Hau?"

"He said he contacted the firm, sent them some documents. Apparently they confirmed receipt, but I don't know the outcome." I paused. "I got a message from Charles, actually. But not about, you know, the client issue. He said Arthur's left the firm."

The fact I'd resigned had come as a bombshell to my friend circle. Explaining the reason why had made them so raucous in their indignation that we'd come close to getting kicked out of our favourite Korean restaurant, but Zuri now knew everything Arthur had done since I'd moved with him to Swithin Watkins.

"He got fired?" she said, her eyes widening. "Because of what you told HR?"

"Charles didn't go into the details. He only said Arthur's left." I was relieved to note that I didn't feel a twinge of guilt, saying it.

It was strange: After resigning and reporting Arthur to HR, the thought of him and how he'd treated me made me furious, as it had never done before. I kept remembering things he'd said and done, that I'd accepted at the time, and getting mad about them in retrospect.

It was as though I'd blocked that capacity for anger before, in order to survive our relationship. It was only now it was over that I could see how dysfunctional it had been.

"I hope he has to sell all his properties and ends up in a dead-end job where his boss bullies him," said Zuri.

"He'll probably just move to another firm," I said.

"Ugh." Zuri scowled. "What else did Kawan Baik say?"

I shrugged. "That was it. He probably can't say anything about the client issue." I sighed. "I'll be lucky if he doesn't report me to the SRA for breaching confidentiality."

"You didn't break confidentiality. They all assumed Helen Daley was going to get sued already."

I made a noncommittal noise. I didn't regret anything I'd said or done, but it probably was more than I should have. But I didn't want Zuri worrying about it.

"Did you reply to Charles?" said Zuri. "What did you say?"

"'Thank you' lah. What else is there to say?"

"Does he know you're going to Hong Kong?"

I nodded. "Sanson asked me to go the day I quit, so I mentioned it to him."

Zuri and I had been friends for so long that words were not really essential to our communication. I could sense that she was dying to say something.

"What is it?" I said.

"Nothing," said Zuri. After a moment: "I thought he was a really nice guy, Charles."

"He is a really nice guy."

Zuri gave me a sidelong look. "So you do like him?"

There was no point denying it, at this stage. It didn't make much difference one way or another.

"Yeah. But it's not going to work, is it?" I leaned back in my seat, glaring at the advertisement for sleeping pills above the window opposite me. "I don't know why Fate has to do me like this. I have to meet someone nice right when I might be leaving the country."

"You don't have to leave. You could get another job here what."

I had thought about this. "Yeah. But you know, I decided to stay in London for Tom. And I moved to Swithin Watkins for Arthur. I don't want to make another big career decision for a guy, you know? This opportunity at Sanson could really work out for me. And then, when I come back to London—if I come back—I want it to be on my own terms. Because it makes sense for me."

"I can see the logic," said Zuri. "But Charles could move, in that case. He's from Hong Kong, right? He could get a job there."

I gave her a look.

Zuri said, "What? What's so wrong with that? Might as well let the guy chase you for once."

"OK, I'll just suggest that to him, shall I?"

"Well, maybe you should!"

"What, tell a guy I've known for two months he should move to Hong Kong so we can be together?"

"You've known Kawan Baik for years. Anyway," said Zuri, before I could interject, "I'm not saying go propose to the guy or what. But you don't need to shut things down because you're worried about the distance. You could do long-distance."

I had also thought about this. Over the past couple of weeks, I'd spent a *lot* of mental energy on Charles, how I felt about him and what I should do about that. When I'd first seen the notification of his WhatsApp message, my heart had leapt.

Then I'd read it. Charles had maintained a dampeningly professional tone:

I thought you should know that Arthur has left the firm. Hope all's well with you.

I'd seen him be more informal in emails to colleagues and clients he'd never spoken to before. That weekend together in my flat might never have happened.

But then again, I'd been the one to push him away, after that last dinner. And the reasons I'd given him then hadn't changed.

"I'm not up for a long-distance relationship," I said. "Not after Tom."

"The whole point of Kawan Baik is he's not Tom," said Zuri. "We wouldn't have signed off on him if he was Tom."

"You hung out with Charles for, like, an hour max!"

"Yeah, but I got a good feeling from him," said Zuri. "I liked the way he said your name."

Of all the arguments for Charles Zuri might have put forward, I hadn't been expecting that. "How did he say my name?"

"You know. Like it was a little treat that he got to say it," said Zuri. "It was cute. You guys were so cute. The way you kept looking at each other. It was more like you were boyfriend-girlfriend roleplaying being colleagues, rather than the other way around."

This shut me up.

Zuri said, "Just because you couldn't trust Tom doesn't mean nobody else is trustworthy. You have to leave space for life to surprise you."

I stared at the beefy Swiftie's feet. He was wearing bright red trainers.

"If Charles is interested, he could say so," I muttered. "He's got my number."

"And he texted you, no? And all you said was 'thank you.'"

"Yeah, because he was so standoffish!"

Zuri held out her hand. "Show me the message."

I passed her my phone. What did I have to lose? It wasn't like I had any dignity left with Zuri.

Having reviewed the exchange, she said, "OK. I can see your dilemma. But look at it this way. You left the firm because your boss hit on you—"

"And because we were advising the guy who embezzled billions from our country."

"Yeah, OK, that too. But maybe Kawan Baik doesn't want to

pressure you, you know?" said Zuri. "I mean, if you're a decent guy, that's what you're going to be thinking. 'Kriya's dealing with a lot, I don't want to kacau her.' How much encouragement have you given him?"

"I let him stay in my flat for three nights," I protested.

But it was true Charles had taken his lead from me, throughout the time we'd known each other. And I'd left matters with him on an ambiguous note, the last time we saw each other. It had been, I realised, the one time he'd asked for more.

I'd been preoccupied and distracted that night, but maybe I had been a little afraid, too. My life was breaking open. I was getting more than I'd ever dreamt was possible for me. It didn't seem reasonable to want Charles, too, much less get to keep him.

"If you want to hear from him, give him an opening lah," said Zuri. "Give him the chance to put his case."

She stayed with me while I checked in my bags at Heathrow, walking me to Departures. We hugged. I scanned my boarding pass, waved at Zuri, then turned and went through to security.

It took a while to get through security—the downside of travelling on a Sunday during the school summer holidays. I was stuck behind dozens of people who seemed never to have been to an airport before. But finally I was disgorged at the other end, only slightly ruffled by the experience.

I followed the signs through the maze of duty-free shopping, alone among the crowd. I'd always enjoyed travelling by myself—that sensation of being neither here nor there, temporarily cut off from everyday reality. I bought myself a snack, admired the bags in the Mulberry storefront—should have indulged while I was still being paid a salary—then sat down to watch the departure board.

I bit into my cookie and realised I was thinking about Charles. The way he frowned when he was concentrating. His gentleness, the smell of him, and his hands.

I didn't believe in soulmates. There would be other people, probably, if it wasn't Charles.

But I wanted it to be him. Maybe that was reason enough to reach out. To open the door, even if it would be safer and less complicated to keep it shut.

I took my phone out of my bag and snapped a photo of the cookie, with the bite taken out of it. The black screen of the departure board could be seen in the background, out of focus.

Not quite as good as the SW meeting room cookies

The double blue tick appeared almost instantly. I could see Charles was typing.

You're flying to Hong Kong today?

Yes. Can you remind me what the roast goose restaurant you recommended was called?

Yat Lok.

Thanks. Hoping I manage to get there this time around.

When's the interview with Sanson?

I told him. I hesitated, then typed:

I'm going on to Malaysia after. Not sure when I'll be back in the UK, but maybe we could grab a coffee then?

It took a little longer for Charles to respond, this time around. I put my phone down and looked around the departure lounge as though there was anything to see that interested me more than what was happening on my phone.

The phone buzzed. I grabbed it.

Sounds like you'll be busy. Good luck. Have a safe journey.

"Seriously?" I said aloud.

Maybe I—and all my friends—had imagined Charles's interest. Or maybe he'd already had what he wanted from me. Or maybe—this seemed the most likely option—he felt there was no mileage in pursuing a connection that was about to be broken off, since I was flying off that day to interview for a job thousands of miles away.

I fell back against my seat, letting out a breath.

Well. So much for that.

CHAPTER
THIRTY-EIGHT

Charles

Repairs to the flat inevitably took longer than estimated. Ended up living out of my windowless hotel room for three weeks.

It was all right. Being in the flat would have been depressing anyway, with Loretta away. Office was quiet, too, now I was on my own again.

I worked and went to the gym. Great thing about work, there's always something to keep you occupied. Though even there I found myself scraping the barrel after a while, writing case notes for the department blog and doing the cybersecurity training I'd ignored for the past two years.

Client billable work had gone quiet all at once. The Jamaludin case was dead in the water, for us at least—the documents Kriya's contact had sent had tipped the balance with the risk management committee, even with the prospect of losing the work on Blackmount's two hundred million acquisition deal.

Farah had been the one to email Shaw the news that the firm wouldn't be advising further on the suit against Helen Daley. I'd been told to decline any calls and reroute any emails from Shaw upwards, but he hadn't been in touch, not even to respond to Farah's email. Presumably he was exploring other options.

At least the repairs to the flat were done in time for Loretta and Hayley's return from honeymoon. I was back in occupation two days before their arrival. Loretta texted me from Heathrow in the early morning:

At baggage reclaim. Won't see you before you leave for work, but come home for dinner, OK? Hayley's cooking.

Bunked off early, at seven p.m. It was like coming home to a new flat. Loretta and Hayley's suitcases were in the hall. There was a pile of exquisitely packaged Japanese biscuits and cakes on the kitchen counter. (Loretta: "Those are for you. We got the local speciality in every city we went to.")

The dining table was laid, with wine glasses and napkins and a vase of flowers at the centre. Didn't even know we had a vase.

Dinner was veggie moussaka with garlic bread and salad on the side, and a bottle of red wine, with tiramisu for dessert. Change from the Sainsbury's meal deals I'd been subsisting on for the past few weeks. Lifted my head when I was finished and said, in quiet awe:

"Loretta, you are going to get so fat."

Loretta, smugly: "I know."

Hayley: "The tiramisu was from M&S. I can't take any credit for that."

Loretta: "We're giving you the credit, babe, whether you like it or not."

They kissed. I looked away. Entirely correct of them to be visibly in love, but I wasn't in the mood to be the light bulb to a blissful romance just then.

Conversation focused on Japan: pictures from their trip and so on. It was only after dinner, once Loretta had collected our plates and dumped them in the sink, that she said:

"What have you been up to, while we were away?"

CG: "Mostly trying to sort the flat. Someone's coming to

look at the stain on your bedroom wall on Friday. I'm planning to work from home—"

Loretta: "I meant with Kriya!"

Hayley looking polite, as befit an in-law who was going to have to live with me for an indefinite number of weeks. But she was definitely listening.

Knew what Loretta had really been asking about, of course.

CG: "Kriya's left the firm."

Loretta's eyes widened. "Oh my God! She got pushed out by that partner who was harassing her?"

CG: "Essentially. But I don't think she was happy even before the issues with him began. It sounds like it's been the right move for her. She messaged yesterday from the airport, she's flown off for a job interview in Hong Kong."

Was pleased by how that came out: neutral, professional. Sounded like I wished her well in her future endeavours. Well, I do.

Loretta sat up. "She messaged you? You've got her number?"

CG: "She wanted me to send her food recommendations, since she was going to Hong Kong."

Loretta: "Oh, so she gave you her number? And she texted you? Let me see."

CG: "What? No."

Scuffle ensued. Loretta cheated: licked my arm. I dropped the phone trying to get away from her.

CG: "That's disgusting! What's wrong with you?"

Hayley, admiring, to Loretta: "You really will stop at nothing."

Loretta: "At least I didn't bite you. Charles, you should lock your phone, anyone could pick it up and go through your shit."

She scrolled through my messages while I was sputtering.

Loretta: "She asked you out! Babe, she asked him out!"

CG: "She didn't ask me out." Assailed by doubt. "Did she?"

Loretta: "What's this bit about having a coffee, if it's not meant to be a date?" She handed my phone to Hayley. "And he turned her down! Charles, what's your problem? I thought you liked her."

CG: "She just wanted to keep in touch, as colleagues. She wasn't asking for a date." Was she?

Maybe I should have asked. I'd assumed Kriya wanted information—the details of Arthur's departure from the firm, and whether we'd decided to take Shaw's case on, or not. Could understand her curiosity, but I hadn't wanted to prolong the exchange of messages unnecessarily.

I'd spent enough time pining for Kriya. Experience had shown proximity and regular contact didn't help. I'd thought I'd see what distance could do.

Hadn't done much so far, it was true. But it had only been three weeks.

Loretta rolled her eyes. "Poor Kriya. Reacting with a thumbs up emoji was more than you deserved."

Hayley: "I can see why Charles thinks it's ambiguous, to be fair. It could be a networking thing, especially if she's job-hunting now. It depends on the context."

Perhaps Hayley would be a salutary influence in our flat. There were times I had felt Loretta could do with some moderation.

Hayley: "What actually happened when you stayed over at Kriya's? Did you guys, you know." She gestured. "Mess around?"

Loretta: "Of course they messed around. Wait, didn't you?"

CG, stiffly: "It doesn't matter. She isn't interested in anything more. She's going off for this job now anyway."

Loretta and Hayley exchanged an extremely married look.

Loretta: "Charles, seriously." Tapped phone screen. "This is solid evidence she's interested. She wants to see you again. If it was about networking so she could get another job, why wouldn't she network with all the former colleagues she *hasn't* slept with?"

Hayley: "That's true. It's not like she doesn't know what straight men are like. She has to expect you'll be thinking, 'She wants to hook up again.'"

They were both so serenely certain it shook me. Recovered my phone from Hayley so I could review the messages.

There still didn't seem much in them to encourage hope. Loretta and Hayley hadn't been there when Kriya had said, *It's complicated.* She could have messaged me before she left the country, if she'd wanted to meet up.

But she'd said other things, too. *You're so lovely.*

Heart lifted at the memory of the look in her eyes.

Maybe Loretta and Hayley were right. It was hardly an area in which I had much expertise. I was very willing to concede the point.

Loretta: "It's awkward that she's going to Hong Kong. But you know, LDRs are a thing." Looked at Hayley, who took her hand and squeezed it. "I don't know, Charles. I know you think I'm being this hopeless matchmaking auntie, but you really seem to vibe with Kriya. That never happens. It's worth fighting for, isn't it? At least tell her how you feel. Maybe you'd be giving her a reason to stay."

Stared at their joined hands, resting on the dining table. Light gleamed off the opal in Hayley's engagement ring.

CG: "I wouldn't want to persuade her to stay, if she's keen on this role. It sounds a good fit for her. She knows the business well. She's on good terms with the internal stakeholders. The work is likely to be less technical, more about providing strategic guidance to the business. That wouldn't suit me, but it would play to Kriya's strengths. Not that she lacks technical skills, but her soft skills are particularly strong. The hours should be better and the pay will be comparable, at least to start out with. It might not rise at the same rate, but I doubt she would have wanted to make partner anyway."

Hayley: "You sound like a legal recruiter."

Loretta: "I told you, he's obsessed with Kriya. Every time he talks about her, he does this super detailed analysis. He's like a one-man Kriya Rajasekar subreddit." To me: "I can't believe you're just going to let her go. Are you really happy working all the time and going to the gym and not having anybody to smooch when you come home?" She smooched Hayley, who laughed.

Loretta turned back to me. "There's more to life than your job, you know, Charles."

That was true for them. There wasn't much more to *my* life than my job.

And there wouldn't be, so long as I failed to do anything to change it.

CG: "I know."

Loretta: "So what are you going to do about it?"

Put down my phone. I'd come to a decision. Seemed to me I didn't have much to lose, except face.

How much face did I have left with Kriya, anyway? She'd seen me in my *Duke of Badminton* cosplay.

CG: "I'm going to take a holiday."

CHAPTER THIRTY-NINE

Kriya

When I came out of the Sanson office, Charles was there.

I spotted him at once, amid the crowds of central Hong Kong. He was leaning against a lamppost, dressed in a cream linen shirt, light brown trousers, boat shoes, and sunglasses. He looked like something out of a magazine, probably *Monocle*, untouched by the heat of the Hong Kong summer.

If you'd asked me before I saw him, I would have said I had mixed feelings about the idea of seeing Charles again. I'd archived my WhatsApp chat with him, so I wouldn't keep going back to look at his last message.

But in the moment, all I felt was uncomplicated pleasure. It was like seeing an old friend unexpectedly, among a crowd of strangers.

"Charles!" I went up to him. "Look at you. You look so cool!"

Charles's ears went pink. He took off his sunglasses. "Hi."

I gave him a hug. He allowed it, a little awkwardly. He smelled incredible, which made me feel both horny and sad.

I squashed down both sensations.

"I didn't know you were in Hong Kong," I said. It was odd

he hadn't mentioned it when I messaged him. Maybe some-thing had cropped up at work. "What brings you here?"

Charles looked embarrassed.

"Well," he said. "You."

I gaped. He squirmed.

"Really?" I said.

"Loretta said I should give it a shot. I wanted to talk to you, and what I have to say is better said in person." He squared his shoulders. "You mentioned having a coffee, on WhatsApp. Could I take you up on that? Are you busy now?"

"Er, sure. I don't have any plans for the rest of the day." I paused. "Though I might go for yuenyeung instead. Do you know where's good for lunch around here? Something local."

Charles reflected. I'd forgotten how furious his face got when he was thinking.

My chest squeezed. I wanted to protect him from anyone who might ever be mean to him.

"There's a famous cha chaan teng not far from here," he said. "It was one of my recommendations. Shall we go?"

"It's a date," I said lightly.

We started walking together, close enough to hear each other over the noise of the traffic and the bustle of the crowd. Not quite close enough to touch.

"Is it?" said Charles, not at all lightly. He glanced at me before looking away. "I came here to tell you, I—I really like you. I'd like to explore—I mean, it would be good to—I mean, we could try dating and see how that worked, if you were open to that. Really dating, I mean. Not just what we were doing before."

"Oh," I said.

My tone must not have been very encouraging. Charles looked worried.

"It's fine if you want to think about it first," he said.

"That's not it," I said. "It's just . . . I thought you weren't interested. You know, you were put off because of the distance, or because I breached privilege, or all of the above."

I laughed, though it wasn't a joke. I had passed a couple of jet lagged nights since arriving in Hong Kong, dwelling on all the possible reasons why Charles had decided he didn't want to see me again.

"No. I could understand your concerns about the Helen Daley case," said Charles. "The firm's decided not to act, by the way. I wasn't sure if your contact would have told you."

"He mentioned it." I hesitated. "I think I stopped short of breaking privilege. I told him as little as I could, but they already knew it was coming. I'm sorry if it made any trouble for you."

Charles shook his head. "It wasn't an attractive case. Farah was keen to have a good reason to push for us to step away. The documents your contact sent us were helpful, in that regard." He paused. "I've thought about how I would have felt, in your position. I'm sorry I wasn't very supportive, especially given you took the work on as a favour to me."

"Well, you offered the work as a favour to me. I could see your point too. Sometimes it's hard to know what's the right thing to do." It was an observation that applied to more than ethical dilemmas about work. I said, "Sanson are going to make me an offer."

"I thought they would," said Charles. "Congratulations. Are you pleased about it?"

"Yeah. I'm planning to take it. But it means I'll be in Hong Kong for the next two years, at least. Possibly longer, if it all works out." I looked at Charles, wistful. "I like you so much, Charles. But I don't know if I can do a long-distance relationship, at this point in my life."

"About that . . ." Charles cleared his throat. "I've set up a meeting with the Head of Litigation at Swithin Watkins's

Hong Kong office. I'm seeing him tomorrow. We've spoken before. He knows I've got an interest in the region. It sounds like there may be an opportunity."

I came to a stop in the middle of the pavement. A Chinese auntie almost crashed into me, but swerved off, grumbling in highly profane Cantonese.

"You'd move here for me?" I said.

Charles took my arm to shift me out of the way of the people streaming down the street.

"I've thought about moving back before," he said. "You know, my mum's here. And my dad." He grimaced. "But so are my half-siblings. It would be good to be able to spend more time with them, and the food's better . . . But it would mostly be for you, yes."

He looked nervous. "I hope that's not too much. Loretta said to work up to it. I probably should have let you have your yuenyeung first."

"It's OK," I said. Warmth filled my chest. I reached out and took his hand.

Charles looked up, startled. After a moment he smiled. His fingers curled around mine. His palm was warm and dry.

We were waiting at the cha chaan teng for our pork chop buns, holding hands under the table, when it occurred to me to ask. I said:

"So what happened with Arthur? Did he get asked to re-sign?"

"I assume so. I only saw the announcement that he was leaving," said Charles. "They kept it to a line in the internal newsletter. The last email about a partner departure ran to five paragraphs, so that said something in itself."

"He'll probably pop up again." I made a face. "It's a good thing I'm getting out of the London legal market."

"You don't think you'll be going back?"

"Not for another job in the City. I owe Arthur for one thing, at least," I added. "If it wasn't for him, I might never have found the courage to leave. It was overdue. The job wasn't right for me."

"You think the Sanson role will be a better fit?"

"I hope so." I told him about my meeting with the GC, who'd been as nice as Rosalind had promised. Reassuringly, my impression was substantiated by a chat with the woman who'd held the role I was being recruited to fill. She was moving on promotion to Sanson's Paris headquarters, but she was full of convincing enthusiasm about the GC and the Hong Kong team.

"She had some good insights into the challenges of working here, too. But they all sound like things I can live with," I said. "I guess I'll see."

I hadn't really thought about what moving to Hong Kong would mean for Charles. To be fair to me, I hadn't known that was a prospect until half an hour ago. But I thought about it now.

"Do you have any concerns about it?" I said. I glanced around the restaurant and lowered my voice. "Given the political situation, and so on."

Charles looked sombre. "I did think about that. I know a lot of people who've left. But my mum wants to stay. So long as she's here . . . I'd like to make it work." He took a sip of his milk tea. "What are the next steps with Sanson?"

"They've said I should get the formal offer by email some time today. It'll be an expat package for the first two years. If I want to stay in Hong Kong after, they'd probably look to move me to a permanent local contract. But coming in as an expat means I'll get relocation costs and a housing allowance for two years. If I give up my lease in London, I should be able to save quite a lot— enough to cover my parents' home loan for a couple of years. That means I could take a break from working, potentially."

Charles was watching me with an expression I recognised from his client calls: intent, his brow furrowed with the effort of absorbing and retaining information. "What would you do, if you took a break?"

"In the longer term, I'd like to move out of the private sector, if I can. Focus on work that's more about helping people. I thought maybe I could do a Master's, something that would help me pivot. I'll have to do some research, talk to people."

"I know someone who left the firm to become Head of Legal at a charity," said Charles. "I could put you in touch with her."

"That would be good," I said. "Thanks."

Charles stroked his thumb over mine. Zuri's voice echoed in my head: *It was more like you were boyfriend-girlfriend roleplaying being colleagues.*

I'd have to text her later, and prepare to get roasted at the next group meetup. Part of having friends was accepting that sometimes they were entitled to say, *I told you so,* and there was nothing you could do but take it.

When we came out of the restaurant, I said:

"I'm staying at the Marriott, funnily enough. Do you want to check out my hotel room? It's got a great view."

I watched, charmed, as Charles turned deep red from his hairline to the V at the collar of his shirt.

"Yes, definitely," he said. "I'd love to. But, um." He checked his watch. "Right now I'm due to—I was wondering if—I mean, you can say no. Don't feel you have to, if you aren't comfortable doing it."

"What is it?"

"I was wondering," said Charles, "if you'd be up for coming to meet my mum."

I gave Charles's hand a little tug so he'd lean down, then kissed him. I expected him to give me a peck before drawing back: we were on a busy street in Central. Instead he slid his arms around me, deepening the kiss.

I ran my hands along his back, feeling the linen crinkle over warm flesh and solid muscle. He felt like home.

When Charles finally pulled away, he was breathing heavily, mussed and dreamy-eyed.

"Maybe we could see her another time," he said. "I could text her to push it back."

"Charles! No. We can make out later," I said. "Let's go see your mum."

ACKNOWLEDGMENTS

Thank you to:

The publishing team behind this book, including but not limited to my agent, Caitlin Blasdell; Erika Tsang, Tessa Villanueva, and Desirae Friesen at Bramble; Ellah Mwale and Chloe Davies at Pan; and Bo Feng Lin for another amazing cover.

My family, as always.

The Malaysian literary aunties group chat, especially Ipoh girls Preeta Samarasan and Maureen Tai.

The Idlers by Bamboo, especially Hana Lee, for *Duke of Badminton*.

Rachel Monte for Charles's arm workout.

The people who made being a City lawyer bearable and sometimes even enjoyable: chiefly Ruth Grant, Angela Baker, and Jelena Steponavicius, but also my law school buddies Preetha Gopalan, Shilpa Delaval, and Lim Jian Liang.

Particular thanks to Ashvina Segaran, Sharmilla Ganesan, Sumitra Selvaraj, and Sheena Gurbakhash for reading the manuscript. All remaining errors and infelicities are my own.

ABOUT THE AUTHOR

Ilona Denton

ZEN CHO is the author of the Sorcerer to the Crown novels, *Black Water Sister*, and various shorter fiction. Her work has won the Hugo, Crawford, and British Fantasy Awards, and the *Los Angeles Times* Ray Bradbury Prize, as well as being short-listed for the World Fantasy, Lambda Literary, Locus, and Astounding Awards. Born and raised in Malaysia, Cho now lives in the UK.